Robert Beaken is parish priest of St Mary the Virgin, Great Bardfield and St Katharine, Little Bardfield in Essex. He holds a PhD from King's College London and is a Fellow of the Royal Historical Society.

'Fascinating . . . this important book not only revises views of Lang but also sheds new light on the influence exercised by the Church of England in the wider society in the first half of the last century.'
Paul Richardson, *Church of England Newspaper*

'Highly informative.' Bernard Palmer, *Church Times*

'[Beaken's] research has been detailed and immense and has the advantage of objective judgment and analysis.' *Methodist Recorder*

'Robert Beaken draws on previously unseen material to create a complex picture of Lang' *The Catholic Herald*

'Dr Beaken is to be congratulated on a fine piece of work, well researched, perceptive and clearly and engagingly written' *Anglo-Catholic History Society Newsletter*

'Robert Beaken's study of Lang seeks to show that he responded, successfully in each case (albeit to differing degrees), to the three big crises which occurred during his archiepiscopate: the abdication of King Edward VIII, the rejection of the revised book of Common Prayer by Parliament and its consequences, and the Second World War . . . it is in discussing these three crises that this meticulously researched (and referenced) and eminently readable study comes to life.' *New Directions*

'groundbreaking' The Historical Association

'A Bishop of Decision', 'Spy' cartoon of Lang from *Vanity Fair*, 19 April 1906

COSMO LANG

Archbishop in War and Crisis

Robert Beaken

Foreword by Rowan Williams

I.B. TAURIS

LONDON · NEW YORK

Reprinted in 2013 and first published in 2012 by I.B.Tauris & Co. Ltd
6 Salem Road, London W2 4BU
175 Fifth Avenue, New York NY 10010
www.ibtauris.com

Distributed in the United States and Canada Exclusively by Palgrave Macmillan
175 Fifth Avenue, New York NY 10010

ISBN: 978 1 78076 355 2

A full CIP record for this book is available from the British Library
A full CIP record is available from the Library of Congress

Library of Congress Catalog Card Number: available

Typeset by JCS Publishing Services Ltd jcs-publishing.co.uk
Printed and bound by CPI Group (UK) Ltd, Croydon, CR0 4YY

MIX
Paper from
responsible sources
FSC
www.fsc.org   FSC® C013604

To FDJB, BMB and ACDB

Contents

Illustrations

Foreword

History and biography have not dealt kindly with Archbishop Lang. His predecessor was regarded with affection as a shrewd, serene, patriarchal figure; his successor was a charismatic national leader, a major public intellectual and a theological and devotional writer of unusual quality. Lang's public utterances could be badly judged, and he was mercilessly abused by sections of the media. His own complex personality both fascinated and alienated contemporaries, and his first biographer (who had not known him personally) concentrated on this in ways that were none too helpful. Most people who remember his name at all remember the unfortunate broadcast at the time of Edward VIII's abdication – or perhaps the anecdote about Orpen's portrait of him ('proud, pompous and prelatical').

Robert Beaken has undertaken an immense labour of research in the copious primary materials now available, and has produced a completely fresh picture of Lang. For the first time, we are given a glimpse of his warm friendships with women as well as men; we learn to see him as an insightful and sympathetic counsellor to the English Establishment, not just a moralising observer; and we meet a man who had a far more creative approach to both the social and the religious challenges of his era than we should ever have guessed from earlier treatments. This is a three-dimensional figure; certainly a man of his age and class, with the limitations that implies, but also a thoughtful and courageous leader of his Church. Much in regard of the health and vigour of the Church of England that might have been ascribed to other influences turns out to have owed a great deal to his oversight. Lang helped the Church rise to the challenge of the Second World

War, but he was already thinking forward to the tests of a post-war world.

Dr Beaken organises his material with clarity and vividness. This is a study that will open up some very important new perspectives on the twentieth-century Church of England, and should appeal to a much wider readership as well. Lang stood near the centres of political power at a time of unprecedented change and intense crisis. His contribution to state as well as Church was substantial. This excellent book spells out what he gave to both Church and state and helps us towards a far more rounded appreciation of an unusual, gifted, sometimes tortured, always dedicated Christian pastor.

+Rowan Cantuar:

Lambeth Palace
London SE1

Acknowledgements

I wish to thank Her Majesty Queen Elizabeth II for graciously giving me permission to reproduce material from the Royal Archives. I am also grateful to The Queen for allowing me access in 2004 to the then-restricted royal correspondence in the Baldwin Papers.

I am especially grateful to Her late Majesty Queen Elizabeth The Queen Mother, who received me in audience and took a great interest in my work on the archbishop who had crowned her in 1937. Almost Her Majesty's last words to me were an injunction to write to her if I had any further questions or wanted help.

I should like to take this opportunity to record my immense gratitude to the late Melanie Barber, who placed her detailed knowledge of the archives at Lambeth Palace Library at my disposal, and helped me to decipher Cosmo Lang's handwriting, which was not always an easy task. I should also like to express my thanks to all who have helped me with my research, answered my enquiries, or otherwise been of assistance: the Most Rev. and Right Hon. Dr Rowan Williams, Archbishop of Canterbury; the late Sir Alastair Aird, private secretary to HM Queen Elizabeth The Queen Mother; Miss Cressida Annesley, Canterbury Cathedral Archives; the Right Rev. Dom Aidan Bellenger OSB; Mr David Blake, Royal Army Chaplains' Department Museum; Lord Brownlow; Professor Arthur Burns; Miss Julia Burt; the late Lady Mairi Bury; the Right Rev. Lord Carey of Clifton; the Right Rev. John Cavell; Miss Pamela Clark, Royal Archives, Windsor; Dr David Crankshaw; Ms Jessica Cuthbert-Smith; Viscountess Downe; Lady Alethia Eliot; Dr Dominic Erdozain; the late Sir Edward Ford, assistant private secretary to HM King George VI; Miss Joanna Godfrey; Mr John Green-Wilkinson;

Miss Sharon Hamilton; Mr Robin Harcourt Williams; Mr David Hardy, Federal Bureau of Investigation; the late Earl of Harewood; the Right Rev. Christopher Hill; the late Canon Derek Ingram Hill; Mr Marcus Humphreys; the late Baron Jenkins of Hillhead; Dr Elisabeth Kehoe; Abbot Kyrill of the Community of St John the Baptist, Tolleshunt Knights; the Right Rev. Robert Ladds; Lord Londonderry; Mr David Malcolm; Sir John Maxwell Macdonald; Mr Peter Meadows, Cambridge University Library; Metropolitan Meliton of Philadelphia; the Right Rev. John Perry; Dr Colin Podmore; Herr Rudolf von Ribbentrop; Madame Francesca Roques; Mrs Celia Root; Sir Clive Rose; the Right Rev. Dr Geoffrey Rowell; Mr David Sellar, Lord Lyon King of Arms; Mr James and Mrs Gabrielle Service; the Rev. Dr Jeremy Sheehy; Mr Nicholas Shipman; the Rev. W.A. Simons; Dr Mark Smith; Dr Laurel Spooner; Ms Mari Takayanagi, House of Lords Archivist; Dr Alexander Taylor; Canon Garth Turner; Miss Louise Wardle; Mr Jeremy and Mrs Gudrun Warren; the Rev. Gordon Watkins; Mr Irvine Watson; Mrs Wendy White-Thompson; Professor Sir Colin St John Wilson; Canon Alan Wilkinson.

I should also like to thank the staff of the following institutions: Balliol College, Oxford; the Bodleian Library, Oxford; the Borthwick Institute, York; the British Library; Cambridge University Library; Canterbury Cathedral Archives; Churchill College Library, Cambridge; the Coddrington Library, All Souls College, Oxford; Colchester Library; Durham Cathedral Archives; Essex Record Office; the Institute for Historical Research, London; King's College London Library; Philip de László Catalogue Raisonné; Leeds University Library; Lincolnshire Record Office; The National Archives, Kew; the National Library of Scotland, Edinburgh; Norwich Cathedral Library; Pusey House, Oxford; Rhodes House, Oxford; Ripon College Cuddesdon Library; the Royal Archives, Windsor; University College London Library; University of London Library; the Wellcome Institute Library, London; Westminster Abbey Muniment Room. Above all, I should like to thank the staff of Lambeth Palace Library, London, for all their help, advice and encouragement.

*

Lastly, I should like to record my deep gratitude and appreciation of all the help, advice and encouragement so unfailingly afforded me by my parents and brother over the past seven years.

Robert Beaken

Great Bardfield, Essex

Note on Conventions

To avoid over-cluttering the text with notes, rather than having notes at the end of several consecutive sentences, I have tended to group references into one note. The references in each note appear in the order in which they are cited in the text.

When a book is cited in this work, the short-title system will be employed:
    At first reference:

    J.G. Lockhart, *Cosmo Gordon Lang* (London, 1949)

Thereafter:

    Lockhart, *Lang*

When the cited work is part of a collection of essays or articles, this convention is still observed, except that the title of the essay or article is marked with inverted commas:

    M. Barber, 'Randall Davidson: A Partial Retrospective', in S. Taylor (ed.), *From Cranmer to Davidson: A Church of England Miscellany* (Woodbridge, 2002)

Unless otherwise stated in the notes, all primary material cited in the work is from Lambeth Palace Library. When it is from another archive or in private possession, details are given in full in the note.

When a diary is cited for the first time, details of the diarist are given in full. Subsequently, only the diarist's surname is used. If the diary is not at Lambeth Palace Library, its location is then given:
First reference:

Diary of the Rev. A.C. Don, 18 July 1932

Thereafter:

Don, 18 July 1932

First reference:

Diary of May Ford, 29 June 1898: Family Papers of Sir Edward Ford

Thereafter:

Diary of May Ford, 29 June 1898

When an exchange of correspondence is cited, names and initials of the correspondents are given in full on the first occasion (except when the correspondents are Archbishop Lang and his chaplain the Rev. A.C. Don, who are simply referred to as Lang and Don); subsequently only the surname is used. This is followed by details of the location of the correspondence (unless it is at Lambeth Palace Library), and, if the papers have been catalogued, of the volume and folio number:
First reference:

Lang to Bishop J. Perry, 16 July 1940: LP, vol. 88, f. 29

Thereafter:

Lang to Perry: 18 July 1940: LP, vol. 88, 32

The following abbreviations have been used in the notes:

Bod.	Bodleian Library, Oxford
CUL	Cambridge University Library
IWM	Imperial War Museums
f.	folio
LP	Lang Papers
LPL	Lambeth Palace Library
ODNB	*Oxford Dictionary of National Biography*
MS	Manuscript
MSS	Manuscripts
TNA	The National Archives

The abbreviation *C.C.* for *Cosmo Cantuar:* was habitually used by the Rev. A.C. Don in his diary to refer to Archbishop Lang, and this usage has been retained in this book.

1

Introduction

SINCE HIS DEATH IN 1945, Cosmo Gordon Lang has not enjoyed a good reputation; indeed mention of him can sometimes spark off violent reactions. 'I HATE Cosmo Lang,' exclaimed one clergyman after a paper I delivered at the Institute of Historical Research. That clergyman was aged six when Lang retired, and his opinion seems to have been formed solely on the basis of J.G. Lockhart's 1949 biography of Lang and a couple of recent television programmes. Lang's long career was not unchequered or uncriticised. Hensley Henson, bishop of Durham, for example, had an odd relationship with Lang, and his criticisms of the archbishop in his diary have often been repeated. Lang also attracted much opprobrium with his remark about 'sacred memories' of the kaiser in 1914 and his broadcast at the time of Edward VIII's abdication in 1936. Yet, four years after Lang's death, his old doctor, who had known him intimately and was a member of the Church Assembly, insisted that he had been a good and saintly man, and W.R. Matthews, dean of St Paul's, wrote that if posterity understood the conditions of the time in which Lang lived, it would certainly say that Lang had been a great archbishop of Canterbury.[1] History has failed to be as generous towards Lang as his doctor and Dean Matthews. In the sixty years since Lang's death, his reputation has steadily declined. The clergyman at the seminar who hated Lang had come to hold an image of him as a snob, an appeaser, a repressed homosexual and an ineffectual spiritual leader.

From the point of view of his reputation, it was Lang's misfortune that his biography was not written by his chaplain Alan Don as he had wished, but by J.G. Lockhart. Lang's was a complex personality. Don, who had been in daily contact with him, might have been able to do him justice. Lockhart is not believed to have met Lang, did not have access to his official papers, and had a tendency sometimes to exaggerate or to simplify things for the sake of a good tale.[2] The result was a biography that might be described as fairly good but rather limited. Sixty-five years after his death, one criticises William Temple at one's peril, but the future judgement of history may prove to be that Temple was not quite such a flawlessly great archbishop of Canterbury as he has sometimes been portrayed, and that Lang was not nearly as bad as his reputation would imply.

The time is now ripe, twenty years after Lang's papers were first made available to the public, for a reappraisal of Lang and his archiepiscopate. Lang's was a difficult and torn personality, in turn sophisticated and simple, and very far from the cardboard figure he has so often been depicted as. This book will endeavour to get behind the layers of half-truth, misunderstanding and prejudice, and give Lang the fair hearing he deserves. Some of the myths that have circulated about him will be shown to be unsustainable. The truth as it emerges may be less dramatic than the myths, but it is far more interesting. Lang, like all men, was a mixture of good and bad. Some of the criticism aimed at him was richly deserved; some was not. The view that Lang represented the past, whilst Temple represented the future deserves to be challenged. In some ways, Lang was the first modern archbishop of Canterbury – for example, by making use of modern media such as radio and film – and with his finger in many ecclesiastical pies. Historians have unfairly overlooked Lang's long years of hard slog, much of it routine and unspectacular, simply to keep the Church of England going. Many of the issues with which he had to grapple remain live within the Church of England – for example, churchmanship and liturgy. If Lang was not quite the great archbishop of Canterbury envisaged by W.R. Matthews, he was at least a shrewd and hardworking occupant of the throne of St Augustine. Lang made mistakes and blunders, but he also enjoyed triumphs, and he successfully steered his rather complicated and sometimes mutinous Church through some very choppy waters.

This book examines Lang's ministry as archbishop of Canterbury in the Church of England between 1928 and 1942. Although reference will be made to his influence on foreign affairs, these are outside the scope of this book, but it is hoped they may be the subject of a subsequent work. As Lang's years at Canterbury were marked, more than those of most archbishops, by ecclesiastical, national and international crises, this book will examine in depth his handling of three of them: the crisis surrounding the abdication of Edward VIII in 1936, the ongoing crisis following the House of Commons' rejection of the Revised Prayer Book in 1928, and Lang's role during the Second World War until 1942.

The popular perception of Lang's role in the abdication of Edward VIII is that he was an uninvolved bystander until the end, when he intervened with a disastrous radio broadcast which appeared to be kicking a man when he was down. Lang was involved in the abdication of Edward VIII from a much earlier stage and pressured Stanley Baldwin, the prime minister, to ensure that the king abdicated in favour of his brother Albert ('Bertie'), who thereupon became George VI.

A crisis which rumbled on in the Church of England between the wars concerned Prayer Book reform, particularly after the Commons' rejection of the 1928 Revised Prayer Book. Adrian Hastings' view of Lang was critical:

> As Archbishop of Canterbury he provided no effective leadership for the Church in either its ecclesiastical or social dilemmas . . . Lang's response to the malaise of the Church was to do as little as possible: *après moi le déluge.* Hold on as long as possible to the way we have known it . . . Lang stood as a final sentinel to the *ancien régime.*[3]

In truth, Lang provided a very great deal of leadership during his years at Canterbury. Some of it was effective and some was not, but this was as much due to circumstances as to Lang. The image of him as a sentimental old buffer, resisting change, is so wide of the mark as to be a caricature. Lang was a pastoral archbishop, a shrewd judge of men and situations, with his finger on the pulse of parish life in his diocese and in the wider Church. His conversations with William Temple, archbishop of York, show that he was conscious of the problems of the future and of the danger of allowing the Church merely to drift.

Alan Wilkinson, writing about Lang's role during the Second World War, adopts a similarly critical view to Hastings:

> Archbishop Lang by contrast [with Temple] had nothing original left to say. He was too identified with appeasement. Almost 75 when the war broke out, he was old and tired. He represented an earlier age . . . By 1939 Lang had become an embarrassment.[4]

Lang may have represented an earlier age, but he had much left to say and he guided the Church well during the worst years of the Second World War. Lang responded with unexpected vigour and clarity to the new conditions thrown up by the war. The demands upon the archbishop of Canterbury, far from contracting, actually expanded under Lang during the war.

These three crises were very different from each other, but one theme running through all of them was the relationship of the Church of England to the state. Hastings has portrayed Lang as having a somewhat simplistic view of the establishment of the Church of England which it would have been too awkward to abandon. In fact, Lang had a far more subtle and nuanced understanding of the establishment and of the relationship of the Church to the Crown and state.[5] He believed himself to be the archbishop of a Christian country, albeit one in which the practice of Christianity had been 'crowded out' of many busy lives. He was not an Erastian in the sense that he thought the Church subservient to the state. He rather conceived of the Church as something like a partner – admittedly a junior partner – with the state in the life of the nation. Thus Lang felt justified in putting pressure on Baldwin to encourage the abdication of a king who, for a variety of reasons, he felt was unsuitable to occupy the throne. Lang further believed that the main priority of the Church of England was to maintain its ministry and the spiritual life of its people. If after 1928 this meant ignoring aspects of the Commons' rejection of the Revised Prayer Book, Lang was fully prepared to risk 'extra-legal' action and to weather the consequences. Likewise, although Lang firmly supported his country's cause during the Second World War, he was keen at times that there should be some distance between the Church and the state.

He did not wish the Church to emerge sullied and damaged from the conflict.

The Church of England under Lang was not some sort of ecclesiastical dinosaur, stuck doing the same old thing in much the same old way, whilst the forces of secularisation grew and gnawed away at the edges of its ecclesial life. Rather, the Church of England under Lang was a lively and dynamic organisation that sought to respond to the pressures of societal change on various levels, from the national to the parochial. Lang played a key part in this through his central role in the Church's administrative machinery, his balance of appointments to high office, his influence in Church and state, and in his daily work of untangling problems, keeping things running, and encouraging groups and individuals.

A major preoccupation during Lang's archiepiscopate was the clash of churchmanships and Lang's attempts to contain them and keep the Church of England going. Seen from a slightly different vantage point, the clash of churchmanships may be understood as the members of a complex and lively Church seeking how best they might engage with, and minister to, contemporary English society, with different Anglicans tugging away in different directions. Anglo-Catholics stressed the Eucharist and an associated *cultus* not merely because they drew inspiration from contemporary Roman Catholicism, but because they believed this to be normative Catholic worship and a means whereby they could reach out to people and make them holy. Evangelicals and more Protestant-minded Anglicans objected to Anglo-Catholic practices, not merely because they saw them as Romish mummery which undermined Reformation principles and the national Church, but because they believed that preaching the pure Word of God was the best way to evangelise the nation. Modernists contended that the best means of reaching contemporary, scientifically minded men and women was through a version of Christianity purged of the 'superstitious' and miraculous.

The Church of England during Lang's archiepiscopate was a Church in transition. It was still woven into the fabric of English society in the 1930s in much the same way that it had been in 1918. Yet there was a gradual unravelling of that social fabric, with many people falling away from the practice of Christianity. Lang recognised this development, which is one reason why, for example, he was a keen supporter of parish preaching missions whilst at York. As archbishop of Canterbury, Lang felt that there was still a widespread instinct of religious faith amongst the people of England, and from time to time he called upon them in sermons and events such as the 1937 Recall to Religion to give expression to that faith by churchgoing. Yet, it would be a mistake to picture the Church of England in the 1930s as panicking or sliding consciously into doom and gloom. Numbers of Easter communicants peaked at the start of Lang's archiepiscopate, and other statistics indicated that the Church was holding its own, or at least declining only very slowly. If Lang had to appeal for vocations to ordination, it is significant that in the aftermath of an economic depression he had no doubts about the ability of his Church to pay the stipends of more clergy.

What light will this reassessment of Lang's archiepiscopate shed on the question of the place of the Church of England in the 1930s and early 1940s? We shall see that, during Lang's time at Canterbury, the archbishopric *mattered* in England. On one level, Lang dealt on a daily basis with the nation's governing elite. A conversation or a letter to the right government minister or civil servant often got a problem cleared up, and they were often pleased to receive Lang's support and approbation. In 1936 pressure from Lang upon Stanley Baldwin successfully helped ensure the abdication of Edward VIII. It is harder to judge what ordinary people thought of the archbishopric, because unless they wrote diaries or letters, their views and opinions seldom survive. However, there is some evidence to show that the archbishopric still mattered to many ordinary people, whether they were churchgoers or not. A local newspaper, to take one example, printed a verbatim report of Lang's lunchtime address to their local rotarians rather than a brief summary, which indicates at the very least that they thought him good 'copy'. The files at Lambeth show that parishioners complaining about their vicar or bishop, conscientious objectors suffering ill-treatment, government ministers planning wartime regulations, and even German Jewish emigrés all turned to Lang in the expectation of help. Indeed, the scope of his archiepiscopal ministry actually expanded during the Second World War. Similarly, the furore over Lang's abdication broadcast is explicable not just in terms of what was said about Edward VIII, but because it was said by the archbishop of Canterbury. At the very least, all this was a recognition of the significance of the great and ancient office that Lang occupied. On another level, it was a recognition of the spiritual, pastoral and teaching role of the archbishop, and thus implicitly of Christianity itself. Those people in England who believed they did not have to go to church to be good Christians still related to the archbishop of Canterbury and felt they could turn to him in trouble or perplexity. They also believed they could fittingly criticise him. The archbishop evidently was not ignored by those outside his flock. As we shall see, Lang was an important figure in 1930s Britain.

2

From Fyvie to Lambeth: The Making of an Archbishop

WILLIAM COSMO GORDON LANG, THE second son of the Rev. Dr John Marshall Lang and Hannah Lang, was born on 31 October 1864 at Fyvie, a remote village in Aberdeenshire. John Lang had gone there in 1859 as the Church of Scotland minister after over-working himself in Aberdeen. Lang's first few hours were not easy: 'Puir wee lamb, it'll be a mercy if the Lord takes him,' remarked the nurse at his birth, but Lang survived and was duly baptised 'William Cosmo Gordon' after the local laird, Colonel William Cosmo Gordon. 'William' appears to have been an oversight by the officiating Church of Scotland minister, and Lang later dropped it, though it reappeared from time to time on official documents such as Letters of Orders.[1]

Cosmo Lang was descended on both sides from Church of Scotland ministers in Lanarkshire. His ancestors also included the occasional merchant, surgeon and small property-owner. Lang's forebears were not minor Scottish gentry, like the family of Archbishop Randall Davidson, but were from the growing Scottish middle class. One can speculate about some of the values of this class that a son of the manse such as Lang may have imbibed: an emphasis on respectability and hard work, a high regard for education, a belief in 'getting on' in life, a serious approach to religion, and frugality to ensure every shilling went a long way. Lang retained what Scots sometimes call a *keen* streak all his life.

Shortly after Lang's birth, John Lang returned to more strenuous parish work in Anderston, Glasgow, and then in 1868 moved to Morningside, Edinburgh. Here, Lang showed the first signs of a vivid imagination:

The world I remember is the garden – the trees behind which robber-knights were stalked and slain; the earth under a shrub where on a cold day, unknown to all I sat, self-stripped, indulging in all the pathos of a beggar-child; the bundle of sticks on which I stood enduring the fancied flames as a Christian martyr; the great black roaring cat, who was to me the Devil walking about seeking whom he might devour – I can see him now, stealthy and sinister, creeping along the wall – at whom I threw every missile of fervent and pious wrath. In all that world I reigned supreme, fancy free . . . These were the years, never to be repeated, when I was master of my own realm, the glorious realm of imagination, the 'land of make believe'.[2]

In 1873, when Lang was nine, his father returned to Glasgow to be minister of the Barony Church, and the family lived at 5 Woodlands Terrace. Lang had an older brother, Patrick, and five younger siblings, Douglas, Marshall, Hannah, Norman and David. In later years, Lang used to like to tell the dramatic tale of the rise of the boy from 5 Woodlands Terrace to Lambeth Palace, but in truth the family were more comfortably off in Glasgow than Lang's story-telling might imply. John Lang's stipend was £900, two or three times the stipend of a Church of England incumbent, and he was later granted a coat of arms.[3]

John Lang's ministry during these years had a great influence upon his son. The Barony Church, Glasgow under John Lang had twenty-one elders, 2,098 members on the Communion Roll, 1,290 children in the Sunday School, 310 young people in Guilds, and eighty-four Bible Class scholars. It is interesting to note, in the light of Lang's later development, that his father was a much-admired preacher and was suspected of high church liturgical practices.[4]

Lang attended Park School, a day school, in Glasgow. Here, the schoolboy with a vivid imagination was a bit of a loner. John Lang was academically minded and both parents pushed their children.[5] Fortunately, Cosmo Lang showed signs of great promise. He entered Glasgow University aged fourteen in 1878 and in 1881 obtained his Glasgow MA. He then tried to secure a place at an English university. The senior tutor at King's College, Cambridge, commented: 'You really should try to improve your handwriting. I had great difficulty in making out much that you wrote, and the fault will stand in your way considerably if you do not mend it.'[6]

To the regret of historians, Lang's handwriting never did improve. His weakness in mathematics precluded a place at King's College, Cambridge, where he would have had to pass an examination in mathematics as part of the tripos, so he secured a place at Balliol College, Oxford, where there was no such requirement. Lang's parents and grandmother scrimped to pay his fees and he went up in October 1882 to read Greats (Classics). Lang won the prestigious Brackenbury Scholarship in his first term and this success, combined with a newfound freedom, went to his head. He neglected his studies, joined various Oxford clubs, spoke often in the Oxford Union and played rugby. The crash came following his examinations in 1884 with a postcard sent to Scotland, 'Sir, you have got a Second.' Lang thought he had ruined his life.[7] He set to with a will and the next year sat the examination in Modern History. This time, he obtained a very good First.

ORDINATION

Lang travelled in Germany after Oxford, and spent the summer of 1887 studying German at Göttingen University. When challenged one day to fight a duel by some Prussian students, Lang named a horsewhip as his weapon, and the challenge petered out.[8] Despite this incident, Lang enjoyed his few weeks at Göttingen, and returned there briefly on holiday in 1888, but his visits to Germany appear to have had no lasting influence on him.

In the autumn of 1887 Lang began to read for the Bar and was taken into the London chambers of W.S. Robson. In 1888, on his second attempt, he obtained a fellowship of All Souls College, Oxford. A distinguished career in the law beckoned (indeed Asquith once told Bishop Winnington-Ingram that if Lang had stuck to this profession he would have become a judge) but in the spring of 1889 Lang's plans were disarrayed by the growing conviction that God had given him a vocation to ordination in the Church of England. Lockhart rather oversimplifies this in his biography for the sake of a good tale, but Lang's own notes – allowing for a dramatic streak – suggest that this discovery was long, complex and difficult.[9] In the late nineteenth century it must have taken great strength of character to leave the Church of Scotland for the Church of England. Lang's parents were troubled by this change in their son's plans and his mother was particularly anxious about his acceptance of the eucharistic Real Presence. In the end, Lang's father appears to have accepted his son's vocation more easily and completely than did his mother.[10]

After Presbyterianism, Lang was attracted not to Anglican evangelicalism but to Anglo-Catholicism. The Anglo-Catholicism Lang encountered in the late 1880s and early 1890s was a vibrant and growing force within the Church of England. It principally expressed itself through more careful and sacramental worship and spirituality. There was also a strong social concern amongst Anglo-Catholics, whose parishes were frequently to be found in poorer districts. Anglo-Catholics such as Stewart Headlam and James Adderley, moved by concern for the poor, founded Christian socialist organisations such as the Guild of St Matthew (1887) and the Christian Social Union (1889). Anglo-Catholicism also inspired the revival of the religious life, and by the 1880s nuns and even the occasional friar or monk belonging to Anglican communities were to be encountered in the Church of England.

Liturgically, Anglo-Catholicism was continuously evolving. In most Anglo-Catholic churches in the 1880s and 1890s the celebrant at the Eucharist usually wore only a surplice and a coloured stole, but simple vesture and a restrained ceremonial was accompanied by a high view of the sacrament. By the end of the nineteenth century, some Anglo-Catholics had begun to find inspiration in late-medieval English and north European Catholicism.[11] The early years of the twentieth century saw a further evolution in Anglo-Catholicism with the development of a group who looked to contemporary continental Roman Catholicism and to Rome for an example. Dom Anselm Hughes OSB[12] and subsequent historians have tended to stress the difference between the two groups, but there is anecdotal evidence that the boundaries were blurred, and that many early twentieth-century and inter-war Anglo-Catholic clergy and parishes borrowed freely from both traditions. There can be no doubt, however, that the group that was inspired by

contemporary continental Catholic practice and looked increasingly to
Rome for an example formed the vanguard of Anglo-Catholicism from
about 1910.

This, though, was never the Anglo-Catholicism of Lang. He later
recalled that he had once experienced a vivid dream of Cardinal
Newman urging him to travel in a third-class railway carriage, but
he overcame this solitary incident of Roman fever and seems never to
have been troubled by it again.[13] He remained a gentle, restrained 1890s
Anglo-Catholic all his life. His Anglo-Catholicism seems neither to have
increased nor decreased when he became a bishop and later archbishop.

In June 1889, Lang was confirmed by Bishop Edward King, in time to
commence at Cuddesdon Theological College in Oxfordshire in August.
Cuddesdon entered Lang's life in a similar way to All Souls: he used to
refer to it sometimes as 'my Mecca' and in later years as an archbishop
would try to spend Holy Week there, where his humility attracted the
attention of the ordinands.[14] Lang was ordained a deacon in Cuddesdon
Parish Church by Bishop William Stubbs of Oxford on 1 June 1890, on
the title of his fellowship. He was ordained a priest in the Church of St
Mary the Virgin, Reading, on 24 May 1891. Lang almost returned to All
Souls as chaplain and bursar, but in the end he decided he needed to leave
Oxford and accepted a curacy at Leeds Parish Church in Yorkshire. The
vicar was Edward Talbot, formerly warden of Keble College, Oxford,
who had a great influence upon Lang over the next three years and
nudged him in the direction of 'modern [Biblical] criticism joined with
equal insistence upon Catholic tradition and practice'.[15]

Talbot's daughter May kept a diary continuously between 1887 and
1932, and the entries for 1891–92 (when she was 'fifteen and three-
quarters') paint a fascinating picture of Lang preaching sternly, singing
carols, visiting schools, taking part in parish entertainments and carrying
out all the duties of a curate. Lang seems to have enjoyed May's company:
they played tennis together, went boating and on walks, had tea and
supper, and he daringly showed her his room in the clergy house, which
she pronounced 'very cosy'. Her son, Sir Edward Ford, believes that his
mother fell a little in love 'with this dark, handsome Scotsman' and in
later life their friendship meant much to Lang. During his three years
in Leeds, Lang worked hard in the parish and gained the reputation of

being the most eloquent and influential of all Talbot's curates. They were amongst the happiest years of his life.[16]

During this time Lang began to be approached with offers of other posts. In June 1893 Sir Herbert Warren, the president of Magdalen College, Oxford, unexpectedly invited him to become the college's dean of divinity. He accepted after a struggle, but left Leeds feeling very low. Lang turned out to be quite a success at Magdalen. In 1894, he was also appointed vicar of the University Church of St Mary, where he tried to revive the worship and was conscious of treading in Newman's footsteps.[17] He later reflected upon this period of his life:

> But alas! All this work, together with my duties at Magdalen, finally knocked out all my hopes for systematic study. I shall never cease to regret this failure. No such opportunity has ever come again: and I have always deplored my lack of a basis of real theological learning. It is useless to complain – one has not wholly the ordering of one's own life. But this lack of real knowledge of the habit of concentrated study and thought, of the discipline of the mind and memory have made much of my work slight and superficial, and remains as one of the many reasons which force me to realize how ill-equipped I am for the great offices which have come to me. It is pathetic to remember that I had intended at Oxford to write a book on the Mind of St Paul and had actually entered into a contract with Rivingtons for its publication. But I could never make any headway with it and had finally to ask the publishers to release me.[18]

In 1896, Lang accepted First Lord of the Treasury A.J. Balfour's offer of the parish of Portsea in Hampshire. As it had been in Leeds, this departure was a struggle. Portsea was a complete contrast to Magdalen. Lang found himself the vicar of a parish of 40,000 people with six churches and a staff of fourteen curates, mostly all living in one clergy house with a single lavatory. Discipline had been rather lax under the previous incumbent, Edgar Jacob. All that changed with Lang, who expected high standards of others as of himself. Curates were recruited from a variety of churchmanships, though the parish itself was very gently catholic. Lang initiated a daily Eucharist and opened an oratory in the clergy house, but forbade the wearing of cassocks in the streets. Lang soon became known as 'a live wire', preaching courses of sermons to ever-increasing congregations and conducting men's conferences and large Bible study classes.[19] There are echoes in Lang's Portsea ministry of his father's ministry at the Barony Church. It was during this period that he was invited to visit Queen Victoria at Osborne House on the Isle of Wight, beginning a life-long connection with the British royal family.

BISHOP OF STEPNEY

In March 1901 Lord Salisbury offered the thirty-six-year-old Lang the suffragan see of Stepney and a canonry of St Paul's Cathedral. This preferment originated with A.F. Winnington-Ingram, the previous bishop of Stepney, who apparently accepted the see of London on the condition that Lang were offered Stepney. Lang consulted Randall Davidson, bishop of Winchester, but there was never any doubt that he would accept. He moved into 2 Amen Court and was consecrated a bishop by Archbishop Frederick Temple in St Paul's on 1 May 1901.

Lang was immediately confronted with an immense task. As bishop of Stepney, he had care of 208 parishes, staffed by 550 clergy, who ministered amongst a population of 670,000 people. Unlike Portsea, which had a stable population, Lang soon discovered that the East End of London had a fluctuating population, which often lived in the depths of poverty and degradation. An immense gulf existed between the Church and the bulk of the population. According to Bell, Lang brought an 'extraordinary vivacity . . . and zest' to the East End. He travelled largely by bus and worked hard to understand his parishes and their problems. He later recalled that he was always impressed by the cheerful patience of the East Enders, but added that at times 'it almost *hurt* to go into the West End' and see the contrast. He concluded, in the face of so many problems, that the only thing for the Church to do was simply to 'carry on'. He played a central role in the formation of the Church of England Men's Society, believing it would help ordinary working Christian men. In these years Lang's reputation grew further as a preacher; indeed, he had to stomp the country preaching sermons to raise money for the

East London Church Fund. In 1905, he published *The Opportunity of the Church of England: Lectures Delivered in the Divinity School of the University of Cambridge in 1904*, in which he described the problems of the poor and the ways in which they might be helped, and tried to stir up vocations to ordination.[20]

ARCHBISHOP OF YORK

Lang proved to be a very successful bishop of Stepney. In November 1908 he was startled to receive a letter from the prime minister, H.H. Asquith:

> I have the great pleasure of proposing to you that you should be nominated for election to the Archbishopric of York, which will become vacant at the end of the year. It is not without careful consideration of the claims of others, and of possible criticism on the ground of your not having administered a diocese as its responsible head, that I have come to the conclusion that you are the best man for the post. I think it of highest importance that the Primacy of the northern Province should be held by one whose Churchmanship is beyond suspicion, and who at the same time possesses the advantage of comparative youth, of fresh and vital contact with the people, of accessibility to and frank sympathy with new social ideals, and of a broad outlook upon the large and growing area of questions where the interests and activities of Church and State are intermixed.[21]

Lang saw Asquith and consulted Davidson and Winnington-Ingram. On 12 November 1908, he wrote to Asquith allowing his name to be sent to the king. Lang was forty-four.[22]

In his biography, Lockhart chronicled the applause which greeted Lang's elevation and described his enthronement on 25 January 1909. At no point, however, did he explain the meteoric rise of the suffragan bishop of Stepney to become the second figure in the Church of England. Lockhart ignored information on the subject furnished by George Bell. Similarly, in 1950 Don also ignored information supplied by Bell for an entry about Lang for the *Dictionary of National Biography*.[23] As chaplain to Davidson, Bell was well informed and had access to many sources. He recorded that he understood that Asquith had appointed Lang because the prime minister felt that the Church was in for a difficult time during the next twenty years, including possible disestablishment, 'and it was most important that York should have a man of great strength and vitality who would cope with the Church's problems for a great number of years'. Bell also mentioned, 'you might also refer to the outstanding impression this young, black-haired Bishop of Stepney made on the fathers of the Lambeth Conference in 1908.' Lang presumably had his backers – Asquith, for example, would hardly have nominated him in the teeth of opposition from Davidson or other senior figures – but I have failed to find any trace of them. Asquith, like Lang, was a Balliol man, and the two may have known each other via the college. It is probable that Lang's preaching made him better known than many other suffragan bishops; he had connections through his fellowship of All Souls College; and it was recognised in southern clerical circles that Lang was a great help to the unworldly Winnington-Ingram. Not for nothing did a 1906 issue of *Vanity Fair* contain a Spy cartoon of Lang, captioned 'A Bishop of Decision'.[24]

When Lang arrived in York, the bishops of Liverpool (Francis Chavasse) and Manchester (Edmund Knox) were staunch Evangelicals. The bishops of Newcastle (Edgar Jacob), Ripon (William Boyd Carpenter) and Wakefield (George Eden) were of broad churchmanship. The northern province contained no Tractarian or Anglo-Catholic bishops, unlike the southern province, where Edward King and Charles Gore were the bishops of Lincoln and Birmingham. Lang's arrival was awaited with some apprehension and there were anti-ritualistic Kensitite demonstrations outside York Minster before his enthronement. In the event he wore convocation robes rather than a cope and mitre – which he quietly introduced later on – and this sartorial sensitivity was emblematic of the tactful way in which Lang dealt with all shades of churchmanship. With time, he won the support and trust of the clergy and bishops; perhaps not the least of Lang's achievements is that he made Anglo-Catholic churchmanship more widely acceptable.[25]

The papers and correspondence which survive at York from Lang's day paint a picture of a busy man who was first and foremost a diocesan bishop, taking interest in the minutiae of parish life, appointments, educational work, charitable appeals and so on.[26] Lang again tried hard to get to know all the parts of his diverse diocese and to visit all 465 parishes. He was the first archbishop of York to go down a coal mine. He tried to break the terrible isolation of many clergy through visits, quiet days, invitations to meals and children's birthday parties at Bishopthorpe, his archiepiscopal palace. The knowledge that a young and enthusiastic archbishop might descend on the sleepiest parish apparently had quite a revitalising effect. Lang found that his clergy were badly underpaid and he did what he could to increase stipends. Lang was also anxious to encourage the highest standards of priestly ministry, to foster vocations to ordination and to encourage lay work.[27]

Early in his archiepiscopate, Lang realised that the York diocese was too unwieldy, and he was instrumental in the creation of a separate diocese of Sheffield in 1914. He was further involved in the creation of the dioceses of Bradford in 1920 and Blackburn in 1926.[28]

Bell believed that one of Lang's more noteworthy accomplishments in these years was to improve the relationship between the archbishops of Canterbury and York which had previously been 'courteous and polite rather than completely co-operative'. Archbishop and Mrs Davidson gave Lang two rooms at Lambeth Palace, and for twenty years he was almost a member of their family. The two primates spent a week together at Canterbury each January and made a point of meeting before each of the three annual bishops' meetings, when they would talk over the items on the agenda and 'a hundred other things as well'.[29] Davidson would also ask Lang to travel to Lambeth or Canterbury when a special problem arose. Bell contrasted the two thus:

> When Davidson met conferences of Free Churchmen and tried to find a solution of the educational religious problem, he would open the proceedings by explaining to the company the difficulties of the situation with his own constituency and invite their help. He then let them do all the talking – but in the end got out of them the lines of the solution on which he himself had

determined. When Lang held similar conferences (he then being at Canterbury) he did all the talking and propounded his solution at the start. He was the cleverer and academically the abler man; but though much trusted at the end, he lacked the sympathy of his elder and the elder's capacity for winning as much as could be won from the other side.[30]

Lang was profoundly grateful for Davidson's help and later recalled: 'I can never be sufficiently thankful for those twenty years during which I watched him at work and for his goodness and generosity to me, for the lessons I learned from his mind and above all from his character.'[31] Davidson tended to select chaplains and then to groom them for high office and he may similarly have been preparing Lang to succeed him at Canterbury.

Lang was with Davidson at Lambeth on 4 August 1914 when war was declared. The conflict appears to have brought the two men closer together. Lang was Davidson's right-hand man and helped him deal with difficult issues such as wartime prayers, the ban on combatant service for the clergy and negotiations about National Service and the clergy. In 1915, at the request of Admiral Jellicoe, Lang spent ten days with the Grand Fleet and in 1917 he made a similar visit to the Western Front. Lang played a central role in the 1916 National Mission of Repentance and Hope, the Church of England's wartime campaign to evangelise the nation. In 1918, he went to the United States of America at the request of the Foreign Office and conducted a lengthy preaching and speaking tour. Throughout the war, he remained 'in intimate touch' with many of the bereaved in his diocese.[32]

The war took its toll on Lang: in 1914 an unwise reference to a 'sacred memory' of the kaiser (kneeling beside Queen Victoria's coffin) in a speech of an hour and fifty minutes about the aims of the war was taken out of context by the press and brought Lang a deluge of opprobrium. As a result of stress, he aged prematurely, much of his hair fell out and what remained turned white.[33]

Lang was aged fifty-four at the Armistice in 1918. Post-war reconstruction kept him busy and he played an important role in the 1920 Lambeth Conference, where he secured the 'Appeal to All Christian

People' for reunion. In the post-war years, Lang took a great interest in the Cathedrals Commission, the report on ecclesiastical courts, and was obliged to take an interest in Prayer Book revision. In 1927, Lang presided over the celebrations marking the thirteen-hundredth anniversary of York Minster.[34] There is, however, a sense when reading Lang's papers from the 1920s in the Borthwick Institute in York that if he was not exactly stale or stuck in a groove, he was sometimes close to it. His most exciting work at York had been between 1908 and 1914, when he was in his forties. Lang still carried out important work, but as he entered his sixties he began to flag a little and lost some of his previous zest.[35]

APPOINTMENT TO CANTERBURY

A few weeks after Parliament's second rejection of the Revised Prayer Book in 1928, the eighty-year-old Davidson announced his resignation as archbishop of Canterbury. The choice of a successor lay with the prime minister, Stanley Baldwin. Davidson pulled strings to try to ensure that he was succeeded by Lang.[36] In fact, Baldwin was already thinking of Lang as a potential successor, as he had made clear to Lord Irwin, the viceroy of India, in 1927:

> I think it not unlikely that I shall have to find a new Archbishop before I go out. I should value your views very much. The Court will probably press for York. Of course it would be the line of least resistance. York to Canterbury, Oxford to York. Oxford might do for Canterbury. I shall rule out every Bishop who appeared with the Industrial Christian Fellowship during the Coal Strike, because not to see what Cook was denotes a lack of that wisdom essential for the position. There is no obvious man.[37]

I have not managed to trace Irwin's reply, but the Anglo-Catholic viceroy and son of the second Viscount Halifax, president of the English Church Union, was unlikely to oppose Lang's candidacy. By 1928, Baldwin must have become convinced that Lang was the right man for the job, for he arrived at Lambeth Palace the day after the announcement of Davidson's retirement and told Lang, 'It is inevitable.

I won't hear of any refusal. You are the only man. Your one and only duty is to say "Yes" at once before I leave.'[38] At Lang's urging, William Temple was translated from Manchester to York. It was an inspired move: in temperament and age, Temple balanced Lang and both men got on extremely well. Temple visited Lang at his house at Ballure, in the Scottish Highlands, in the late summer of 1928, where both men knelt in prayer in Lang's oratory, the Cell, and vowed to do their utmost to serve the people of the Church of England. Something of Lang's attitude towards his translation to Canterbury is revealed in his reply to a letter from Dick Sheppard, who had evidently wished for a more exciting appointment to Canterbury:

> When I saw a letter in your handwriting lying among the hundreds which are crowding my table, I opened it with special interest, not only because of my love for you, but because I wanted to see whether you had been able to bear with Christian fortitude the appointment of an Archbishop so different from the one you had in your dreams beheld.
>
> I am sorry that I cannot play the part of the new St Francis or Savonarola; but I did not choose myself, and when the choice came from those who had the right to make it, I could not refuse, could I?, merely because I did not answer to the Archbishop of your dreams? So you will have to make the best of it!
>
> After all I think I have some invincible youth hiding within me, and a late lark singing; and I look to you and others to keep me in touch with youth and spring. Anyhow, I know I shall have your prayers, and that they will be given the more earnestly because, as no one knows better than I do, I fall so far short of what the great trust at the present time demands. I send you my heart-felt thanks for your letter, and my love and blessing.[39]

After twenty years, Lang found it a wrench to leave the north and particularly the gardens at Bishopthorpe.[40] Lang was confirmed as archbishop of Canterbury at Bow Church, Cheapside, and subsequently enthroned at Canterbury on 4 December 1928, though the illness of King George V somewhat marred the celebrations.

LANG'S PERSONALITY

What was the character or personality of this ninety-seventh archbishop of Canterbury? Lockhart described him as 'a strangely unintegrated person, a jangle of warring personalities which never really reached a working agreement among themselves . . . at the dinner-table for example, a click could almost be heard as one Lang went off and another came on.'[41]

Lockhart has exaggerated Lang's character in order to weave the strands of his book to a conclusion, but there is more than a grain of truth behind this overstatement. Lang's was a complex personality and the basic fault line was caught unintentionally in the naive entries in May Talbot's diary in the early 1890s. Having recorded Lang's hard work amongst the poor of Leeds, she went on to record a family holiday in Oxford. One day 'Mr Lang turned up, quite bright and very much in his element.' He took May to lunch and tea with prominent academics, showed her around some colleges and they went punting.[42]

The two sides to Lang's character which pulled him in different directions throughout his life were his deep Christian faith and desire to serve the Church and the poor, and his ambitious streak, which knew he had gifts and wanted to use them to get on. Lang had a powerful, over-riding sense of duty and discipline. He was personally very frugal and for years slept on an old bed that he had used in Leeds – one without a mattress and with a blanket thrown over the springs – until his chaplains at Bishopthorpe sneakily replaced it.[43] It should also be remembered that Lang was a clever Scotsman from a home where much emphasis was placed on academic success.

There can be no doubt that Lang was also ambitious. In his youth, he wrote an imaginary entry in *Who's Who* (see Appendix 1), which is a record of unparalleled success ending with himself as prime minister. At Portsea, he once penned a spoof archiepiscopal signature at a staff meeting, and the curates noticed he enjoyed the company of important people and was determined to climb to the top.[44] One may speculate that Lang's inner drive to attain high office in the Church may have stemmed from a need to demonstrate that his conversion to Anglicanism and ordination had been right.

Lang possessed great gifts and great flaws; often they appear to have been two sides of the same coin. Sir Lewis Dibdin, dean of the Arches, described him as very 'self-sufficient', and Don – also from Scotland – called him 'an undemonstrative Scot' and observed that he could be strangely detached. Lang sometimes gave an impression of effortless superiority, though Don believed this was far from true and discovered that he liked people to stand up to him.[45] Ian White-Thomson, Lang's last chaplain, recorded that he was struck by Lang's humility, especially in Lambeth Palace chapel early in the mornings. Lang was never heard to swear or to tell a risqué story. He had great charm and a gentle sense of humour, often telling funny stories against himself. Everyone who knew Lang to whom I have spoken has talked, quite unbidden, of his kindess. Lang was a pastorally minded bishop and would arrive, unannounced, on vicarage doorsteps when he learnt that any of his clergy had problems or illnesses. He would discretely meet in Oxford senior clergy with problems. Significantly, apart from one lapse in 1891, Lang is not recorded as saying anything caustic or gossipy in any of the diaries or papers which I have examined. Lockhart never mentions this and perhaps it never occurred to him to do so.[46]

Lang could also be a bit odd at times. White-Thomson noted that he had a shy streak which would sometimes break through during refreshments after parochial services. When Lang climbed into his car, he would switch off the light in the back to avoid being observed. He hated being surprised by press photographers, being fussed over, and any celebration of his birthday. Lang long suffered from what he called 'surface irritation' – 'this is *intolerable!*' was his usual exclamation – and this was often directed at his housemaid Martha Saville, who by all accounts was a bit of a trial. He sometimes appeared grumpy in public, particularly when something went wrong during a service. Another of Lang's foibles as he aged was a hatred of novelties, staff changes or anything that threatened his established routine. He learnt to type, but never mastered a fountain pen. He did not go to a cinema until 1935, and when Don and his wife took Lang to see a film in 1939 he complained about the accompanying Disney cartoon, 'What a waste of my time.'[47]

Lang's vivid boyhood imagination remained with him all his life.[48] In 1895, he rather improbably published a romantic novel, *The*

Young Clanroy, a tale of the 1745 Jacobite rebellion of the boy-meets-girl, loses-girl, gets-girl variety. He could be dramatic about himself and enjoyed wrapping things up in a good story. For instance, Lang described his dog, James, who accompanied him to church in Portsea and was 'addicted to pious practices' until Lang forbade him to enter the vicarage oratory.

> This was the end of James's Church life. Deprived of Church privileges . . . he took to evil ways. He would vanish for days and return from these orgies 'smelling 'orrid' and with bloodshot eyes. As he was no longer fit company in a vicarage, I banished him to the country, to Norfolk, and there, alas! he ended his days as a victorious fighter and poacher.[49]

The truth is more prosaic: the dog James went because Lang was too busy to take him for walks.[50] From time to time, Lang let his tongue run away with him. Lang's biggest oratorical error before he went to Canterbury was his 'sacred memory' speech during the Great War, but he still occasionally exaggerated things for the sake of a good sentence. In 1935, for example, he told the Church Assembly that he had received many messages from all over the world about Italian aggression in Abyssinia. A dismayed Don confided in his diary that Lang had merely received half a dozen messages from Europe:

> All over the world, indeed! His habit of hyperbole was never more glaringly displayed! I wish he wouldn't exaggerate in this way – it gives a false impression of what he is doing – and one of these days he will be caught out![51]

Lang had a slightly snobbish streak, which Lockhart attempts to exculpate.[52] Archbishops must move amongst the important, the powerful, and the leaders of society. The intellectual and romantic Lang seems sometimes to have enjoyed this a bit too much. But he was aware of this failing: he himself nicknamed his annual journey to Ballure via several stately homes the 'Snob's Progress'. His snobbery, though it may offend modern sensibilities, was arguably only a minor foible rather than a guiding principle, and should be viewed against the background of a more highly class-conscious society. Lang never talked-up his own middle-class roots.[53] It should also be remembered that he twice left the congenial surroundings of Oxford to work amongst the poor in Leeds and Portsea, and his book *The Opportunity of the Church of England* (1905) reveals a close understanding of their problems. Lang's maiden speech in the House of Lords in 1909 was in support of Lloyd George's reforming Finance Bill. In his earlier years he had a great rapport with the poor – in 1912 a working man once cycled thirty miles from Leeds to hear him preach and shake his hand – and throughout Lang's years at Canterbury, former parishioners from Leeds would visit him annually at Lambeth. In the 1930s, Lang spoke in the Church Assembly and House of Lords about social problems, and Sir Edward Ford remembers him being concerned about the unemployed, but not being quite sure what he could do to help them.[54]

Although Lang had a spell as a don at Magdalen College, he could not really be called a professional academic or theologian. The three books he published whilst at Stepney are perfectly competent, but they are collections of sermons or addresses rather than works of systematic theology.[55] Lang's greatest gift lay in what would have been his career had his vocation to ordination not arisen: the law and advocacy. He remained something of a canny Scots lawyer all his life, with a penetrating mind which went straight to the heart of a problem or issue and then worked out how to deal with it, writing letters in plain and unambiguous English; there are no replies at Lambeth seeking elucidation because he had not made himself clear. His opinion and aid was sought by George V and George VI, prime ministers and government ministers not simply because he was the archbishop of Canterbury, but because of his intellect and gift with words. For these reasons, he was invited in 1933 to sit on a joint committee on the Indian constitution. Lang was also a shrewd judge of character and a good administrator. He possessed both physical and moral courage and if he believed something was wrong, he would say so. Lang's shortcoming was that he was a workaholic who did not find it easy to delegate and never took a day off.[56]

Lang's other great gift was as a preacher and speaker. He was perhaps slightly better as an after-dinner speaker; Don used to remark that it was just like turning on a tap, but even he, who knew all Lang's oratorical skills, was still impressed from time to time by what he heard. Although physically small, Lang had an impressive presence with 'eyes like a hawk's and a voice like a bell'.[57]

SPIRITUALITY

What inspired or motivated Lang? Apart from his journals at Ballure, Lang kept no daily prayer diary, nor did he speak much about his hidden life of prayer, but it is possible to reconstruct a little of his spiritual life and outlook. Lang came from a Presbysterian background and this appears to have left a lasting impression upon him. All his life, Lang retained a strong sense of sin, and during his annual trips to Ballure he spent much time examining his conscience and listing his sins. After becoming an Anglican, he made use of sacramental Confession. From Lang's sermons, it is clear that he had a deep knowledge and love of the Bible, and this too can probably be traced back to his Scottish childhood. Lang frequently made use of poetry in preaching, and it may be surmised that poetry meant much to him.[58]

The picture of Lang's spiritual life that may be discerned from Don's diaries is very much that of someone who at heart was a gentle, prayerful and unfussy Anglo-Catholic. Lang said Mattins and Evensong each day with his chaplains. He also had a daily Eucharist in the chapel, and it is clear that he believed the Eucharist to be the highest form of Christian worship, but Lang's preference appears to have been for quiet and prayerful celebrations. He celebrated the Eucharist at 8 a.m. in Canterbury Cathedral on many Sundays, and he is recalled celebrating in the Cell at Ballure clad simply in a linen rochet.[59] His eucharistic spirituality meant that he would have understood the liturgical concerns of a later generation of Anglo-Catholics after Parliament's rejection of the 1928 Prayer Book, even if they were not quite his own. Lang does not appear to have had any great devotion to the Blessed Virgin Mary, though he turned a blind eye to complaints about the revived shrine at Walsingham in Norfolk. His outlook was what might be called a Christ-centred Trinitarianism. Lang frequently spoke about looking beyond that which was seen and temporal to that which was unseen and eternal, and he seems to have been strongly conscious of the sovereignty and transcendence of God.[60] John Cavell, a Canterbury curate and later a bishop, recalled:

> He [Lang] was a deeply spiritual man and disciplined in his pattern of worship and his personal prayer life. He was a High Churchman . . . nevertheless he was respected by the Evangelicals, and my Low Church Vicar in Deal thought very highly of him . . . [at the bishop's charge before my ordination] Cosmo, speaking without notes, and almost in a trance, spoke of the Johannine passage of the True Vine, and *especially* on the text 'Abide in Me – except ye abide in me, ye can do nothing.' He then spoke very movingly on the times in his long ministry when he had *not* abided in the Vine, and felt he had achieved nothing. It was a revelation of his humility: altogether a moving experience.[61]

Lang was long inspired by an Anglican nun who worked tirelessly in South Africa, Mother Cecile CR, as he recalled in 1934:

> I have a very special personal association with Mother Cecile which may perhaps surprise you. I never, alas! saw her in the flesh; but I was so greatly impressed by a picture of her, that I kept the photograph in my study for many years, as a vivid revelation of the depth and beauty and serenity and joyfulness of a truly consecrated life. How little could Mother Cecile, in the midst of all her activities, have known that the mere picture of her was being used to quicken and sustain the ideals of a young priest and bishop wholly unknown to her.[62]

In retirement, Lang wrote a final little book, *Tupper: A Memoir of the Life and Work of a Very Human Parish Priest* (1945), about his old friend Darwell Tupper-Carey, with whom he had once been a curate. *Tupper* reveals as much about Lang as it does about Tupper-Carey. It is a paean of praise to a certain sort of late nineteenth-century Anglo-Catholic slum ministry. As Lang traced Tupper-Carey's work in Leeds, Poplar, Lowestoft, York, Huddersfield, and finally the very un-slumlike

Monte Carlo, he wove a picture of systematic visiting, 'full and reverent ritual' at the Eucharist, careful preaching and evangelistic work, care of the sick and dying, parish clubs and societies, vicarage hospitality and parish outings.[63] It is hard to resist the temptation to see reflected here Lang's work at Portsea and indeed his father's work at the Barony Church. The impression is given that God is to be served and found in lives of careful busyness – perhaps another Presbyterian hangover. This, in many ways, seems to have been Lang's ideal of ordained ministry and one may surmise that Tupper-Carey was the sort of parish priest that part of Lang secretly wished to be. Yet, there are a few surprises. Lang realised that this pattern of ministry was hardly possible in 1945 and he pondered the future impact of lay evangelists.[64] He also looked to the post-war world:

> Multitudes in our cities, towns and industrial villages have been compelled by circumstances beyond their control to live on a level which the community ought not to tolerate. Here, looking back, it must be confessed that the generation of clergy and churchpeople to which Tupper belonged did too little to rouse the whole community to face and fulfil its own responsibility. We may well be thankful that now the Church is being called to insist upon the duty of the community to change social conditions which make it a mockery to expect human life, cramped and often crushed by these conditions, to rise to higher levels.[65]

Chapter 7 will show that during the Second World War Lang himself called for such change, and that he never appeared backward-looking, nor bemoaned the loss of some golden age. He may have had a fairly static monarchical ideal, but in other respects he spent much time and thought preparing for the future.

Another key theme running through *Tupper* is Lang's clear belief in the importance and dignity of each and every person. His vision was of 'a Church catholic enough to embrace people of every sort' and in which there was a welcome for the 'rough outsider' as well as the devout.[66] He recalled an incident from his curacy that had remained with him for over fifty years:

When I began my ministry . . . at Leeds, part of the district assigned to me was inhabited by homeless people of the lowest class living in common lodging-houses. In many of these lodging-houses the most elementary decencies of life and the restraints of what we call morality were unknown. Into one of them there came once a young man from the country, seeking work, ignorant of the pitfalls of a town, and in an advanced stage of consumption. When there his illness overcame him and he was at death's door. Among the denizens of this lodging-house was a young 'woman who was a sinner.' She took pity on the homeless, friendless, dying lad, protected him, nursed him, paid for his few necessities by the earnings of her own manner of life.

As death drew near, knowing, as she told me, that he had been well brought up in the country, she came one night to me and asked me to see him. I did so then and for a day or two after, and was able even in these surroundings to minister to him. When he died I committed his poor worn body to the earth and his soul to God. As I did so, I caught sight of the young woman who had befriended him standing alone at a distance. When all was over I asked her why she had not come nearer. This was her answer, made with passionate intensity: 'I wouldn't let my black soul be near to spoil his white soul at its passing.' Black soul! Surely whiter in her self-forgetting charity than many an outwardly respectable soul filled with jealousy or uncharitableness or the deadly sin of self-righteousness . . . A trace of the image of God her Creator and Father was visible in the soul of this poor girl, defaced indeed, but not obliterated.[67]

The truly human parish priest, Lang concluded, would be found amongst his people at whatever level they were to be found, and the most important thing was that they knew he loved them.[68]

SEXUALITY, HOPES OF MARRIAGE, AND LONELINESS

There has been a tendency amongst some modern authors and biographers to write, and sometimes to speculate, about their subjects' sex lives. Lang has not been immune from this, and in recent years claims have been advanced in print and on television that he was a repressed homosexual. These claims are of peripheral concern to this book, but it is necessary to say something about them for two reasons. Firstly, because upon closer examination the evidence cited is slight, whilst stronger evidence exists which tends to a different conclusion. Secondly, because of the danger that such claims may overshadow Lang's very real achievements as archbishop of Canterbury, and all that many people may remember about Lang may be what they recall from watching television documentaries.

A.L. Rowse first aired speculation about Lang's sexuality in his 1989 autobiography, *Friends and Contemporaries*.[69] Seven years later in 1996, Channel 4's series *Canterbury Tales* about the twentieth-century Church of England quoted Lang's correspondence with his chaplain Wilfrid Parker, and suggested that the archbishop might have had special reasons for remaining a confirmed bachelor, adding that it was widely believed in the Church of England that Lang was a celibate homosexual. Lang's letters to Wilfrid Parker, which he began writing when Parker was his chaplain and continued on and off until his death in 1945, were made available to the public at Lambeth Palace Library in the 1980s. *Canterbury Tales* based its suggestion on selective extracts from Lang's letters to Parker, but offered no other evidence. By the time of David Starkey's 2002 television programme *Reinventing the Royals*, this was treated as accepted fact. Starkey enlarged it:

> But there was a secret irony to this new family monarchy, for its architect, Archbishop Cosmo Lang, was a homosexual, though unlike Esher, he was a repressed one. He had a series of intense relationships with his young chaplains and with his male secretaries, one of whom proclaimed that he loved Lang better than the East End boy. But Lang never laid a finger on any of them, but paid the price for this repression with lifelong insomnia and an extraordinary episode of premature ageing.[70]

It was the newly ordained Dick Sheppard who told Lang he loved him more than the East End boy in an effusive letter of good wishes following Lang's translation to York in 1908. Lang's alopecia resulted from the 1914 'sacred memory' episode, and there is no evidence that he suffered from insomnia.[71]

Is it true that Lang was a repressed homosexual? The answer may be sought in the wider history of Lang's relationships, as well as in the detail of Lang's relationship with Wilfrid Parker. Lang did not always find human relationships easy. At school he had been a solitary boy. Lang's brother, Bishop Norman Lang, said Cosmo 'buttoned himself up tightly in an impenetrable reserve'. For some years after his conversion to Anglo-Catholicism in the 1880s, Lang believed priestly celibacy to be the highest ideal.[72] Celibacy, however, may seem exciting and possessed of a certain religious glamour when a priest is in his twenties or thirties. He may come to view celibacy rather differently by the time he is in his forties or fifties, and loneliness has begun to bite. In 1900, Lang wrote to Stafford Crawley that 'I wish I had time to have a wife,'[73] which presumably means he wished he had a wife but could not bring himself to admit it in such bald terms to an ordinand. Lang's loneliness was increased when he became bishop of Stepney. Perhaps the Confirmation classes for well-to-do girls from the West End which Lang held at 2 Amen Court ('Number 2 Company') were in part an attempt to find a suitable bride. Winnington-Ingram visited Lang at Bishopthorpe after his translation to York and found Lang's loneliness palpable; he believed it aged Lang.[74]

As a bishop and later as an archbishop, Lang was entitled to have domestic chaplains. Davidson tended to select promising young priests such as Bell and Haigh whom he could groom for high office. Lang, by contrast, chose chaplains who would be congenial company. They appear to have provided what a later generation would call his 'support network'. The chaplains provided companionship and sometimes food after the day's work. Lang would sometimes let off steam at them in safety.[75] Not surprisingly, Lang became very fond of his chaplains, rather as generals can become fond of their ADCs, and up to a point he seems to have regarded them as surrogate sons. There were also other young men of whom he thought in this way. The married but childless Hensley Henson similarly had several surrogate sons.[76]

In 1905 Edgar Sheppard, sub-dean of the Chapel Royal, wrote to Lang, who was then bishop of Stepney, to ask if he knew of a secretarial post which might suit his son, Dick Sheppard, who had graduated from Cambridge and was presently working at Oxford House, a university settlement in Bethnal Green.[77] Lang appointed Dick Sheppard as his lay secretary, in place of a chaplain, between 1905 and 1906. During this time Lang helped Sheppard resolve his difficulties about being ordained, and Sheppard cheered up Lang's rather gloomy residence at 2 Amen Court. Sheppard was possessed of a dynamic and caring personality, as well as a tendency to pull Lang's leg, and had a very deep love of the poor and dispossesed, rooted in his experiences in Bethnal Green. Lang soon began addressing Sheppard in his correspondence as 'my dear Dick', and with time Sheppard became 'almost as a son' to him.[78] Lang was very moved when Sheppard wrote to him in December 1905 announcing that after a long struggle he had finally decided to seek ordination. Lang replied:

> Your letter was the best Christmas present I have received: many thanks for it. But I really don't know *what* 'I have done for you'! I have ragged you and kicked you and hustled you: what else? I know well what I have left *un*done – it is so very hard to give time and thought to oneself and to those who share one's life in this crowded existence. But you know how much I care for you: how warmly I thank you for all your loving service: and how earnestly I pray that God may lead and guide you into the work He has in store for you in the greatest service in the world.[79]

This letter is significant because it shows that as early as 1905 the pattern of Lang regarding some of his younger colleagues as quasi-sons and caring for them was beginning to establish itself. Sheppard evidently came to regard Lang with great affection, as is shown in the gushing letter he sent Lang shortly after his translation to York and his own ordination to the diaconate:

> Take nearly all my heart with you to York. I expect even Archbishops need human love at times, and since you can never realise what East London is to me without you, I must tell you that I shall never cease to pray for God to give you the greatest power

and the biggest 'guts' in Europe and the knowledge, in times of
depression, that a young freak of a deacon, who owes the intensest
joys of his life to you and who finds he loves you even more than
he loves the East End boy, is often on his knees, trying to switch
on a little light and love to penetrate the loneliness of His Grace's
study at York.

This is written as I think it off the reel and it may sound all rot.
Like my rotten sermons, it admits of no reply.[80]

Lang continued to support Sheppard during his subsequent ministry
at St Martin-in-the-Fields, Canterbury Cathedral, St Paul's Cathedral,
and also during the long periods of illness and asthma which blighted
the last twenty years of Sheppard's life. On 31 October 1937 Lang
received a letter and a bunch of flowers from Sheppard to mark his
birthday, and was distressed an hour later to receive a telephone call
to say that Sheppard had been found dead. When Sheppard's papers
were gone through, it was discovered that he had carefully preserved the
letter Lang sent him for his ordination thirty years earlier, in which he
counselled him often to recall the love of God and to pray the words, 'O
Love I give myself to Thee, Thine ever, only Thine to be.'[81]

Wilfrid Parker was the grandson of Charles Longley, archbishop of
Canterbury 1862–68. He was also a friend of Dick Sheppard, and after
ordination and a curacy, he joined Lang at 2 Amen Court, shortly before
the latter became archbishop of York. Lang seems particularly to have
been able to relax in Parker's company, and Parker, in addition to his
other duties, took over many of the household and domestic chores at
Bishopthorpe. The busy Lang communicated in part with Parker by
letter, and his correspondence contained a mixture of official business
and personal matters, such as accounts of his enthronement in York, the
Privy Council, Edward VII, the House of Lords, and a trip to Ireland.
The letters are affectionate in tone: Lang mostly addressed Parker as 'my
dear Wilfrid' and sometimes 'dearest Wilfrid'. Lang pulled Parker's leg
from time to time – for example, about a letter from a female admirer.
It is clear that Lang developed a degree of emotional dependency upon
Parker, possibly to an unhealthy extent. It may have been mutual. In
1912, for example, Lang wrote to Parker, after he had gone to South

Africa: 'And now it is midnight: I must go to bed. No Wilfrid to rag at his fireside or to pummel after his bath in the morning. Ah me!'[82] One letter which has been mentioned in connection with Lang's relationships and sexuality is that of ten pages which the archbishop wrote from Bishop's House, Iona, on 17 September 1911, where he had received an unexpected letter from Parker, announcing that he wished to go to South Africa. Lang began:

O Wilfrid, my heart is sair, my heart is sair. I used to try, foolishly perhaps, to [*indeciph.* thrust or push away?] the thought of the coming evil day: I did not think it was near: and when the shadow of it came into sight it made me, makes me, very desolate. I daresay you think I am weak and foolish to make so much of it; and I daresay you would think me even more foolish if I tried to put my feelings about it into words. You can't understand – how could you – the strange way in which you have got into my heart and fitted into my life. You see, or rather I think you don't see, for these are not things one ought to wear on one's sleeve – my life is really rather a lonely one. It needs not friendships, I have plenty of those: not work – I have too much of it: but just that simple human thing – someone in daily nearness to love. The fact that for reasons sufficient to me I am not and do not propose to be married, does not make this need less.[83]

Lang continued that Parker must think him an old fool and selfish. He added that he would bear Parker's departure cheerfully and twice said, 'I do not doubt that you *are* right,' going on to suggest ways in which the move would benefit Parker and fit him for more important work in the Church. He dealt with a number of items of purely diocesan business, sent a greeting to Parker's parents – who were leaving their old home – and concluded, 'I shall always eagerly look forward to seeing my old callous, imperturbable, beloved chaplain. Forgive this long letter, even if it bores you to read it. It has made me feel better to write it.'

The usually buttoned-up Lang was using this letter to pour out his shock at Parker's bombshell and his fear of more loneliness ahead. Later in 1911 Lang wrote to Parker's mother about her son:

But – oh dear! – it is *very* hard to let him go. He has been something in my life which I cannot express without seeming to be foolish. But perhaps you can understand that in my necessarily rather lonely and public and heavily-burdened life, it was a real blessing to me to have in Wilfrid a combination of the elements of son, younger brother, wife and friend. In his work as chaplain he has been the greatest help. He has a genius for managing a hospitable and large household. I can never get another chaplain who will save me as much as he has done from all domestic cares and who will be so tranquil and unruffled . . .You will always know that my love for your boy is only next to yours – and perhaps next to that of the wife who somewhere may be waiting for him.[84]

It is, admittedly, a rather strange outpouring, and the temptation is to read into it the conclusion Rowse and Starkey have advanced, but perhaps it might mean exactly what Lang had written and no more, namely, that he had become very dependent upon Parker and would miss him terribly. Mrs Parker continued to correspond with Lang until her death in the 1930s. Other correspondence reveals that Lang – whom one suspects could not boil an egg – was grateful to Parker for shielding him from domestic worries. It should also be remembered that Lang hated any staff changes: he was, for example, 'desolate' at the departure of the bishop of Dover in 1934.[85] Certainly Lang wrote to Parker using terms no modern archbishop would employ, but the vocabulary men use to each other has changed over the past century; Parker's letters to Lang have not survived, so the historian must make the best of a one-sided correspondence.

Despite Lang's protestations to Parker, he became equally fond of his next chaplain, Edward Gibbs. This time it was the chaplain who developed something of an emotional dependency upon Lang, the archbishop helping him with sermons and the life of prayer. Gibbs volunteered as an army chaplain in 1917 and on the eve of his departure sent Lang an emotional letter full of love, gratitude for Lang's patience and help, and of self-reproach for his temper and lack of respect.[86] Gibbs was killed on Good Friday 1918. Lang wrote to his close friend Nancy Crawley:

You know that I loved the boy with my whole heart, really as a
son and a younger brother both. I can't quite feel that anyone felt
quite for him as I did. I always feared – I think *he* felt, though he
did not fear – that he would be killed: but it is very hard to bear.[87]

I have discovered no contemporary references suggestive of Lang's
alleged repressed homosexuality in any of the diaries or letters I have
seen. Don, who knew Lang very closely for the last fourteen years of his
life and who could be critical of him, never once expressed any suspicions
of homosexuality in his diary, and in the 1930s Lang was perceived as a
celibate. Sir Edward Ford, who as a lawyer, soldier and private secretary
to two monarchs might be reckoned to have a wide knowledge of men,
was very surprised to be told in 2001 that some people believed Lang to
have been a repressed homosexual: 'I was alone with him many times
from the age of eleven and I never once suspected anything like that.
Don't forget he had close friendships with women, one of whom was my
mother.'[88]

Canon Derek Ingram Hill, who was ordained by Lang and saw quite
a lot of him in the Canterbury diocese, also thought it improbable
that Lang was a homosexual, observing, 'He loved his chaplains in
the way a happily married man might love the music of Bach' (Canon
Ingram Hill was a widower with a love of Bach). He added that he was
once interviewed by Lang after he had just dismissed two priests for
homosexual acts, and he had never forgotten how upset Lang was, nor
his sense that the priests had let him down.[89]

Historians and writers have hitherto ignored Cosmo Lang's relationships with women. In his teenage years, Lang wrote a spoof *Who's Who*
entry, in which he expected to marry and father a large family.[90] As a
twenty-seven-year-old curate, he seems to have found his vicar's teenage daughter attractive, though hardly a potential bride. Don noted that
he was susceptible to beautiful women and repelled by ugly ones.[91] It is
worth pondering what sort of young woman Lang might have seen as
a potential wife. As bishop of Stepney and later as archbishop of York,
he stayed at Windsor and Balmoral as a personal guest of the royal family. He needed a wife who would fit in, for she might suddenly find
herself talking with the kaiser or the prime minister and would need to

be unfazed by the prospect. Similarly, he needed a wife able to preside over social events as châteleine of Bishopthorpe. So, the dull but worthy daughter of some country parson or suburban doctor would probably, in Lang's eyes, be unlikely to fit the bill. His opportunities to find someone suitable after his consecration in 1901 were limited, and all men must face the fact that when it comes to marriage, they are dependent upon whoever is prepared to marry them. Perhaps there was simply no young woman prepared to take on Lang, and whom he would have considered a suitable bride.

I have discovered that in his early years at York, Lang fell in love with Norah Dawnay, the third child of the eighth Viscount Downe, a Yorkshire landowner. She was twelve years his junior and just the sort of well-born woman one might have imagined him wishing to marry. Lang proposed marriage twice – which indicates that he was serious – but Norah declined his offers. It is believed that this was because her family felt the match to be inappropriate. Norah Dawnay never married anyone else and died in 1947. Lockhart knew this from George Bell, but at the insistance of Norah's sister he did not mention it in his biography. Lang's reputation might have been different had Lockhart done so. Lockhart's assertion that 'there is no evidence that he ever thought seriously of marriage'[92] is misleading. If Lang's proposals were rejected by Norah Dawnay, and then a year or so later he received Parker's sudden resignation, that might supply an alternative explanation of his assertion that 'for reasons sufficient to me I am not and do not propose to be married.' Lang may still have loved Norah. He might not have wished to suffer the emotional pain of further rejection. Or he might finally have realised that, aged forty-seven, he was unlikely to marry, and had started to cope by embracing a celibate outlook.

Towards the end of his life, Lang unexpectedly fell in love one more time. Don recorded on 6 December 1933:

> C.C. remarked the other evening at dinner (in the hearing of Dowding and the footmen) 'I have fallen in love again' – on our asking who it was this time, he said 'Ann Todd – I am going to marry her.' This startling announcement was doubtless reported downstairs by the garrulous Dowding, amid titters from the maids.[93]

Ann Todd was a petite, blonde, Scots actress who had dined at Lambeth on 24 November 1933. Lang was immediately attracted to her and a correspondence and some sort of platonic relationship ensued. Todd seems to have destroyed Lang's earlier letters, but I have discovered nineteen from 1937–45 which survive in private hands. The lonely Lang clearly became hooked. In 1939, for example, he wrote: 'You can never go away. My love for you remains: and I can never forget all the love you have shown to me. It has been like a touch of Spring in the Autumn of my life.'[94]

Lang frequently told Todd that she was like a daughter to him and began his letters with 'My very dear Child', but there is a slightly obsessive feel to some of the letters which suggests his feelings were more than simply paternal. In 1938, he wrote: 'I must tell you that I was at *She Too Was Young* on Monday evening. I expect your eyes did not detect me, but I did not keep my eyes off you!' which is not a normal remark from a father to a daughter. He enjoyed learning that she said 'goodnight' across the Thames in the direction of Lambeth Palace each evening. He told her to mark her letters 'Private' or 'Personal', and all his letters to her are hand-written – 'I could not dictate a letter to *you*' – save for two bland ones about changed arrangements. Interestingly, he appears not to have mentioned Todd to his friend and female confidante Nancy Crawley, though Don realised what was going on and recorded how much Lang enjoyed seeing Todd. Lang sought Todd's company at moments of stress: he asked her to visit him as he struggled with the Euthanasia Bill in the Lords, he took refuge in her flat at the height of the abdication crisis, and she stayed with him in Canterbury during the Dunkirk evacuation. Todd went on to marry Victor Malcolm, the son of Lang's old friend Sir Ian Malcolm, and Lang officiated at their wedding, despite harbouring secret forebodings about the match. He died in 1945 on his way to see Todd.[95]

It is unlikely that Lang would have married Todd had there been no Victor Malcolm, for he was too conscious of the dignity of his office, and actresses and bishops are a comic combination. Nor had he very much to offer her in his old age. Yet he craved her company and showered her with invitations. What comes across is his terrible loneliness, his need to give and receive love, and for someone to relate to him other than as 'a dull and old prelate'.[96] In 1939, after nearly six years of marriage, Todd divorced Victor Malcolm and married Nigel Tangye. Lang was afraid that Todd's divorce and remarriage would sever her from him and was delighted when it did not. In view of the abdication crisis, his letters to her about divorce and remarriage are interesting because they reflect both his religious views and also his compassion:

> I was afraid you might have been pained by my last letter. You see I *had* to explain my position about your second marriage. Principles are principles however hard they may often be either to maintain or to apply: and my very love for you compelled me to be frank. And now, instead of the silence of resentment, comes your delightful letter, full of such generous and warmhearted affection. What principles can't do is shut my 'daughter' out. And of course I can't but be pleased to learn of your happiness, even though I don't think happiness is the only aim of life, and sometimes the way of sacrifice is higher. But, but, having made this clear, I am only human: and I realise so fully all your former disappointment and unhappiness that I realise the more all this new love and happiness must mean.[97]

Todd later wrote that Lang showed her love and understanding such as she had received from no one else, save an old aunt, and that she minded his death very greatly.[98]

Lang's sexuality was perhaps jumbled up – sexuality by its nature is complex – and one will never be entirely certain, but the weight of evidence would suggest that Lang was probably some sort of heterosexual, who liked beautiful women, and at times would have liked to marry. Lang found relationships difficult, indeed one may speculate that a personality as complicated as Lang's would have found marriage – where ultimately there can be no acting or posturing – not very easy to begin with. Yet, had Lang married Norah Dawnay, his life and reputation would have been very different. He found instead a refuge from his cancerous loneliness in chaplains as companions and surrogate sons, in friends like the Crawleys, and in Ann Todd. There is a very great difference between regarding chaplains as companions and surrogate sons – including becoming unhealthily emotionally dependent upon some of them and writing over-the-top letters when they leave or are killed – and being filled with repressed homosexual passion for them. Historians are just as capable as Biblicists of eisegesis rather than exegesis, and, unless some new historical evidence comes to light, the claim that Lang was a repressed homosexual cannot be said to have been demonstrated. Lang recorded that in his youth he never 'went wrong,' and there is no good reason to doubt that he remained chaste all his life and thought of himself as a celibate for much of it.[99]

HEALTH

Lang became archbishop of Canterbury at an age when many modern men are preparing for retirement. On 23 December 1928, a few days after his enthronement, the new primate was taken very ill whilst dining with the ordinands. He recorded that 'I was seized with a sudden internal pain, a pain more acute than I had ever experienced.'[100] A small clot of blood had passed through his heart and it was a wonder he did not die. A local doctor summoned the king's surgeon, who was later joined by another eminent royal physician, Lord Dawson of Penn. Plans for an operation were abandoned and all they could do was wait. Lang pulled through, but he was a very ill man for at least the next three years and periodically throughout his primacy. He was confined to bed for many months in 1929.[101]

One consequence of Lang's illness were mood swings and depression. 'Cosmo Cantuar, Cosmo Cantuar,' he once muttered, 'what's the point in calling yourself that when it's all dust and ashes,' and he talked of resignation. The one thing guaranteed to get Lang out of depression was the company of children. With the arrival of Alan Don as his chaplain and secretary in 1931, his health slowly started to improve. Lang remained subject to illnesses throughout his primacy, including duodenal ulceration, fifth nerve neuralgia, shingles and fibromyalgia. He was often ill after times of stress: in October 1934, after anxiety about Germany; in May 1935, after George V's jubilee; in January and February 1937, after the abdication; and in August 1937, after the coronation of George VI. He hated to be thought ill and would drive

himself on and not rest when he ought.[102] Curiously, Lang's health seems
to have improved towards the end of his primacy and he stood up well
to the stress of the Second World War, but for quite a lot of his time at
Canterbury he was a sick man struggling to cope with a heavy workload.

BALLURE

No analysis of Lang is complete without a mention of Ballure and the
light it sheds on his character. Whilst at Magdalen, Lang made friends
with John Morton Macdonald, an undergraduate from Largie Castle
in Kintyre. In 1894, Lang holidayed with Winnington-Ingram at
Machrihanish and they visited Macdonald at Largie. Lang fell in love
with the area. According to family tradition, Lang and Macdonald
visited Canada in the 1890s and upon their return Macdonald built Lang
a small Canadian-style cottage, which still exists, called Tav-an-Taggart.
Lang came every year, sometimes twice, and graduated from Tav-an-
Taggart to Ballure House, an early nineteenth-century Macdonald
dower house at Tay-in-Loan. His nickname was 'Taggart', which means
'Bishop', and he is still fondly remembered there today.[103]

Using a modern car on modern roads, it takes over five hours to reach
Ballure from Edinburgh. It is very remote – even Inverary seems a long
way away – and the landscape feels prehistoric, with great lumps of stone
staring out to sea and more sheep than people. The guest books for
Largie Castle show that although Lang brought friends here, he did not
usually bring clergy or important people from the Church of England.
For the most part, Lang walked and spent time praying, examining his
conscience and celebrating the Eucharist in the Cell, a small oratory he
built at the end of the library. Ballure is significant because here Lang
escaped London for six weeks or so – though digests of information
were still sent to him from Lambeth and he usually spent a few days at
Balmoral – and he was able to relax, think and reflect. At Ballure, the
prayerful and almost mystical aspect of Lang's character is most evident.

The Cosmo Lang who emerges from a closer inspection of historical
records is rather different to the popular caricature of him. He had flaws,

notably difficulties with relationships and a tendency to overwork to ward off loneliness. He had a fondness from time to time for aristocratic or well-educated company, though this should not obscure his pleasure in contact with former parishioners from his Leeds days, nor his interest in the ordinary people he met in the parishes of his diocese and his wish to help them.

Lang's occasional tendency to exaggerate things and to let his tongue run away with him would prove a significant flaw. It should be stressed that this was occasional, and that for the most part he was a very accomplished preacher and public speaker, who was keen to use his gifts of speech to offer Christian witness and help. His other great gift was that of a wise adminstrator, patient and seldom flustered, getting on with the daily grind of an archbishop. If his legal mind went straight to the heart of a knotty problem, he also retained a canny streak which usually helped him avoid obvious pitfalls. Lang could sometimes come over as aloof and prelatical, but far more often he was a wise and caring pastor, with a quiet, self-mocking sense of humour. These important aspects of his character and ministry have largely been forgotten or overlooked.

3

The Archbishopric of Canterbury Between the Wars

THE ARCHBISHOPRIC OF CANTERBURY HAS its origins in the mission to England in 597 of St Augustine, who established the provinces of Canterbury and York. The archbishopric of Canterbury is thus the oldest continuous office in England. Archbishops have included scholars like Anselm, martyrs like Becket, reformers like Cranmer, and political figures like Laud. In the table of precedence in the twentieth century, archbishops of Canterbury ranked immediately after dukes of the blood royal and before the lord chancellor.[1] Like many another ancient office, the archbishopric of Canterbury has continuously evolved and adapted over the centuries. As archbishop of Canterbury between 1928 and 1942, Lang had to shoulder a heavy burden of responsibility and an even greater burden of expectation. This, however, was not accompanied by a commensurate reservoir of power. Lang had to exercise influence obliquely and to try to govern his Church with consent. In order to be fair to Lang in later chapters of this book, it is first necessary to familiarise the reader with the scope of his archiepiscopal office and its constraints.

THE BACKGROUND TO LANG'S ARCHIEPISCOPAL MINISTRY

The parameters of Lang's archiepiscopal ministry were largely established in the three or four generations before his translation to Canterbury in 1928. By then, although the Church of England remained a significant presence in the countryside, it was predominantly an urban and suburban Church. The Church over which Lang presided was largely formed of structures, organisations and buildings which had their origins in the attempts by nineteenth- and early twentieth-century Anglicans to respond to the changing needs of the day. Most significant from the point of view of the archbishops of Canterbury were the revival of the Convocations of Canterbury and York in 1851 and 1862 respectively, the creation of new dioceses and suffragan sees, the revival of cathedral life, and the 1919 Enabling Act, which led to the establishment of diocesan conferences and the Church Assembly.

The nineteenth century had witnessed the expansion of the British Empire. Anglican churches, mission stations and eventually dioceses began to be established throughout the empire, as well as in places which were not subject to British control, such as China. Archbishops of Canterbury, especially Archibald Tait (archbishop 1868–82), Edward Benson (1883–96) and Frederick Temple (1897–1902), began to be accorded an additional responsibility for these overseas Churches. In 1867, the first Lambeth Conference was held so that bishops from around the globe could meet for brotherly counsel and fellowship. Thereafter, the archbishop summoned a Lambeth Conference every decade, and this began to be seen as a sign of membership of the burgeoning Anglican Communion. The archbishopric started to become a focus of loyalty for overseas Anglicans and began to be looked to for help and advice.

A further development during the three or four generations before Lang became archbishop was the growth of Church parties. Since the Elizabethan Settlement, the Church of England had aspired to be the Church of the nation, providing a broad religious home for Englishmen of varied theological outlooks and spiritualities. This was facilitated by a certain studied ambiguity: the Communion rite in the Book of Common Prayer after 1559, for example, was open to several different interpretations. The Church of England had long contained different churchmanships.[2] The late eighteenth and early nineteenth centuries witnessed the Evangelical Revival amongst evangelicals in the Church of England and Nonconformist churches. This deepened the life of many parishes and individuals, led to greater expectations amongst the clergy, and inspired missions at home and overseas. This revival was emphatically Protestant in character. Renewal of a very different sort began in 1833 with the Oxford Movement and subsequent Catholic Revival. This startled many in the Church of England by claiming that their Church was not Protestant, as many had long believed, but that its formularies might be interpreted to show that it was a part of Catholic Christendom. The Catholic Revival led to a renewal of liturgical worship and sacramental spirituality amongst its followers, and to the revival of the religious life.[3] One result of the Catholic Revival, however, was an increase in conflict as more Protestant-minded members of the Church of England came to believe that their Reformation identity was being undermined and that erroneous doctrines were being reintroduced by Anglo-Catholics. Archbishops began to find themselves having to attempt to maintain the peace.

ECUMENICAL AFFAIRS

Matthew Grimley has pointed out that the inter-war period saw the decline of English Nonconformity and the end of Nonconformist attacks upon the Established Church over matters such as education. He suggests that it was thus easier for the Church of England – and by extension for its primate – to project a national voice and claim to be speaking for the whole nation. Lang cultivated good relations with the English Nonconformist leaders, and on several occasions invited them to Lambeth Palace to discuss international peace, the work of the League of Nations, and the Italian invasion of Abyssinia. He also sponsored conversations about unity between the Church of England and Nonconformists, and on one occasion celebrated the Eucharist in the chapel at Lambeth Palace and gave Holy Communion to Presbyterians as well as Anglicans.[4] If Lang played only a peripheral role in the conversations themselves, it was at least significant that an archbishop of Canterbury was involved at all: Davidson had sought cordial relations with Nonconformists, despite disagreements about schools, but it is hard to imagine Frederick Temple or Benson taking a similar attitude.

The conversations ground to a halt over the subject of episcopal ordination of the clergy. Many in the Church of England held that

Nonconformist pastors would have to undergo episcopal ordination to take away any doubt that might be held about their sacramental actions, whilst Nonconformists sought an assurance of the already-existing validity of their pastors' ministry as a basis for further discussions. In July 1934 Lang delivered a speech about ecumenism to the Canterbury diocesan conference, which he knew would be reported outside his diocese, and which was entirely his own composition.[5] Lang told his diocesan conference that he conceived of the Church of England as a sort of bridge church: 'At one end it has an affinity with the great Latin Church of the West and the Orthodox Churches of the East; and at the other end it has an affinity with the Protestant Churches.' Lang paid tribute to the non-episcopal ministry of the Nonconformists, but he nevertheless asserted that, historically speaking, episcopacy occupied a position analagous to the canon of scripture and the creeds. He claimed that the functions of episcopacy were the guardianship of the faith and sacraments, and the provision of a duly qualified ministry, and he drew the conclusion that 'the episcopate and the episcopal ministry must be maintained in any united Church of which the Church of England can form a part.' Anglo-Catholics were delighted with Lang's speech, though Nonconformists were less happy: 'Cold water from Canterbury', commented the *Christian World*.[6]

Lang retained a strong affection for the Church of Scotland, the Church of his Baptism and upbringing, though his relationship with the Kirk once he became archbishop of Canterbury tended to be more cordial than fruitful. All of Lang's family remained members of the Church of Scotland, with the exception of his brother Norman, who also converted to Anglicanism, was ordained and eventually became suffragan bishop of Leicester. In the words of J.G. Simpson, one of Lang's fellow curates at Leeds and also a Scotsman, Lang still 'had the Kirk in his bones'.[7] Many years after becoming an Anglican, Lang recalled:

> With all my experience of English ecclesiastics, I am bound to say that I have not met among them many men of the personal dignity, impressiveness, elevation of tone and manner, which I associate with the great Scottish ministers whom I can remember in my youth.[8]

Like Davidson before him, Lang remained a keen observer of
the Scottish ecclesiastical scene. One gets the impression that some
members of the Church of Scotland, though, were rather wary of this
former Presbyterian who had metamorphosed into a Catholic Anglican.
In 1929 Lang attended the the reunion in Edinburgh of the Church
of Scotland and the United Free Churches, but privately felt that he
had been sidelined and not treated very well during the celebrations. In
1932 Lang addressed the General Assembly, and, with great tact, invited
them to discuss possible future reunion with the Church of England on
the basis of the 1921 Lambeth Conference's ecumenical appeal. 'Pulpits
and newspapers have been humming', reported the *Church Times*,
'with opening negotiations with the "sacerdotal Church of England".'
Lang's overtures met with a polite but somewhat chilly reception from
the General Assembly. At its meeting the following year, the General
Assembly passed a resolution against episcopacy, proposed by Archibald
Fleming, minister of St Columba's Church of Scotland church in Pont
Street, London.[9] When Fleming met Lang in 1934, he asked if he was
still *persona grata* at Lambeth Palace. 'Yes, *grata*,' replied Lang, 'but not
gratissima as heretofore.' It made little difference when Lang's younger
brother Marshall became moderator of the General Assembly in 1935.
Wags may have quipped that Cosmo and Marshall Lang had stitched
up the ecclesiastical Establishment between them, but in truth Lang and
his brothers – with the exception of Norman – do not seem to have got
on very well. Cosmo found Marshall irritating and nicknamed him 'His
Solemnity'.[10] He did, however, travel to Edinburgh to support Marshall
when the General Assembly met in May 1935, and was persuaded to
leave the public gallery and make an impromptu speech, which amused
the members of the General Assembly. Lang seems to have made himself
scarce afterwards, when the General Assembly debated how it might best
combat the spreading influence of Roman Catholicism across Scotland:
symbolic, perhaps, of the difference between the Church of Scotland
and the Church of England.[11]

When Lang became archbishop of Canterbury in 1928, an ecumenical
dialogue was already established between the Church of England and
the Old Catholic Churches of Europe. In 1932 Convocation approved
intercommunion between the two Churches, with the support of Lang,

who noted that 'this was quite an historic occasion being the first instance since the Reformation of the Establishment of formal intercommunion with another section of Christian people.' On 24 June 1932 the Old Catholic bishop of Haarlem took part in the consecration of the Anglican bishops of Kensington and Jerusalem in St Paul's Cathedral, laying his hands on the bishops and repeating the Old Catholic formula of consecration, *accipe Spiritum Sanctum*, at the same time as Lang repeated the Anglican formula from the Prayer Book.[12] Thus, Old Catholic orders percolated into subsequent Anglican ordinations.

Lang's happiest ecumenical relationship was probably with the Orthodox Churches. The late nineteenth and early twentieth centuries had seen the growth of interest in Eastern Orthodoxy amongst Anglicans, and Lang was kept in touch with developments in the Orthodox Churches by enthusiasts such as Canon John Douglas, a south London vicar and member of the Church Assembly, who had developed close connections with the Orthodox world. The Ecumenical Patriarch sought Lang's help from time to time, as did other Orthodox patriarchs and bishops.[13] An Orthodox delegation attended the 1930 Lambeth Conference, and Lang regularly received Orthodox visitors. In October 1931 Lang hosted discussions about reunion at Lambeth Palace between representatives of the Church of England and the Orthodox Churches, though the hopes of some on the Church of England side that a meeting of the Pro-Synod of the Orthodox Churches 'will lead to the various Orthodox Churches following the example of the Ecumenical Patriarch in pronouncing Anglican Orders to be valid (βέβαιος) and that intercommunion κατ' οἰκονομίαν will be permitted' were never fulfilled.[14]

Lang's relationship with the Roman Catholic Church in England was slight and rather formal, and reflected the rather withdrawn and inward-looking stance of English Roman Catholicism between the wars, after centuries of persecution and marginalisation. In 1896 Pope Leo XIII had declared Anglican orders null and void in the encyclical *Apostolicae Curae*, and, according to Don, Cardinal Francis Bourne of Westminster was 'stiff' in his dealings with the Church of England. For his part, Lang always spoke respectfully of the Roman Catholic Church, though he regretted the failure of the Vatican to participate in ecumenical dialogue. There was something of a thaw after Arthur

Hinsley became the Roman Catholic archbishop of Westminster in 1935. From 1937, Father (later Bishop) David Matthew kept in touch with Don, establishing an informal link between Lambeth Palace and Archbishop's House, Westminster. Although Lang felt unable to invite Hinsley into Lambeth Palace after accepting a lift home in the cardinal's motor car – he was probably wary of an evangelical backlash – Lang met both Hinsley and Archbishop William Godfrey, the apostolic delegate, on a number of occasions in the neutral territory of the Athenæum Club in London. There were no talks about church unity between the Church of England and Roman Catholic Church, but it was felt at Lambeth Palace that Hinsley was genuinely anxious to be on terms of friendship with the Church of England, and in 1940 Don noted that there was much more cooperation between Lang and Hinsley than there had been with Bourne.[15]

Lang's work and influence overseas are beyond the scope of this book, but some reference to foreign ecclesiastical affairs will help to create a rounded picture of the archbishopric between the wars. The great theological influence exercised by German Protestantism in the nineteenth and early twentieth centuries quickly dwindled away after the outbreak of war in 1914.[16] The Roman Catholic Church continued to hold aloof from other denominations, whilst the popes remained 'Prisoners in the Vatican' until 1929. The rest of the Christian world had been unbalanced by the Great War, and in the 1920s and 1930s it was coming to terms with the consequences of the conflict. The Russian Orthodox Church was traumatised by Soviet persecution.[17] The 1919 Treaty of Versailles gave Great Britain a Mandate to administer Palestine and thus have oversight of the Holy Places, whilst Egypt, Mesopotamia and other parts of the Eastern Mediterranean and Middle East containing ancient Christian Churches remained or became subject to British influence. After 1918, many more people outside England took notice of the Church of England and of its archbishops. Some foreign Christian leaders saw in Lang an archbishop who cut a patriarchal figure (he was presented with a patriarchal staff when he visited the Ecumenical Patriarch at the Phanar in 1939), who was treated with great deference, who knew many influential people, who made speeches in the House of Lords and who was a close friend of George V. Not quite fully grasping the nuances of the Church of England, they sometimes over-estimated the archbishop's influence in both Church and state and they often sought Lang's help when seeking redress from the British government.[18] Because there was no World Council of Churches until after the Second World War, international Christian ecumenism may perhaps have tended to focus a little more on individual Christian leaders such as the archbishop of Canterbury.

An Overview of Lang's Role

Although there are references to the archbishop of Canterbury here and there in Canon, Common and Statute Law, his role has been nowhere codified. This flexibility probably helped the archbishopric to evolve down the centuries. The papers of twentieth-century archbishops at Lambeth Palace would seem to suggest that Lang had several clearly defined and overlapping roles:

(a) He was a diocesan bishop and had to administer his diocese of Canterbury.

(b) He was the Primate of All England and Metropolitan. To use one of Lang's expressions, he had to have *solicitude* for the whole Church of England.

(c) He was expected to be an exemplar of Christian and of priestly life.[19]

(d) The Church of England was a National Church by Law Established, and the archbishop was a national figure. As Grimley has said of the 1920s and 1930s, 'The senior clergy still *mattered*, commanding significant national respect and attention as political players.'[20] Lang was expected to speak with a Christian voice to the nation. He was sometimes expected to express a Christian viewpoint to the government, and to request it to right wrongs. By custom, he was present at the great ceremonies of state such as the opening of Parliament. He was usually present at national liturgical functions in Westminster Abbey or St Paul's Cathedral.

(e) A further aspect of their national role was that archbishops had a special relationship with the British monarchy and crowned the sovereign.

(f) The archbishop was a teacher and preacher. Through sermons, broadcasts, booklets, newspaper articles, etc., Lang was expected to teach the Christian faith and to reflect upon contemporary events from a Christian perspective.

(g) The archbishopric was surrounded by great prestige. The archbishop became a figure around whom Anglicans could rally and in whose name committees might be established. One aspect of this was the role of the archbishop as a focus of unity in a Church containing a complicated range of churchmanships. Mid-nineteenth-century archbishops had tended to dislike the growth of Anglo-Catholicism – or at least the trouble it caused – though Tait eventually came to view it in a more positive light. Both Benson and Frederick Temple accepted a certain diversity within the Church, but nevertheless laid down rules and expected to be obeyed. Davidson coped by adopting an attitude of being above the fray. Holding the Church together in the late 1920s and early 1930s after Parliament's rejection of the 1928 Revised Prayer Book was a significant and large part of Lang's work in his early years at Canterbury.[21]

RESTRICTIONS ON LANG'S USE OF POWER AND INFLUENCE

In order to understand the tools available to Lang in fulfilling these various functions, it will be helpful first to examine the constraints on his power and influence. The position of the archbishop of Canterbury in the twentieth century was frequently misunderstood. The public sometimes saw a figure at the head of the Anglican hierarchy who was treated with great deference, and assumed that he was a sort of Anglican version of the pope. In fact, although modern archbishops can sometimes wield considerable influence, they have relatively little formal power over the Church of England. The twentieth-century Church of England did not teach that any special *magisterium* attached to the archbishopric of Canterbury. The archbishops did not claim to be the universal ordinary, nor did they assert that the apostolic succession was derived only via them.

Why do modern archbishops of Canterbury have comparatively little formal power? Henry VIII's separation of the Church in England from the papacy in 1534 created a large hole in the fabric of the Church. Petrine ministry was replaced by royal supremacy. Some pre-Reformation archbishops of Canterbury had exercised considerable power as papal legates. This disappeared with the Act of Supremacy, and although Cranmer announced in 1534 that he was replacing his title of 'Legate of the Apostolic See' with 'Metropolitan', he and his successors wielded very much reduced power. By Lang's time, although the king retained a certain residual power and bishops were appointed in his name, the royal supremacy effectively meant that Parliament was the ultimate authority.[22] This situation was to prove controversial in 1927–28.

One element in the evolution of the archbishopric is of older powers falling into desuetude. In 1904, for instance, Davidson worked hard to secure a Royal Commission on Ecclesiastical Discipline instead of a Select Committee of the House of Commons, on the grounds that a Royal Commission undertaken in the name of the king would be more acceptable to the Church, whilst a Commons' Select Committee might make a difficult situation worse. By the time Lang came to Canterbury, such a use of residual royal power was no longer possible. Although there was nothing to prevent it, in reality widespread anger over Parliament's second rejection of the Revised Prayer Book in 1928 effectively precluded any use of royal power because many in the Church would not have trusted the move and some might have rebelled. Similarly, until the late seventeenth century, archbishops had undertaken metropolitical visitations of dioceses, during which they enjoyed the powers of the ordinary and could rectify wrongs. Lang contemplated a visitation of the diocese of Birmingham in the 1930s, but was advised that this power of visitation had effectively lapsed and could not easily be revived except in 'a grave impasse.'[23]

Lang was further restricted by the relationship between the archbishopric and the other bishops. To a large extent, Lang was a *primus inter pares*. He could not impose his will upon the bishops, but had to work alongside them, which often meant convincing and cajoling them. Lang's experience was that if the bishops dug their toes in, it was impossible for him to get them to do anything they did not wish to do.

Another reason why Lang had very limited power was a practical one: he had a tiny staff comprising two chaplains, a male and two female secretaries, and certainly not the 'curia' he would have needed if he were to exercise wide and considerable power. Expectations of him were high, but his resources were limited. 'This job is really impossible for one man, yet only one man can do it,' he observed in 1935, adding the next year that his life was 'incredible, indefensible, and inevitable'.[24]

ARCHIEPISCOPAL INFLUENCE

Having ascertained the restrictions upon Lang and shown that he did not possess much direct power, it may nevertheless be claimed that he was a figure of considerable influence. Indeed, one might reasonably ponder at what point influence turns into power. If people *think* someone is important, that person becomes important.

The Bishops

There were many ways of exerting influence open to Lang. A very considerable one was his influence amongst the bishops. It is useful to begin by thinking about the sort of house of bishops of which Lang was a member, because the role and expectations of bishops changed during the nineteenth and twentieth centuries. By Lang's time, bishops, like their clergy, had become more professionalised. Bishops were no longer partly Whig or Tory political appointees, positioned at the apex of the social structure, governing huge dioceses and remote from their clergy, as they had been in the early nineteenth century.[25] The number of diocesan and suffragan bishops grew during the nineteenth and early twentieth centuries. The diocesan bishops of Lang's era exercised considerable authority within their dioceses. They were untrammelled by their diocesan conferences, in contrast to the way that their successors are constrained by their diocesan synods. They chaired most diocesan committees, of which there were far fewer than later in the twentieth century. It was easier for them to exercise patronage or to move their clergy around the dioceses than it was for many of their successors. In the words of one episcopal survivor from Lang's era, there were 'forty-three diocesan bishops, forty-three oracles, each with his own Delphi'.

Correspondence at Lambeth Palace shows that the bishops treated Lang with great respect and even Barnes of Birmingham was courteous, albeit through gritted teeth.[26] They sought his help and advice, and were glad to receive his approbation. Once a man was installed as a diocesan bishop, he was subject to few checks and the archbishop had very limited powers over him. The controversial appointment of Henson to Hereford in 1918 had shown that the archbishop could not refuse to consecrate a properly nominated bishop. Lang could not interfere with the administrative action of a bishop in his own diocese. In theory, as metropolitan, he was expected to correct abuses in other dioceses, though it is not entirely clear how he was supposed to do so.[27] He had his archiepiscopal court, which last sat in 1889 – to try Bishop Edward King – after being in abeyance since 1698; this was hardly a happy precedent.

Despite this, several ways remained in which Lang could exercise influence amongst the bishops. For a start, Lang had great sway over appointments. This had not always been the case: some prime ministers had rarely consulted the archbishops or merely informed them once episcopal appointments had been made. Queen Victoria ensured that the archbishop should always be consulted, and in the later years of her reign she arranged that episcopal appointments should not be made without the consent, though not necessarily the good wishes, of the primate. According to Ramsey, the influence of the archbishop grew under Davidson, peaking under Lang and in Fisher's first years. Lang took great pains over appointments and sought to gather a balanced bench of bishops. It is possible that some clergy may have been wary of getting on the wrong side of Lang for fear of ruining their chances of preferment; this would have provided him with one element of leverage.[28]

Lang exercised a sensitive pastoral care of the bishops and most days involved exchanges of correspondence or meetings with bishops, who would seek his guidance or refer problems to him. Lang was also a quiet influence amongst the bishops in Convocation and the Church Assembly, sometimes persuading individuals not to table or to withdraw amendments liable to cause trouble. Occasionally, he would have to issue a courteous but firm reproof to a bishop.[29]

Speeches, Sermons and Addresses

Speeches, sermons and addresses have long been a significant means of influence for archbishops of Canterbury. The House of Lords was traditionally an important forum for archbishops in the late nineteenth and early twentieth centuries because an archiepiscopal speech there might be heard by people of influence and reported in the press. Bromhead has suggested that under Lang the quality of archiepiscopal interventions increased and he ascribes this to Lang's personality and to a change in perception about the episcopate, which may tie in with Grimley's observations about the decline of Nonconformist hostility towards the Established Church.[30] In the sessions of 1934–36, for example, Lang spoke on the Government of India Bill, government policy towards the League of Nations and Abyssinia, slavery, defence, Special Areas, the Education Bill, the persecution of the Assyrian community in Iraq, the Tithe Bill, social services, and redundant public houses. He spoke so often in 1934–35 that he became one of the most regular contributors to debate. He also used the Lords to condemn Soviet persecution, Italian foreign policy, Nazi oppression of the Churches and persecution of the Jews, and in retirement to oppose blanket bombing of German cities.[31]

Two other fora in which mid-twentieth-century archbishops' speeches could carry weight were the Church Assembly and the Convocation of Canterbury. Lang was chairman of the Church Assembly and president of Convocation, though these positions had their drawbacks, as he told the Assembly:

> *The Times* remarked the other day that there was no soft cushion on the Chair of St Augustine. There is certainly no soft cushion on the Chair of this Assembly. There is, for example, always a certain conflict of duty. On the one hand, if the Chairman keeps to his proper business, which is to get things done, he is apt to be criticised for forgetting the responsibilities of leadership which may belong to his office of Archbishop. If, on the other hand, he intervenes in the discussion, he is apt to be criticised for having unfairly used the authority of the Chair. Or again, if moved by natural impatience at the waste of time and confusion of issues he

interferes with some asperity, he is apt to be accused of resorting to dictatorial methods in the Assembly.[32]

Lang did not much enjoy some of the long debates in the Church Assembly and Convocation. The minutes reveal that he rarely intervened from the chair. When he did so, he was usually concerned to pre-empt problems and to calm things down – for example, during debates about clerical co-respondents in divorce cases and about extremist Anglo-Catholic clergy. Lang similarly smoothed things in Convocation – for example, in 1929, when his legal skills avoided a tangle during debate on the Lausanne Treaty.[33] Lang evidently did not feel the need to confine himself to purely ecclesiastical affairs and used both the Assembly and Convocation to make important statements and speeches. In 1932, he used the Church Assembly to mention the round table conference on India, relations between Great Britain and the Irish Free State, economic depression, the World Economic Conference and a League of Nations discussion about the Far East. In 1934, Lang expressed grave concern in Convocation about the condition of the Churches in Germany, and in 1935 he used the Assembly to criticise Nazi persecution of the Jews.[34]

Preaching and public speaking was another means of influence available to twentieth-century archbishops. The majority of Lang's sermons were delivered in his diocese and were about the liturgical year, the Bible, the sacraments, and so on. Lang also preached at royal and state occasions, at funerals and memorial services, and sometimes delivered addresses at conferences. In 1935, for example, he used a speech at the Church Congress in Bournemouth to attack Italian aggression in Abyssinia and defended the rights of conscientious objectors. Some of Lang's sermons were reprinted in part or in full in the newspapers and so may have reached a wider audience.[35]

Lang was the first archbishop of the mass media age. Davidson had made a limited use of radio after 1923.[36] Lang, however, with his love of words and touch of the actor, made considerable use of the radio. He regularly broadcast at New Year and during Sunday evening religious programmes. Some of Lang's regular sermons in churches and cathedrals were broadcast by the BBC. He also broadcast on special occasions, such as the five-hundredth anniversary of Henry VIII's vernacular 'Great

Bible' in 1938.[37] Lang spoke three times on the radio during the 1938
Munich Crisis.

Personal Influence

An important way in which archbishops have been able to affect things
in modern times is by personal influence, a point recognised by Tait in
1859:

> A Bishop's authority is of two kinds. Within a certain range defined
> by law, he has power to give orders and enforce obedience to them
> by penalty of law. Over a much wider range, he has authority from
> the good feeling of all well-disposed members of the Church, who
> voluntarily accept his paternal advice and guidance. It is not too
> much to say that by far the greater part of a Bishop's government
> of his Diocese is carried on through the willing deference which
> good Christian feeling suggests to the members of his Church,
> both lay and clerical, that he is entitled to claim on account of the
> very nature of his office.[38]

In order to exercise personal influence, an archbishop has to know
people and to be known, and he must quite literally be familiar with the
corridors of power. Lang, if not quite so skilled as Davidson, devoted
much time and effort to this aspect of his work and became quite effective
at it. It must have helped that by the time Lang came to Canterbury he
had already been an archbishop for twenty years, knew many people and
had observed Davidson at close quarters. Lang usually spent weekends
in his diocese and weekdays at Lambeth Palace. Don's diary reveals that
Lang received a constant stream of visitors, including parish priests,
bishops, leaders of other Churches, prime ministers, Cabinet ministers,
diplomats, royalty, exiles, writers and society figures. Lang enjoyed
being a host at Lambeth. He would provide bishops with overnight
accommodation, frequently entertained guests to meals and regularly
held large dinner parties. When Lang wanted, he could be extremely
charming. Mervyn Haigh, who was chaplain to both Davidson and
Lang, observed that Lang invited a slightly wider selection of people to
dine at Lambeth than Davidson.[39]

Lang also enjoyed dining out – a bit too much, in Don's opinion – but it was a way for him to meet people of importance in their own environment.[40] He developed skills as an after-dinner speaker and in this way sometimes exerted a certain influence, as Don recorded:

> The *Cinematograph Times*, commenting on C.C.'s speech at the Cinematograph Exhibitors Association the other night says that the C.E.A. have had many distinguished guests, but C.C. 'just towered among them all with the interest he excited and the impression he made'. 'This single visit of the Archbishop has done far more to deepen our sense of duty and responsibility to the public and to raise our ideals of worthy entertainment than all the criticisms and censorious faultfinding that have been directed against us throughout our history.' That is high praise – another feather in Cosmo's cap.[41]

The Diocese of Canterbury

Lang's work as a diocesan bishop was another way of influencing the bishops and the wider Church. He could set an example in the diocese of Canterbury for other bishops to follow – for instance, by liberally giving permission for Reservation of the Sacrament. The *Canterbury Diocesan Chronicle* was a tool for getting his message across because it was read outside the diocese and sometimes quoted in the local and national press. He could also use his diocesan conference to address issues outside the diocese: in 1934, for example, he delivered an address on 'the heritage of Catholic faith and order entrusted to the Church of England and the whole Anglican Communion' as a riposte to recent sacramental controversies in Birmingham and problems in Liverpool, where a Unitarian had preached thrice in the cathedral.[42]

Correspondence

Late nineteenth- and early twentieth-century archbishops exerted a wide personal influence through their correspondence. In Lang's day, although telegrams and the telephone were used, letters were the primary means of communication. Throughout Lang's archiepiscopate there was a constant stream of mail into Lambeth Palace. The bound volumes of Lang's correspondence reveal that, though his chaplains dealt with many letters, especially those from the general public and the parish clergy, a large number still ended up on the archbishop's desk. Many of Lang's letters to people were pastoral – letters of congratulation, encouragement, or sympathy – but the majority were reactions to incoming mail. It was not uncommon for him to dictate thirty letters a day on different subjects, as Don recorded:

> Another desperate array of letters on subjects such as the King's Jubilee, the deputation to Roumania, the misdoings of the Orthodox clergy in Antioch, the suppression of the Russian Student Christian Movement in Latvia, the imprisonment of Lutheran pastors in Russia, the Christian minorities in Austria, the forthcoming meeting between Hitler and the *Reichsbischof,* the schism in South Africa, the slaughter of seals in the Arctic regions, etc., etc. Is there another man in England who is expected to switch his mind on to so many different subjects in the course of a single day? – and all the time he is interviewing individuals, advising, consulting, disciplining them or deciding their careers for them. If C.C. were a man who worried, he would crack under the strain.[43]

The sheer number of letters sent to Lang are an indication of the extent to which the archbishop was believed to be influential. If Lang received an appeal for help which he thought important, his habitual practice was to get his chaplains to research the details. He would then write a courteous letter to whoever was responsible, usually a Cabinet minister, civil servant or a bishop, setting out the problem and inviting them to look into it. One example was Lang's action on behalf of a number of elderly people from his diocese who were evacuated and allegedly ill-treated in 1940.[44]

Lang used newspapers in order to convey a point. In 1934, for instance, he wrote to *The Times* protesting against the anti-Jewish propaganda in the Nazi newspaper *Der Stürmer.*[45] During the Second World War, he wrote to the press in order to communicate information to the clergy. He also used the *Canterbury Diocesan Chronicle*, pastoral letters and the publication of his 1936 Charge to express his views.

Commissions and Committees

Since Benson set up the Archbishop's Assyrian Committee in 1886, nineteenth- and twentieth-century archbishops sometimes established committees and commissions to investigate, manage, or reform various things.[46] Lang set up committees to deal with spiritual healing, Church reform, dispensations, kindred and affinity, spiritualism, lawful authority, work overseas, and new churches in the Canterbury diocese. Together with the archbishop of York, he inherited a commission on Christian doctrine and established committees to deal with moral welfare, war damage, Canon Law, Church and state, ordination training, women's work and evangelism.[47]

What was Lang's role in commissions and committees? If the 1937 Commission on Kindred and Affinity is a representative example, it is evident that his involvement was peripheral. The 1935 *Church and Marriage* report had urged reconsideration of impediments to marriage, following Parliamentary marriage legislation between 1907 and 1931 which was at variance with the *Table of Kindred and Affinity* in the 1662 Prayer Book. The *Table* was causing difficulties in missionary dioceses, and in 1937 the Lambeth Conference Consultative Body requested Lang to establish a commission to examine consanguinity and affinity.[48] Lang devoted great pains to securing a balanced commission: he sought to obtain the services of a Hebraicist, a canon lawyer, an anthropologist, a church historian, a moral theologian, someone with missionary experience, an Anglo-Catholic and an evangelical. He advised that it would be preferable to interview an expert in eugenics than to have one on the commission. Lang offered the commission a room at Lambeth Palace for a meeting and dinner, and guaranteed the members' expenses. Lang authorised the circulation of a questionnaire to Anglican metropolitans and bishops of extra-provincial dioceses, sent the commission details it had requested about discussions of kindred and affinity at bishops' meetings in 1924 and 1931, and offered some advice about publication. Lang was sent a copy of the final report in December 1939 and played no further role.[49]

No *magisterium* attached itself to Lang, but his ancient office had great standing in both the Church and nation, and was a rallying point for Anglicans. It is clear that archiepiscopal commissions were not so much the archbishop exercising power as the Church using the name and prestige of the archbishopric to find a way of resolving problems or disseminating teaching. Lang was tasked with the responsibility of forming these commissions, largely because he was one of the few people who could. He subsequently advised some of the commissions from time to time by their request, but that was usually the extent of his involvement.

Lang's View of the Archbishopric

How did Lang view the archbishopric? Unlike Davidson, who periodically kept a diary and wrote two memoranda about being the archbishop of Canterbury, Lang neither kept a diary nor set down his thoughts. Fortunately for the historian, Lang gave a talk on 'My Job' to the Croydon Rotarians in 1935 and an enterprising journalist from the *Croydon Times* took down his words.[50] Lang began by referring to his solicitude for all forty-three dioceses in England. He reminded his audience that each diocesan bishop was 'supreme, save for certain legal restrictions, in his own diocese', but said it was 'the custom of one and all to appeal to the Archbishop for advice or counsel upon all sorts of subjects', which were usually very tangled by the time they landed on his desk. There were also a 'vast number of clergy and laity' who tried to go behind the backs of their bishops and make an appeal to the archbishop.

Lang spoke of his work in the Canterbury Convocation and the Church Assembly and of the work involved in steering important matters through them. He mentioned having to decide whether colonial clergy should be allowed to minister in England, and also having to discipline priests and sometimes deprive them of their ministry.

Lang spoke of his work with the Anglican Communion overseas, comprising some 350 dioceses in independent provinces or Churches and twenty-five missionary dioceses in his own jurisdiction:

> The Archbishop must needs keep abreast with all their affairs and be ready to give counsel wherever any request is made to him from any part of the world . . . In this matter, the Anglican community is very like the British Empire. There are a number of nations linked

together only by union with the Crown, and here are also these free Churches linked only by their union with the Archbishop of Canterbury. It is impossible to convey what an immense amount of work all this involves.[51]

Lang next spoke of his domestic role in England, and it is interesting to see how he perceived himself:

Then you must think of his work as a leading citizen of the country, particularly in the leadership of Christian citizenship. He cannot escape that responsibility, whether he is worthy of it or not, from his great position as first subject of the Realm. It demands him taking part in all that appertains to the welfare of the people – housing, education, public morality, public health, and, not least in these difficult times, maintenance of peace. It is to me very touching to know how ready the leaders of other denominations in this country are to receive and accept the leadership of the Archbishop of Canterbury. It is one of the most remarkable indications in recent times of the growing cooperation between all Christian citizens.[52]

He elaborated this point when talking of his work in the House of Lords, where the archbishop 'has to be consulted' about very varied subjects. He said he hoped the day would be far distant when the archbishop concerned himself exclusively with Church affairs. The archbishop had to concern himself in all that belonged to the public life of the nation, including art, science, music, drama and the cinema: 'I think it would be a sad and great misfortune if he ever allowed himself, in spite of pressure on time, to be side-tracked into the purely ecclesiastical region.'

Lang spoke of his own diocese of Canterbury, which he said kept him earthed in the real life of the Church of England. He added that he was also a 'common target' at which 'every partisan, crank and enthusiast throughout the country is entitled to shoot'. Impossible schemes were proposed to him, which would immediately spring into fruitful life if he would but support them. 'They convince the Archbishop of one thing, that if it be true the King can do no wrong it must equally be true the Archbishop can do no right.' He mentioned his extensive daily correspondence, and that he only had his chaplains and secretaries to help him deal with it all. His was a solitary job, where responsibility was not shared with others, but 'nevertheless, I like my job.'

Reading the newspaper text cold, Lang could come across as grumpy and somewhat precious. This is perhaps to miss the twinkle in his eye in the photograph and the touches of self-deprecating humour. At times he appeared to be gently teasing the good Rotarians of Croydon, who interrupted his talk with applause and cries of 'hear, hear'. The psychologist may be tempted to contrast Lang's very exalted concept of his office – the first subject of the realm, with a seemingly unquestioned right to be involved in all that appertained to the common good, accepted by other denominations as the principal leader of Christianity in England – with his stated reluctance to draw attention to himself, because 'if there was one thing he hated more than another it was publicity and talking about himself and his own affairs.' Was Lang being artificially humble, or engaging in some artifice to win over his audience, or was he genuinely in awe of his office and of the responsibility it brought, and perhaps conscious of his limitations and failings? If the latter, it may be another manifestation of the fault-line discernable earlier in Lang's life: ambition for success and preferment, trying to co-exist alongside the desire to serve God. Lang was certainly conscious of being the latest in a long succession of archbishops of Canterbury: 'Lanfranc, Anselm, Becket, Laud, Davidson, and then, at the end, my unworthy self'. He felt that the Church of England was summed up in the person of its archbishop, its 'chief officer'.[53]

What were Lang's priorities? Lang's papers and Don's diaries suggest that reacting to events and issues formed a major part of his work. In fairness, Lang did not have the necessary secretariat to do very much more than to react; and reacting may have been a fair and legitimate part of Lang's ministry. Despite this, some trends in Lang's work may be discerned. He feared the collapse of the Church of England, telling Don, 'I wonder how long the C. of E. can hold together – I can only hope disruption does not come in my time.' Like Davidson, who made 'comprehension' a major plank of his archiepiscopate, Lang spent much time and effort trying to ensure that the Church rubbed along together. He once quoted Newman to Don: '"This is what the Church is said to want – not party men, but sensible, temperate, sober, well-judging persons to guide it through the Channel of No – meaning between the Scylla and Charybdis of Aye and No",' adding, 'That is the "Lambeth Touch", isn't it?'[54]

Another important area of Lang's work was evangelisation and renewal. Lang believed in the value of the establishment of the Church of England, though as events would show after 1928 he was far from being an Erastian. He also believed that England was a mostly Christian country in which there was a widespread 'instinct of religion', but he felt that God was 'not so much denied as crowded out' of many lives. A regular theme in Lang's preaching and radio broadcasts was a call to make a firm personal commitment to God and to express this by attending worship.[55]

Lang spent much thought and effort on providing a Christian witness and commentary on public events. He evidently did not believe that religion and politics should be kept separate. From time to time Lang publicly criticised Mussolini, Hitler and the Soviet Union. He occasionally voiced public criticism of the British government, but one may speculate that he may have felt that this was a policy of last resort, which could potentially backfire. Perhaps he remembered the 1926 General Strike, when the government forbade the BBC to let Davidson broadcast.[56] Lang's correspondence with government ministers, lawyers and civil servants suggests that he felt he could more easily influence things behind the scenes with a letter or a discreet word.

Advancing Christian unity broadly across all fronts was another clear priority for Lang. In 1930, Lang preached in Canterbury Cathedral about the importance of ecumenism, using very generous language about the Roman Catholic Church: 'There can be no fulfilment of the Divine purpose in any scheme of Reunion which does not ultimately include the great Latin Church of the West,' though he admitted the problems caused by some of the Roman claims, adding, 'But meanwhile in the quest of Unity we cannot refuse to enter a door which is opening because another door is for the present closed against us.' Bell, in a private letter to Don in 1950, described Christian unity as an 'absorbing interest' of Lang's and recalled the encouragement he gave to the ecumenical movement in 1937 when he celebrated the Eucharist for all the delegates at the Oxford ecumenical conference.[57] Lang made a point of improving his relationship with the archbishop of Westminster, saw the recognition of Anglican Orders by some Orthodox, and smoothed the way towards inter-communion between the Church of England and the Old Catholic Churches. Less fruitfully, he hosted theological conversations with the Orthodox Churches, addressed the General Assembly of the Church of Scotland and helped resume conversations about unity with the Free Churches.[58]

At one point during his talk to the Croydon Rotarians in 1935, Lang drew a parallel between the Dominions of the British Empire, held together by their common loyalty to the king, and the Churches of the Anglican Communion, held together by their loyalty to the archbishop of Canterbury. If one extends this to include the forty-three dioceses of the Church of England, the parallel may not be so much with King George V as with the Emperor Franz-Joseph of Austria-Hungary. Day after day, Franz-Joseph sat at his desk in Vienna, dealing with a stream of paperwork, attempting to hold together his polyglot empire with its many nations and races tugging in different directions, trying to enable a very imperfect dual-parliamentary system to function and endeavouring to provide a focus of loyalty for all his subjects. Lang's archiepiscopal ministry was broadly similar.

Unlike Franz-Joseph, however, Lang could not command or insist. If he thought something should be done or a particular line followed, he could commend it by word and example, try to cajole reluctant bishops and promote men who would do it. But, in the end, Lang's archiepiscopal ministry depended upon consent and had to be received by the Church. It was not worth his while to go out on a limb, advocating a hopeless cause or a policy that no one would follow, for that might lead to loss of face and impair his leadership on other issues; like an ecclesiastical juggler, he had many different issues to keep in the air at the same time.

Mention has already been made of the fact that the ministry of the archbishop has nowhere been codified or laid down. In the early twentieth century, this gave the archbishops considerable leeway. They could not determine the issues they had to deal with, but they could to a large extent determine the manner in which they would tackle them. To later generations, from a more committee-filled age, it seems surprising that Lang had no cabinet or standing committee which he could consult. This left him in a lonely prominence. Perhaps it gave him greater ease of action, but it also deprived him of a possible avenue of help and support. It also meant that Lang was subject to few checks and balances. In fairness, however, there is no evidence that Lang ever unfairly exploited his position for his own ends or to favour any individuals or groups. Himself an Anglo-Catholic, he was scrupulously fair to all shades of churchmanship.

Between 1928 and 1942, the archbishopric of Canterbury was filled by an elderly Lang who did not always enjoy good health. He had considerable gifts, particularly when it came to teasing out intricate or legal problems, assessing individuals and public speaking. Above all, he had been a bishop since 1901 and an archbishop since 1908. He knew from observing Davidson how the Church of England worked and he had a wide aquaintance amongst senior figures in the royal household, in the government, civil service and judiciary. However, Cosmo Lang, a workaholic with an overriding sense of duty, came to occupy an archbishopric with few boundaries, an almost impossible workload and heavy expectations. Lang's life, in consequence, was relentless.

4

Lang and the Monarchy

'I THINK LANG DID A BIT more for the Royals than other archbishops.'[1] Thus Sir Edward Ford, assistant private secretary to King George VI, mused in old age upon the relationship between Cosmo Lang and the British royal family. Lang did indeed do 'a bit more' for the royal family than other archbishops of Canterbury during the twentieth century. This chapter will chart his relationship with the royal family and will show how he came to have a coherent and deeply held view of Christian monarchy, which would subsequently prove highly significant in the events surrounding the abdication of Edward VIII and the accession of George VI in 1936.

LANG'S CONNECTION WITH THE ROYAL FAMILY

Lang's view of the monarchy was shaped over time, but his experience of the household of the elderly Queen Victoria laid a highly formative foundation, upon which rested his subsequent relationships with members of the royal family.

In 1896, Marie Mallet, a lady-in-waiting to Queen Victoria, heard Lang's Holy Week addresses and was much impressed. Mrs Mallet mentioned Lang to Queen Victoria and in 1898 he was invited to preach before the queen at Osborne House on the Isle of Wight, conveniently just across the Solent from his parish of Portsea. Lang left two accounts of his visits to Osborne: firstly, a set of notes made at the time of his visits or shortly thereafter, and secondly a fuller account written after his retirement in 1943.[2] Lang wrote shortly after his first visit in January 1898:

The invitation was to dine at Osborne on Saturday and stay until the following day after the service . . . Next morning breakfast at 9.30 – the Royal Household has not yet advanced to the primitive custom of regarding the Holy Eucharist as *the* Divine Service. At breakfast, the Ladies of the Household – I forget at this moment who they were, but all very pleasant and unaffected. I can't help thinking these companies must get somewhat tired of one another – *drilled* by the obviously dominating thought of a Personage unseen yet everywhere at the centre of all minds! At 11 a.m 'Divine Service' according to the Court. The company assembles in a long room, used as a chapel. Rows of chairs facing the small and well-furnished altar – cross, candlesticks, flowers, etc.; at its side the reading desk and pulpit – a small organ behind. Punctually at 11 the door opens – 'The Queen' – all rise. I was conscious of a little black figure supported by an Indian servant, followed by children. The little figure sat down at once, opposite the priest, and scanned the text placed on her table . . . The service then proceeded as follows: Hymn, the Litany, another hymn, the 'Ante-Communion Service', a third hymn, and then the sermon. Liturgically, a somewhat mangled office (the 'Supreme Head' certainly would be guilty of 'Carelessness'!) but gaining in dignity through its circumstances, the 'great Queen' paying reverence to her King, and a certain pathos – the pathos of a simple good old woman whom the marks of the so-called 'Church Revival' had not touched. It was an experience which has ever since given a new reality to the 'State Prayers'. To be offering them for 'our most gracious Sovereign Lady' knowing that she was *there* only a few feet distant. I preached a short sermon on a text which has *almost* always meant much (would that it had meant more!) for me – 'Lord, to whom shall we go: thou hast the words of eternal life.'[3]

Queen Victoria noted in her journal:

Service . . . performed by Mr Lang . . . preached exceedingly [well], the matter and delivery both so very good . . . spoke to [him]

for some time after dinner. He is [a] very interesting and clever
man, a Scotchman, and was at Oxford. He has a very hard time at
Portsea, having 40,000 parishioners and the population is not very
pleasant, particularly the artisans, who are very difficult, sceptical,
and full of prejudices. The sailors are true and warm-hearted, but
as well as the soldiers, somewhat difficult to manage. Mr Lang has
thirteen curates to assist him and they all live together.[4]

Lang visited Osborne next in August 1898. After dinner, Lang had
another conversation with Queen Victoria, who recorded that 'Mr Lang
is very agreeable and spoke most sensibly on many subjects, amongst
others of the sad position of the sailors' wives whom they left behind
for so long.' On 8 January 1899 Lang preached what the queen again
thought 'a most excellent sermon'.[5]

Several things may be noted about Lang's early visits to Osborne.
Firstly, he was not intimidated by the atmosphere of the court, but he
appears to have enjoyed himself and retained his powers of observation
and of criticism. Secondly, Lang was not cold to his opportunity and he
seems to have taken pains to make himself agreeable to the queen. In
1898, for example, when the queen advocated quarterly Communion, he
prudently forbore to mention that there was a daily Eucharist in Portsea
Church.[6] During the Boer War Queen Victoria recorded:

> [Lang performed the service and preached] a very fine sermon on
> sacrifice and the war . . . [He dined and] spoke very interestingly
> and wisely about the war, and about the loyalty of the people. He
> is much impressed with the personal feeling they have towards me.
> He is a very clever, agreeable man.[7]

The queen concluded that Lang was 'a man of broad and sound views
and very sympathetic' and rewarded him with a royal chaplaincy on 1
June 1899.[8] Lang was asked to go to Osborne to assist Randall Davidson
with the funeral arrangements following the queen's death on 22 January
1901. He spotted Edward VII and Kaiser Wilhelm II kneeling for a
moment in prayer by the queen's coffin – the 'sacred memory' which was
to land him in such trouble in 1914.[9]

Lang did not care much for the more relaxed atmosphere of Edward VII's court, which would imply that his experience of Queen Victoria's court was formative. He wrote to his mother from Balmoral in 1902:

> After dinner the drawing-room where I had a long conversation with H.M. on the sofa – this sitting so easily is a strange contrast to the serenity of the old Queen's rules. Indeed, the whole spirit is different: I almost think that I preferred the old.[10]

Many of Edward VII's papers were burnt after his death. The surviving correspondence between Lang and Edward VII concerns official business and their relationship appears to have been affable rather than close.[11]

Lang's friendship with George V and Queen Mary was the deepest and most sustained of all his relationships with members of the royal family. All three were of a similar age: Lang was born in 1864, George V in 1865, and Queen Mary in 1867. Lang first met George V, then the duke of York, in Portsmouth in June 1898. The duke seems to have been impressed when Lang stood up to him over a sermon and afterwards went out of his way to make Lang welcome at Sandringham. By March 1900, the duke was writing to 'My dear Lang' about a charity.[12] Six weeks later he wrote again about more personal matters:

> Just one line to thank you for your kind letter congratulating me on my dear father's providential escape [from an assassin in Belgium] and on the birth of our third son. I hear that my father and mother were sitting close together in the carriage when the man fired through the window and the ball was found embedded in cushions just behind their heads, and my mother felt the bullet whizzing past her face. We can only thank God that in his mercy he has preserved their precious lives. I am glad to say the Duchess is making a very good recovery and the baby is flourishing.[13]

Two things may be noted about this letter. Firstly, the duke wrote a chatty, personal letter in his own hand, which was an indication of his burgeoning relationship with Lang. Secondly, the duke's letter was in reply to an earlier letter of Lang's. A great many of the letters to Lang from members of the royal family in the hitherto-restricted 1923–45 volume of royal correspondence at Lambeth Palace are replies to Lang's letters.[14] This would suggest that Lang regarded letters as a means of exercising pastoral care, but perhaps also as a way of bolstering his links with the royal family.

Whilst he was prince of Wales, George V had been delighted by Lang's appointment as archbishop of York: 'His only regret', wrote Arthur Bigge (later Lord Stamfordham), his private secretary, 'is that he feels he will not see as much of you in the future as he has done in the past.' The prince had discovered in Lang a confidant to whom he could unburden himself. This relationship continued after his accession to the throne.[15] In December 1911, for example, George V consulted Lang about the crisis in the House of Lords. George V wrote warm and friendly letters to Lang in his own hand and usually signed himself, 'Your sincere friend, G.R.I.' The king fussed about Lang's health, wrote about his family and shared his private thoughts. Many years later, the duke of Windsor – as Edward VIII became after his abdication – wrote: 'My father's simple but sturdy views upon religion could scarcely have held for long the interest of so subtle a mind [Lang's]. Yet there was no doubting the sincerity of the friendship between them.' The king's religious views were not as two-dimensional as the duke of Windsor hinted. George V was proud to be the first monarch since James II to perform the rites of Maundy Thursday, he favoured the Revised Prayer Books, enjoyed hymns and read a chapter of the Bible every night. He insisted that his Accession Declaration be amended to avoid offending his Roman Catholic subjects. Following his illness in 1928, he told a priest, 'I know you won't believe me, but throughout my illness I felt buoyed up by the prayers of my people.'[16]

Queen Mary also regarded Lang as a friend. She was easily the best-educated member of the royal family, and an intellectual bishop such as Lang would perhaps have appealed to her.[17] Lang's conversational skills may have helped overcome her initial shyness. She had a great devotion to the monarchy and to its history, and she would doubtless have appreciated Lang's support of the king. Queen Mary, although not a ritualist, was by nature a deeply religious woman. She enjoyed a good sermon, and Lang's talented preaching would probably have pleased her. Like the king, Queen Mary sought Lang's guidance from time to time.[18]

In 1911, Lang submitted a memorandum to George V about the role of the monarchy. He recorded:

> I urged the importance of his [the king's] coming into contact with the masses of his people, that it was not enough that they should assemble in the streets on ceremonial occasions to see him, but that he might, so to say, go to see them – move about with as little ceremony as possible through their own towns, villages and workshops.[19]

In consequence, the king and queen undertook the first modern royal tour of a part of their kingdom in 1912, when they visited the north of England, accompanied for much of it by Lang. There was a temporary coolness between George V and Lang during the First World War on account of the controversy surrounding Lang's 'sacred memory' speech in 1914, but the king soon relented.[20]

In the winter of 1928–29, when George V and Lang were both ill, Lord Dawson arranged for them to convalesce at Bognor, Sussex. Once Lang had recovered a little, he ministered to the king. George V's private secretaries knew of the king's friendship with the archbishop and made sure they kept Lang informed about the king's health. Sir Clive Wigram, the king's private secretary, knowing how anxious George V was about the 1931 economic crisis, solicited a supportive letter from Lang to the king. George V was the first monarch to speak to his people by radio. Lang wrote the text of four of the king's broadcasts and most of his 1935 jubilee address.[21] Don wrote an account of a private visit by George V, Queen Mary and the princess royal to Lambeth Palace in 1931, which is both amusing and revealing:

> M. [his wife, Muriel Don] and I lunched with C.C. who was much put out by the vagaries of the weather in view of the fact that he was expecting a private visit from their Majesties. I rang up the Equerry in Waiting after lunch to enquire whether the King and Queen were coming – he knew nothing of the matter nor could he

find anyone who did – no orders had been given and their Majesties were still engaged at luncheon. Had the Queen forgotten about it? Then to the relief of His Grace came a message at 2.40 that all was well – the Royal Party would leave Buckingham Palace at 3.15. I warned Woodward, the Porter, to be ready – Dowding the butler and the two footmen threw open the front doors. I donned my frock coat and Muriel a hat. C.C. paced the corridor gazing at the clouds. At 3.15 it started to rain – C.C. in the depths, bemoaning his ill fortune – the long-anticipated inspection of the garden would be out of the question. What was he to do? Inspect the Crypt or what? Every door was unlocked in anticipation of a circular tour of the house. 3.25 came – it still rained in torrents. Had they started? 'O dear me, O dear me – how pitiable' was all that escaped the archiepiscopal lips. 3.28 the bell rang – the Royal car rounded the corner of the yard – C.C. hastened to the bottom of the stairs as fast as his poor stiff muscles would allow. The Queen emerged, followed by the King and Princess Mary. M. and I stood at the top of the stairs – C.C. presented us to his Royal visitors and then led them into the Drawing Room. At that moment the rain stopped miraculously and the sun began to shine. *Laus Deo* – the day was saved!

So out they went through the Archbishop's study, the King talking at the top of his voice – 'What a small room' he shouted as he caught sight of the enormous study. M. and I listened in the passage upstairs to the Royal banter and then watched the inspection of the Garden from the windows of the Bishops' Smoking Room. The sun shone merrily and the Archbishop's spirits rose – Budden, the gardiner [sic] was summoned from his lurking place behind the bushes and was introduced all round. An animated conversation ensued – Princess Mary took notes – the King gesticulated – the Queen asked questions. Budden was in his glory, spied upon by envious eyes from the Palace windows. C.C. finally led the party to the steps up to the Vestry and re-entered the House. A tour of the Chapel, Crypt and Library followed – the Visitors Book was signed – the royal car drew up at the front door and at 4.45 they moved off, passing en route

Muriel holding 'Nigel' [pet dog] aloft and A.C.D. [Don] waving his top hat.

We joined C.C. at tea and congratulated him upon the delightful entertainment he had provided for us. It was great fun – and their Majesties quite evidently enjoyed themselves too.

When, I wonder, did the King and Queen of England last pay a private visit to His Grace of Canterbury? C.C. is indeed in high favour.[22]

Lang was not very close to George V's eldest son, the prince of Wales. He seems to have tried to befriend the prince, albeit unsuccessfully. According to the courtier Lord Esher, the prince was a rather immature young man and he cannot have had much in common with an intellectual archbishop, thirty years his senior.[23] Donaldson suggests another trait in the prince which may have played a part:

The truth is the Prince was always unwilling to give his confidence to anyone who owed his introduction to him to the King. He believed that the disposition to please Majesty is limitless and he regarded everyone who was a friend or appointment of his father's as potentially a spy.[24]

Lang's relations were a little easier with George V's second son, Prince Albert, known to his family as Bertie. He possessed a deep Christian faith and his confirmation in 1912 meant much to him in later years. In February 1923, Prince Albert wrote to Lang in his own hand to inform him of his engagement to Lady Elizabeth Bowes-Lyon. Twelve days later he wrote again to say that both he and George V hoped Lang would preach at the wedding, 'as you have always been so kind to me'.[25] Lang hit it off with Lady Elizabeth Bowes-Lyon. Seventy-eight years later Queen Elizabeth The Queen Mother recalled:

He married us, you know. He spoke such simple, beautiful words at our wedding . . . The ring got stuck at my wedding and wouldn't go on. 'Push it on harder,' said the archbishop, and it went on. It is made of Welsh gold. All the family have rings of Welsh gold.[26]

Lady Elizabeth Bowes-Lyon, or the duchess of York, as she became upon her marriage, came from an old Scottish family which maintained an Episcopalian chapel in Glamis Castle. Perhaps from her father, the earl of Strathmore and Kinghorne, the duchess of York learnt a simple Christian faith. She recalled: 'My father was very High Church, he was at Oxford and he knew people involved in the Oxford Movement . . . he wouldn't have liked incense, but we had vestments in the chapel.'[27]

After their marriage, the duke and duchess of York often prayed and read the Bible together. Queen Elizabeth The Queen Mother recalled Lang's 'ease of manner. He liked a laugh and a joke,' adding, 'he was a good communicator, there were no silences, as there were with the one who wrote all the books of sermons . . . Michael Ramsey.'[28] Lang told the duchess amusing things that happened to him:

> He told us one day he was stalking, and he saw some deer, and he fell asleep on a little ledge. He woke up with a loud cry because an eagle was hovering over him. The eagle thought he was dead!
>
> He went to stay with the Londonderrys in Yorkshire and when he went up to change for dinner, do you know what he found? A dicky! A man at the station had gone off [by mistake] with the wrong bag with all his beautiful purple things.[29]

The duchess of York kept up a correspondence with Lang. Her letters were chatty and amusing, and she usually signed herself 'yours always affec.'[30]

Of George V's other children, Princess Mary, the princess royal, was the closest to Lang. Princess Mary often initiated an exchange of correspondence, signing her letters, 'With love, your affectionate friend, Mary'.[31]

LANG'S VIEW OF THE BRITISH MONARCHY

Queen Victoria evidently made a big impression upon Lang and he was able to recall her clearly in 1943.[32] It is not unreasonable to surmise that during his visits to Osborne, Lang constructed an image of what a monarch and royal household ideally *ought* to be like. He felt he had been transported to the very centre of national life. In 1898, for example, he wrote: 'In the garden it was curious to see Lord Salisbury standing discoursing with the Queen. It was a sort of picture of the inner mind of the Empire.'[33]

Lang believed Queen Victoria to be 'the greatest Ruler in English history' and told his mother that the queen 'concentrates and embodies in her own person the history and dignity of the Empire'. Lang was much impressed by the dignity of the 'little black figure supported by an Indian servant' and by the queen's kindliness and simplicity.[34] He observed that although the queen could appear formidable, she also exhibited goodness, a sense of humour, and put him at his ease. He believed that her long reign had resulted in an accumulation of wisdom and tact. Lang also noted the queen's keen interest in the people of his parish, and in her troops in South Africa. He was impressed by the queen's devotion to duty and the way that she often worked at official papers until 1 a.m., 'and all this at 79!'[35]

It should be borne in mind, by way of context, that Lang first visited Osborne in 1898 when, as Dom Anselm Hughes OSB has pointed out, 'the National Spirit [was] so pronounced in the period between the Diamond Jubilee and the disillusionment which followed the South African War.'[36] It should also be remembered that Lang was possessed of a romantic streak, which possibly coloured his view of monarchy. Whilst vicar of the University Church in Oxford, he had published a romantic novel, *The Young Clanroy*, set during the 1745 Jacobite rising. Lang once asked Queen Victoria if he might keep his sentimental loyalty to Prince Charles Edward Stuart? 'Certainly, provided of course that it remains *strictly* sentimental,' replied the queen. There was also, surprisingly, a hint of royal romanticism at one point in Lang's 1936 abdication broadcast, when he spoke of Edward VIII going into exile from 'Windsor Castle, the centre of all the splendid traditions of his ancestors'.[37]

George V, with his sense of duty, consistency, moral probity, conservatism, personal simplicity and love of routine, was in many ways a reflection of Queen Victoria's style of monarchy. At George V's personal suggestion, Lang preached at his coronation in 1911.[38] It is likely that this invitation spurred Lang into reflecting carefully and systematically about the monarchy, its place and purpose:

The King is set to be the leader of his people in the service of God and man. He is the servant of God. From God's altar, in symbols of Sword and Sceptre, Orb and Crown, he receives his rule. It is a trust committed by a Master to his Servant. Pray we for our King, that his strong trust in God may keep him faithful to God's great trust in him. He is the servant of the people. To be among them as he that serves – among the people in this home land, among the multitudes of India, among the strong young nations overseas, as the one man raised above all private and local interests, to think of all, to care for all, to unite all in one fellowship of common memories, common ideals, common sacrifices – this is indeed a kingly life.[39]

Lang's 1911 coronation sermon was reminiscent of an ordination sermon and there are important parallels between the two. Lang envisaged the coronation as the Christian consecration of the king to a life of service, in which the king's 'strong trust' in God was an important factor.

Lang seems to have reflected further upon the role of the monarchy from time to time. As has been mentioned, he submitted a memorandum in 1911 and there may be other memoranda in the still-restricted papers of George V. The king and queen discussed the future of the monarchy in a post-war world with Lang in 1919, and in the 1930s he was sensitive to the fact that the British monarchy survived whilst other European dynasties had been swept away and sometimes replaced by dictatorships.[40] But Lang's central vision of a Christian monarchy, expressing itself through devoted service, never wavered.

In his sermons and radio broadcasts during the 1935 silver jubilee of George V, Lang emphasised the king's personal Christian faith and his ceaseless and devoted service to his people:

His subjects . . . have felt that his life was founded, as they instinctively desire the life of themselves and their country to be founded, on the Faith and Fear of God. Thus in the passage of the years he has come to be not the King only, but the Father of his people; and to loyalty has been added the warmth of love.[41]

I would ask you to think of him at Sandringham (his own special and beloved home) or at Windsor or at Buckingham Palace or at Balmoral, rising early every day, reading with scrupulous care all the State Papers submitted to him, transacting business with his Secretaries, then in the late afternoon returning again to the task, and thus acquiring a store of knowledge and experience for the service of the State.[42]

In these broadcasts, Lang did not merely reflect upon the king, but he also conveyed an image, an expectation, of what a British monarch *ought* to be: exalted, consciously Christian, and devoted to duty. David Starkey has described Lang in 1935 as possessing 'a view of Christianity in which the monarch rather than the Cross stood as the symbol of the nation's faith'. This sentence depends upon the meaning placed upon the word 'symbol'. If Starkey means that the monarch had displaced the Cross in Lang's mind, his suggestion is easily refuted by reference to Lang's Good Friday and Easter sermons.[43] If Starkey means that the nation had come to have a quasi-religious faith in the monarchy in a way it no longer had in the Cross, then there is no evidence in Lang's writings to support such an idea. Lang would probably have agreed that the British state was summed up in the person of its monarch, who was the fount of honour and justice, head of the armed forces and supreme governor of the Church of England. But if Great Britain had become a republic, it would hardly have altered Lang's faith in the Cross. As it was, Lang happened to live in a monarchy, which he perceived in avowedly Christian terms.

This became particularly clear at the coronation of George VI and Queen Elizabeth in 1937, which Lang recorded as being 'the culminating day of my official life, the day on which the Archbishop of Canterbury fulfils his highest office in national life, on which through him the Church of God consecrates that life through the person of its King'. Lang was keen to proclaim the spiritual significance of the coronation. On 27 December 1936, he inaugurated with a radio address an evangelistic campaign called the 'Recall to Religion', which focused upon the coronation:[44]

Within five months, please God, our King will be consecrated to his high office and invested with it as a sacred trust from the

Most High God by the solemn and sacramental rites which have
been preserved for well nigh a thousand years. But let him not
come alone to his hallowing. As the representative of the Nation
he must bear his people with him. The august ceremony will be
bereft of its full meaning, it will be a mere splendid spectacle,
unless the Nation with and through its King consecrates itself to
the remembrance and service of God . . . At this time I am moved
to make a somewhat special and solemn appeal to my fellow
countrymen. I make it not primarily as the chief officer of the
Church of England but rather, if I may presume to say so, as a
representative of the Christian life of the Nation.[45]

Lang saw the coronation service in sacramental terms and his
'Recall to Religion' was an attempt to ensure that its 'hallowing' effect
extended beyond the walls of Westminster Abbey to the king's subjects,
consecrating them alongside their monarch 'to the remembrance and
service of God'.

It is evident that Lang's outlook and actions derived not merely
from a coherent and exalted understanding of the monarchy, but also
from a high understanding of the relationship of the archbishopric of
Canterbury to that monarchy. George VI was king because he had
inherited the throne from his brother, but only the Church could crown
and anoint him to fulfil that vocation, and the Church's task was focused
upon its archbishops:

By his anointing – regarded from the early days as the central
feature of the ceremony – the King is consecrated and invested
with that spiritual character – that care, protection and supervision
of the Church and Religion of his people which has always been
an attribute of his office . . . The King does not crown himself.
His crown is brought from God's Altar and placed upon his head
in token that his Kingship is a solemn trust committed to him by
God.[46]

Lang expressed here almost identical sentiments to those he had
enunciated at the coronation of George V in 1911. Lang could simply have

been reusing some particularly good material from 1911, or he may have been especially emphasising the religious aspect of the coronation after the abdication, but in all probability his overall conception of monarchy had not changed since his visits to Osborne. It is hard to know whether to praise him for consistency or to accuse him of inflexibility. What is evident is that there would be a problem if a monarch arose who had a different concept of monarchy.

THE PRINCE OF WALES AND MRS SIMPSON

According to Ziegler, the prince of Wales showed no interest in Christianity. Baldwin told his niece, a Roman Catholic nun, 'He has no religious sense. I have never in my life met anyone so completely lacking in any sense of the – the – the well, what is *beyond*.' In later years, it seemingly did not bother the prince that he would be barred from Holy Communion if he married a divorced woman, and when, towards the end of his life, the bishop of Fulham advised him that, due to changes in legislation, he might be readmitted to Communion, he tardily replied four months later that he would prefer to leave matters as they stood. He claimed in this reply to be 'at heart, deeply religious', but this was perhaps the private view of his old age; there is little to challenge Baldwin's assessment in the 1930s.[47] Nor was the prince remotely interested in the Church of England. Don recorded an incident in 1934:

> The Prince of Wales, speaking to C.C. about Bishop Barnes, asked if it was possible to unfrock him – this because of the Bishop's views on disarmament, etc. The Prince then enquired, 'Who appoints the Bishops?' – such ignorance on the part of the Heir to the Throne is really rather depressing! Has he never read Queen Victoria's letters? He takes no interest in ecclesiastical affairs.[48]

Another disadvantage, as Baldwin once told the prince of Wales, was that he was unmarried. The prince, however, showed no serious signs of wishing to marry, despite George V's attempts at persuasion. In 1918, he had begun an adulterous relationship with Freda Dudley Ward. He also had other affairs. In 1934 Mrs Dudley Ward was suddenly displaced by Wallis Simpson.[49]

Bessie Wallis Warfield, the illegitimate daughter of Teackle Warfield and Alice Montague, was born in Blue Ridge Summit in Pennsylvania, United States of America, in 1895. Her parents subsequently married, but Teackle Warfield died in 1897. In 1916, largely to escape a restricted and impoverished home life, Wallis married Win Spencer. Spencer proved to be a violent alcoholic and the marriage ended in divorce in 1927. By this stage, Wallis had met Ernest Simpson, an affluent Anglo-American Jewish businessman. They married the following year in London and settled there.[50] Mrs Simpson was first introduced to the prince of Wales at a house party at Melton Mowbray in 1931 and met him socially over the next three years. In 1934 Mrs Simpson took advantage of the absence in the USA of the prince's latest flame to secure his affections. Former girlfriends, including Mrs Dudley Ward, were suddenly excluded from the prince's life. Wallis and Ernest Simpson soon began to be invited to dinner parties and country house weekends, and Mrs Simpson accompanied the prince on continental holidays.[51]

George V's last year of life was blighted by his anxiety about the prince of Wales' relationship with Mrs Simpson. According to his biographer, Kenneth Rose, 'he thought her unsuitable as a friend, disreputable as a mistress, unthinkable as a wife.' On 19 September 1934 the king had a long talk at Balmoral with Lang about the prince and Mrs Simpson. Lang wrote to Don: 'Things look very black. An hour yesterday in the garden with the King – outpouring all his troubles! I like the daughter-in-law very much – simple and unaffected and sensible.'[52] In other words, Lang was contrasting Mrs Simpson unfavourably probably with the duchess of York, or possibly with Princess Marina of Greece, whom the king's third son, Prince George, was shortly to marry. Alec Sargent, Lang's chaplain, recorded that 'we were not told much, but I gathered that there was some "dreadful common American woman" whom the Prince of Wales was always taking about with him.' It is not clear from the text whether it was Lang or George V who called Mrs Simpson a 'dreadful common American woman'. The king was gloomy and depressed: at some point Lang congratulated him on the high standing of the monarchy, to which he replied, 'What use is it, when I know my son is going to let it down.' George V could not bring himself to talk to the prince about Mrs Simpson, except on one occasion, when the prince assured the king that she was not his mistress. George V's private secretary, Sir Clive Wigram, known as Lord Wigram from 1935, later convinced the king that the prince had lied.[53]

THE DEATH OF GEORGE V AND ACCESSION OF EDWARD VIII

George V was left worn out by his jubilee. His letter of thanks to Lang was written by the lord chamberlain rather than by the king. In early June, the king collapsed at Sandringham and was ordered by his doctors to rest. The king's health steadily declined. On 16 December Baldwin told Lang that 'he was troubled by the news from Sandringham about the King's health, adding (privately) that the possibility of a change coming was to him "like a nightmare".'[54] On 12 January 1936 Lord Dawson saw the king at the start of what would prove to be his last illness. Lang spoke to Wigram on 17 January, 'telling him that I hoped that, if the anxiety grew, I might be allowed to come as, apart from the call of personal friendship, I felt the country would expect it'. Queen Mary 'readily agreed' and early on Sunday 19 January Lang was summoned to Sandringham.[55] Don noted that the archbishop was nervous:

> He rather dreads the ordeal, for the views of the Royal Family on religion are rather conventional and the arrival of the Archbishop may cause some embarassment all round . . . It will require all C.C.'s skill and tact to overcome the shyness with which any suggestion of priestly ministrations will be met – but his long friendship with the King and Queen will stand him in good stead.[56]

Lang visited George V in his bedroom that night, but found the king asleep. He returned the next day, prayed with the king and blessed him.[57] Lang had planned to return to Lambeth, but Dawson dissuaded him:

After lunch, during which Queen Mary was still marvellously strong and calm, Dawson took me aside and said, 'You can't go – the end may come very soon.' I had some talk with the Queen, Princess Mary and the Duke of Kent about my celebrating the Holy Communion and giving the King his last Sacrament. The difficulty was that the Queen, anxious to 'keep up' to the last, was afraid that any such service would make her 'break down', and this was a risk she dared not run; and that the King now losing consciousness would not understand and might be bewildered rather than strengthened. I suppose these are always the difficulties with people unaccustomed to the sacramental aspect of religion. But in view of them I dared not press my own wish. But later I went with Lady Elizabeth Motion to the rectory and arranged with the Rector (Fuller) to have a celebration early next morning.[58]

The prince of Wales, the duke of York and the duke and duchess of Kent then arrived at Sandringham. The prince of Wales was annoyed to find the archbishop of Canterbury in the house, and tried unsuccessfully to persuade Lord Dawson to tell Lang to leave. In his memoirs, the duke of Windsor portrayed Lang as 'a noiseless spectre in black gaiters' slipping in and out of the dying king's room. The other members of the royal family, however, appreciated Lang's support. Lang visited the king again during the evening.[59] He was summoned from his bedroom at 11.15 p.m.:

I put on my cassock and went . . . to the King's room. The Queen and Princess Mary were there, with the doctors and nurses. The sons were together downstairs. No one seemed to think of calling them, and for this I was sorry. Then, after some time of quiet waiting, as the King's breathing grew more slow, I read the Twenty-third Psalm, some passages from the Scriptures such as St Paul's great 'I am persuaded . . .' and some prayers at quiet intervals, and then, going to the King's side, I said the Commendatory Prayers – 'Go forth, O Christian soul' – with a final Benediction. Still the King lingered: then the Prince of Wales, the Duke of York and the Duke and Duchess of Kent were summoned. As it was plain that the King's life could only last for a few minutes, I felt that I must leave the Queen and her family alone and retired . . . Finally, within a few minutes, the breathing ceased, and, in the words of the last bulletin, 'Death came peacefully to the King at 11.55 pm.'[60]

Queen Mary's first action was to kiss the hand of the prince of Wales, now King Edward VIII, who became hysterical. Lang was sympathetic: 'I suppose they [George V's sons] had seldom if ever seen death: and that it was the Queen still marvellously self-controlled, who supported and strengthened them.' Within minutes, Edward VIII ordered that all the clocks, which by order of George V were kept half an hour fast, should be put back to real time, which gave offence to some of George V's staff. 'I wonder what other customs will be put back also,' mused Lang. Edward VIII then repeatedly telephoned Mrs Simpson throughout the night, to her irritation.[61]

All the royal household were present when Lang celebrated Eucharist in Sandringham Church at 8.30 a.m. on 21 January, but he was 'rather grieved' that of the royal family, only Princess Mary was present. As Lang returned to the house, he met Edward VIII, addressed him for the first time as 'Your Majesty', and 'spoke a few hasty but deeply felt words about his great responsibility and my desire to give him loyal service'.[62]

The obsequies of George V were attended by controversy. Edward VIII told Lang that he did not wish any religious service at all when his father's body was brought to lie in state in Westminster Hall. Lang 'insisted that, however short, there *must* be some such service.'[63] As the gun carriage bearing George V's coffin was pulled into Palace Yard, Westminster, the cross fell off the crown which lay on top of the coffin and rolled into the gutter. A quick-thinking sergeant-major retrieved it. 'Christ, what will happen next?' exclaimed Edward VIII. The incident was widely felt to be an ill omen.[64]

Lang officiated in Westminster Hall with great emotion. He then went to the House of Lords, where addresses of condolence were passed.[65] In the days following George V's death, Lambeth Palace was the scene of much activity. Lang became ill and refused to go to bed. He recovered, but was in a low state of mind. He said to Don, as he saw the crowds of people flocking into Westminster Abbey to hear him preach on the

Sunday after George V's death, 'I wish I had something to say to them
– what is wanted is some prophet from the wilderness, not an old hack
who is weary and stale from overmuch speaking.' In fact, Don recorded,
Lang rose to the occasion.[66]

Lang used his sermon in Westminster Abbey on 26 January and a
radio address that evening to express once again his vision of a Christian
monarchy.[67] The archbishop paid a strange tribute in the radio address
to Edward VIII. Having praised the qualities of George V, he then said
that the new king possessed very different qualities and prayed that his
character might be enlarged:

> No other monarch, it may be said, has ever come to the Throne
> knowing so well and known so intimately by all classes of his
> subjects. The new King has a personality of his own, in many ways
> different from that of his beloved father, and it is through his own
> personality that he must make his contribution to the history of
> the British Monarchy. We pray that his gifts may be consecrated
> to the service of his people by God, and that his character may be
> deepened and strengthened that he might rise nobly to the height
> of his great responsibility.[68]

Perhaps, with hindsight, Lang may have given away more about
Edward VIII than he intended. Lang again became ill at Windsor on
Monday 27 January. He recovered sufficiently to officiate at George V's
interment the following day. The archbishop reflected that night:

> What a week! From the arrival at Sandringham on the 19th
> to this final scene on the 28th – the strain of the last hours at
> Sandringham – the preparation of the forms of service for
> Westminster Hall and by request of the Privy Council – the
> intruding business of Convocation – four public utterances, at
> Convocation, in the House of Lords, at Westminster Abbey and at
> the Broadcast Service – and the funeral. All of these crowded into
> ten days. . . But I feel that a long and greatly valued chapter of my
> life – associated with the constant kindness and friendship of King
> George – is closed. There is not only a new reign but a new régime.

I can only be most thankful for what has been, and as for what is
to be [sic] hope for the best. God guide the King![69]

The modern reader of issues of *The Times* from the 1920s and 1930s might
be struck by the sheer number of photographs printed each week of King
George V and Queen Mary carrying out their official engagements, often
with a little description of the queen's dress. It has become something
of a cliché, but Britain between the wars was still a deferential society,
with the monarchy at the top of the social pyramid. Newspapers such
as *The Times* contained news stories and advertisements from around
the British Empire, and it was hard to ignore the fact that, as well as
being king of Great Britain and Ireland, George V was also emperor of
India and monarch of the British Dominions and of his other territories
'beyond the seas'. This image was reinforced by the BBC's programmes
linking radio stations around the empire to mark royal events such as
George V's silver jubilee. The British monarchy in the 1920s and 1930s
was treated with great seriousness in the press and on the wireless: not
for nothing during the Second World War were American servicemen
warned against criticising the royal family when they came to Britain.[70]

From the perspective of the early twenty-first century, this seems a
vanished world, the antithesis to the mentality of 'Cool Britannia'; yet
this was the world and mentality of Cosmo Lang. Lang would have
been a part of that world anyway, by virtue of his office as archbishop of
Canterbury, but his long friendship with George V drew him to its very
centre. Lang himself had been shaped by the prevalent, serious view of
monarchy; and indeed, Lang had helped to promote a solemn and sacral
image of monarchy through his sermons and broadcasts. When Lang
was confronted with Edward VIII's desire to marry Mrs Simpson, he did
not find himself merely casting around for an excuse to justify getting
rid of an unsatisfactory monarch and his unsuitable prospective
consort; rather, in his actions, Lang sought to protect the institution of
the monarchy itself, as he had long conceived of it.

5

Lang and the Abdication Crisis

IF THE PROVERBIAL MAN ON the Clapham omnibus knows anything about Cosmo Lang and the abdication of Edward VIII in 1936, it is likely to be that the archbishop delivered a controversial radio address after the ex-king had gone into exile. A poem afterwards circulated:

> My Lord Archbishop, what a scold you are!
> And when your man is down, how bold you are!
> Of Christian charity how scant you are!
> And, auld Lang swine, how full of cant you are![1]

In fact, Lang's radio broadcast was incidental to his role in the abdication. Although Lang was keen to cover his tracks, he was from a very early stage closely involved in the events leading to the abdication of Edward VIII. Newly declassified documents reveal that Lang and Baldwin shared a hope that Edward VIII would abdicate and that both worked to ease him from the throne and to replace him with George VI. This flies in the face of the widely held view that Lang was merely a concerned bystander. In his 1949 biography, Lockhart played down Lang's part in the events of 1936:

> This account should have shown how small was the Archbishop's part in the conclusion. He was deeply concerned; he was kept fully informed; but, except for one occasion, when the result was no longer in doubt and his opinion was asked on a contingent point, he neither influenced, nor tried to influence, the course of events. Satisfied that the Prime Minister's attitude was substantially

identical with his own, he was content to leave him the hand to play, without an ecclesiastical interference which was unneccessary and might even have been embarrassing. This view was confirmed by no less weighty an authority than Lord Baldwin himself. A few weeks before his death in December 1947 he told the present writer that the Archbishop had made no attempt to force the issue, or even to press his point of view, and that the decisive factor was the uncompromising stand of the Dominion Premiers, and especially of the Prime Minister of Australia.[2]

Lockhart's book has been the standard source of information used by historians and biographers, and his account of Lang's role in the abdication has seldom been questioned. Frances Donaldson used Lockhart for her biography of Edward VIII (1974) and repeated his version of events, as did Adrian Hastings in *A History of English Christianity* (1986). Philip Ziegler cited Lockhart in his official biography of Edward VIII (1990). He also had access to Lang's secret notes on the abdication and to Don's diaries.[3] Lang occupied a peripheral role in Ziegler's account of the abdication and he did not question Lockhart's version.

One of the few people to query Lockhart's account of Lang's role in the abdication was H. Montgomery Hyde in his biography of Baldwin (1973). Montgomery Hyde discovered a confidential letter sent by Lang to Baldwin on 25 November 1936. He pointed out that it contradicted Lockhart's account, but did not pursue this further. Sarah Bradford hedged her bets in her 1989 biography of George VI, claiming that Lang had been on the sidelines of the crisis, 'despite a few attempts to intervene'. Alan Wilkinson, in his entry for Lang in the 2004 *Oxford Dictionary of National Biography*, merely observed that Lang had regular consultations with Queen Mary, Baldwin, Dawson and Sir Alexander Hardinge, the king's private secretary, but 'what influence he exerted on them is not known'.[4]

A very different account of Lang's role is to be found in the memoirs of the duke of Windsor, published in 1951:

I never underestimated the weight and authority of the group whose views the Prime Minister represented. His senior Ministers, the men closest to him, were deeply conservative, not alone in their politics but equally in their way of life. Behind them, I suspected, was a shadowy, hovering presence, the Archbishop of Canterbury. Curiously enough, I did not once see him throughout this period. He stood aside until the fateful fabric had been woven and the crisis was over. Yet from beginning to end I had a disquieting feeling that he was invisibly and noiselessly about.[5]

This chapter will show why and how Lang was 'invisibly and noiselessly about'.

Lang's First Audience with Edward VIII

When Edward VIII acceded to the throne in January 1936, many people expected that with time he would become an excellent king. His official biographer has commented, 'If a committee had been devised to set up a pattern for a modern monarch, it would have ended up with something very similar to what the country had now acquired.'[6] Baldwin, the prime minister, saw things differently. As George V lay dying, he told Tom Jones, his friend and confidant:

> You know what a scrimshanker I am; I had rather hoped to escape the responsibility of having to take charge of the Prince as King. But perhaps Providence has kept me here for that purpose. I am less confident about him than Lucy [Mrs Baldwin] is. It is a tragedy that he is not married . . . He had been to see Mrs S. before he came to see me . . . The subject is never mentioned between us. Nor is there any man who can handle him. I have seen Halsey and Godfrey Thomas [members of the prince of Wales' staff] . . . When I was a little boy in Worcestershire reading history books, I never thought I should have to interfere between a King and his mistress.[7]

Baldwin later confided in Clement Attlee at Edward VIII's accession Privy Council that he gravely doubted whether the king would 'stay the course'.[8]

Lang seems to have hoped for the best from the new king. He was summoned to Buckingham Palace to see Queen Mary on the day after George V's funeral and also saw Edward VIII.

The duke of Windsor later gave an account of his audience with Lang in his 1951 autobiography, *A King's Story*. Was the audience quite as the duke portrayed it? Although the duke was officially the author, *A King's Story* was in large part ghost-written by the American journalist Charles Murphy. One of the duke's biographers, Donaldson, has commented that the book is notable 'for the razor-edged skill with which, using the methods both of *suppresso veri* and *suggestio falsi*, he carries the war into the enemies' camp', and its version of events proved controversial. The duke of Windsor – or Murphy – had read Lockhart's biography of Lang, and the account of Lang's audience in *A King's Story* bears more than a passing resemblance to it.[9]

The duke began by saying that Lang called at Buckingham Palace the day after George V's funeral to see Queen Mary, after which he asked to see Edward VIII, and here his account tallies with Lockhart, except that Lockhart adds that Lang also saw Princess Mary.[10] The duke then includes a 'digression' to explain his feelings towards Lang. Having first mentioned the archbishop's friendship with George V, the duke described him as ingratiating, too polished and worldly, 'rather in the tradition of the medieval churchman, accustomed to the company of princes and statesmen, more interested in the pursuit of prestige and power'. Having thus set the scene, he continued:

> When, therefore, the Primate glided into my office that afternoon, I could not bring myself to greet him with perhaps all the warmth to which he had been accustomed in dealings with the Sovereign. Dr Lang opened the conversation by saying how sorry he was over the years that we had failed to come to know each other better. Announcing that he intended to be frank and forthright with me, he said that he supposed that I must be aware that my father had at various times discussed me with him. 'It would be a pity, Sir,' he said, 'if you were to misjudge me in this connection. Believe me, I appreciate that you are different from your father in your outlook and temperament. I want you to know that whenever the King

questioned your conduct I tried in your interest to present it in the most favourable light.'[11]

Lang's contemporaneous account is broadly similar, but the nuances are quite different:

> Then I had quite a long talk with the King. I told him frankly that I was aware that he had been somewhat set against me by knowing that his father had often discussed his affairs with me. But I assured him – which was true – that I had always tried to put the most favourable view of his conduct before his father. He did not seem to resent this frankness, but quickly said that of course there had always been difficulties between the Sovereign and his heir.[12]

The duke gave his own interpretation of this conversation:

> My conduct, I wondered. What was Dr Lang driving at? No man likes to be told that his conduct has provided a topic of conversation between his father and a third person. At any rate the Archbishop's disclosure was an unpropitious note with which to inaugurate the formal relations between a new Sovereign and his Primate. It was unfortunate, but there it was. However, hiding my resentment, I turned the conversation in the direction of my new responsibilities as head of the Church. Even on this subject, I could not seem to impress him; for, when I brought up the names of several clerics whom I knew and liked, his cool almost negative response implied that my acquaintance with Church affairs was too naïve to be pursued. No doubt he was as relieved as I was when the audience came to an end.[13]

Lang's account, again, has a slightly different feel to it:

> He said, naively, that he understood he had to appoint Bishops, and asked me to tell him how it was done! I tried to enlighten him. He spoke of one or two clerics whom he had met; but even

of these his knowledge was very faint. It was clear that he knows little, and I fear, cares little, about the Church and its affairs. But I was impressed by his alertness and obvious eagerness to know and to learn; and he was very pleasant and *seemed* to be very cordial. As I left, I spoke once again, as at Sandringham, about his great responsibilities and promised to give him all the help and support I could. Well, we shall see.[14]

The duke added a final gloss to his account of the audience:

There was nothing more. Yet the air in the room was heavy with portent when the Archbishop left. During the months that followed my mind was to travel back to that conversation many times. Wallis's name had not of course been mentioned, but I knew that the Archbishop intended that I should know she was the hidden burden of his discourse. He was clearly against our continued friendship. He would undoubtedly muster powerful forces in opposition to my project when I came to press it. That encounter was my first intimation that I might be approaching an irreconcilable conflict.[15]

The duke of Windsor may have retained a very detailed recollection of his conversation with Lang fourteen years earlier. But the possibility that he derived his account from Lockhart's earlier version cannot be avoided. The duke may also have deliberately omitted Lang's remark that he 'was aware that he [the king] had been somewhat set against me by knowing that his father had often discussed his affairs with me'.[16] The overall impression of the duke's account is that he is seeking to enhance himself and his version of the abdication at Lang's expense.

Lang's notes on the audience, which were used by Lockhart, have an altogether different feel to them. His account was written a few days after the audience, and the overall impression is that Lang was concerned about Edward VIII, but wanted to help him, and hoped that the king's alertness and eagerness to know and learn might presage a successful reign. This view is confirmed by the description of the audience Lang gave to Don when he returned to Lambeth Palace later that day:

He had a long talk . . . with the King who was evidently very
cordial. So that is good. His Majesty asked if it is the case that
he had to appoint Bishops and C.C. enlightened him as to the
procedure – altogether a very satisfactory conversation which has
cheered C.C. considerably.[17]

Problems with Edward VIII

Within a few weeks of Edward VIII's accession it started to become
apparent to a small circle of courtiers, to the prime minister and to the
archbishop of Canterbury that the king's initial eagerness and admirable intentions were begining to wane. The problems were his attitude
to his work and his relationship with Mrs Simpson. The king initially
set about the administrative side of his work with great enthusiasm and
read and initialled everything in his red despatch boxes. After a while,
he slackened and read very little. Unlike his father, Edward VIII worked
to no system and thought nothing of disturbing his staff at mealtimes
or during the night. As the months went by he stopped reading state
papers altogether and his staff had to cover up for him.[18] According
to Donaldson, the king's tendency to leave red boxes lying unguarded
around Fort Belvedere, his private residence near Sunningdale, Berk-
shire, was also regarded as a grave security risk and the Foreign Office
began screening all documents sent to him and omitting the most sensitive. The king's tactlessness and penny-pinching – contrasted with
his extravagance towards Mrs Simpson – offended many in the royal
household.[19]

According to Ziegler, Edward VIII had long suffered from depression
and self-pity. Baldwin, who despite everything rather liked the king,[20]
described him after the abdication to his niece Monica Baldwin:

He is an abnormal being, half-child, half-genius . . . It is almost
as though two or three cells in his brain had remained entirely
undeveloped while the rest of him is a mature man. He is not
a *thinker*. He takes his ideas from the daily press instead of
thinking things out for himself . . . No serious reading: none at
all.[21]

Alan Lascelles, the prince's assistant private secretary between 1920 and 1928, and later one of his critics, claimed that 'For some hereditary or physiological reason, his mental and spiritual growth stopped dead in adolescence, thereby affecting his whole consequent behaviour.'[22] There are possible parallels between the character of Edward VIII and that of his dead paternal uncle, the duke of Clarence. His maternal heredity was little better: his grandfather, the first duke of Teck, always touchy, suffered from mental problems towards the end of his life; and his uncle, Prince Francis of Teck, was a gambler and roué who caused his family great anxieties. The problems exhibited by Edward VIII were known to comparatively few people. When he wanted to, the king could still impress and excite his subjects.[23]

It might have been possible for courtiers and the government to cope with a wayward and self-pitying Edward VIII, had he not additionally been infatuated with Wallis Simpson. Those who had heard of Mrs Simpson wondered why the king – the most eligible bachelor in the British Empire – was so besotted with her.[24] Mrs Simpson soon came to dominate the king's life. Edward VIII weeded his court of all who opposed his liaison with her. Hardinge reflected after the abdication:

> It was scarcely realized at this early stage how overwhelming and inexorable was the influence exerted on the King by the lady of the moment. As time went on it became clearer that every decision, big or small, was subordinated to her will . . . It was she who filled his thoughts at all times, she alone who mattered, before her the affairs of state sank into insignificance.[25]

Lang's Change of Mind About Edward VIII

As the months passed, Lang became the recipient of a series of disquieting reports about the king. The first of these came in February 1936 from Admiral Sir Lionel Halsey. Halsey had been the head of the prince of Wales' household for twenty years and was devoted to him, but critical of his relationship with Mrs Simpson. Shortly after his accession, Edward VIII told Halsey that there would be no place for him in his new household. Halsey visited Lang in February 1936 and later recalled telling him that 'I was quite sure that if something was not done to make His Majesty realize the great danger he was incurring, there was bound to be trouble.' Halsey, who knew from Wigram – who was continuing as Edward VIII's private secretary for the first six months of his reign until he was replaced by Hardinge – that the king had told Ernest Simpson that he loved Wallis Simpson and wanted to marry her. Halsey possibly also knew that Wigram had warned Baldwin about this. Lord Linlithgow, the viceroy of India, expressed his concern to Lang and Baldwin during a visit to London.[26]

It is worth noting that Lang had deeply held views about divorce and the remarriage of divorcees. Between 1909 and 1912, he served on the Royal Commission on Matrimonial Causes. In 1912, he issued a minority report, dissenting from the Commission's proposals to enlarge the grounds for divorce.[27] In 1939, Lang wrote to his beloved Ann Todd, who planned to remarry after divorce:

> You cannot expect me to approve of the steps, which, so far as I can understand them, you mean to take. For I do indeed believe – quite apart from my official position – that it is against Our Lord's will that the bond of marriage should be voluntarily broken.[28]

Other troubling reports circulated about the king. In early March, Edward VIII refused to subscribe to all the ecclesiastical charities which George V had supported. On 4 March, William Ormsby Gore, the first commisioner of works, lunched with Lang at Lambeth and reported 'difficulties' with the king. Don noted that the king had not attended the Chapel Royal, unlike George V who never missed a Sunday when in London. The king had also fidgeted all through the Royal Maundy service.[29]

Lang had two private sources of information about the king. Prebendary Launcelot Percival, the precentor of the Chapel Royal, spoke to Don about the behaviour of Edward VIII and Mrs Simpson.[30] On 1 November, Don wrote:

> Met Lancie Percival at the Athenæum – he told me sad things about the King. It is a miserable business. And yet H.M. protests

that Mrs S. is not his mistress – but he spends vast sums of money
on her – is he quite normal?[31]

Percival had been the precentor since 1922, and his action could have
been construed as disloyalty. He must therefore have been very anxious
about Edward VIII and probably hoped that his information would be
relayed back to Lang. It is impossible to know what Percival found out
about Edward VIII, although he lived in St James's Palace and knew
many courtiers and members of the royal family.

One of Edward VIII's chauffeurs was the boyfriend of Lang's
chauffeur's daughter. His accounts of 'rowdy parties at the Fort, with
private cinema shows in Windsor Castle from which they return in the
early hours of the morning' were relayed to Lang's secretary, Gwen Fuller.
She in turn passed them on to Sargent, who thought them 'servants'
talk'.[32] Most likely these were indeed little more than disgruntled
accounts of what the king did and occasionally said; but the significance
is that they reached Lambeth Palace. Lang thus probably knew as much
about Edward VIII's behaviour as Baldwin did, if not more.

As time passed, Lang started to receive letters complaining about
Edward VIII and Mrs Simpson, often from Britons living overseas who
read local newspaper accounts of the king's infatuation and speculation
about his proposed marriage. The British press was more reticent.
Margaret Cook, for instance, wrote from the United States to say that
educated Americans were profoundly disturbed and 'would regard the
King's marriage to Mrs Simpson as a disgrace to the honour, a betrayal of
loyalty throughout the British Empire'. Don wrote that Lambeth Palace
was 'inundated' with cuttings about the king from the American press.
An English correspondent, Mabel McCartney, asked Lang to appeal to
Mrs Simpson not to marry the king.[33]

Why did ordinary people write to Lang about Edward VIII? Why
did members of the the royal household and of the government consult
him? Many people wished that the archbishop of Canterbury would do
something, even though they perhaps did not know quite what they
wanted him to do.[34] They felt unhappy and embarrassed by Edward
VIII's liaison with Mrs Simpson. Lang symbolised a Church of England
which affirmed the sanctity of marriage and was known to have been

a friend of George V. His role was not widely understood, and he was probably sometimes credited with greater influence than he possessed. The truth was that Lang could bring relatively little direct influence to bear upon Edward VIII. George V had consulted Lang and thus the archbishop could make suggestions to him. This did not occur with Edward VIII.[35]

Lang seems to have borne no personal animosity towards Edward VIII. He had known him all his life and had a high regard for 'the rich promise of his service as Prince of Wales', but he was dismayed by his behaviour after his accession. Perhaps, like Queen Mary, he hoped that the king's infatuation for Mrs Simpson would simply wear off. At the start of his private account of the coronation of George VI, written in 1937, Lang looked back to 1936 and reflected: 'I had a sense that circumstances might change. I could only pray that they might, either outwardly or in his [Edward VIII's] own soul.'[36]

Lang tried to cultivate Edward VIII, though there were few opportunities. The archbishop wrote to Edward VIII after a madman called McMahon threw a loaded revolver at him and the king appreciated his letter. On 21 July 1936, Lang visited Edward VIII to discuss the coronation, which was planned for May 1937. He tactfully did not mention Mrs Simpson, noting confidentially that he hoped 'to speak to him frankly about his private life and ask him to reconsider it in the light of these solemn words' nearer to the coronation. Lang was pleased when Edward VIII agreed not to make any drastic changes to the coronation liturgy, though he wrote that the king had seemed 'strangely detached from the whole matter' and had asked the duke of York to be present. The king telegraphed his thanks for a 'kind telegram' which Lang sent him for some reason on 23 July. This was the high-water mark of Lang's relationship with Edward VIII; thereafter things worsened. The king let it be known that he was unenthusiastic about Lang's meticulously planned scheme to erect a statue of George V opposite the House of Lords, preferring memorial playing fields instead. Once, when Baldwin was waiting to see Edward VIII, the duke of Kent entered the room and reported 'He [the king] is damning the whole root and stock of the Episcopacy and has just shoo'd the Archbishop of Canterbury out of the house.' It is unclear when this incident took place, but it is surely significant that after their meeting on 21 July, except for both being present at the state opening of Parliament on 3 November 1936, the king and the archbishop did not meet each other.[37] Indeed, the two men appear never to have spoken again.

By the time of the abdication, Lang's chaplains, Don and Sargent, realised that Lang secretly felt that Edward VIII was unfit to be king and wished him to go.[38] Lang himself wrote in 1937:

> But as the months passed and his relations with Mrs Simpson became more notorious the thought of my having to consecrate *him* as King weighed on me as a heavy burden. Indeed, I considered whether I could bring myself to do so.[39]

To Sargent, Lang confided, 'Think of pouring all those sacred words into a *vacuum*!'[40]

When did Lang decide that it would be preferable if Edward VIII were to abdicate? It is impossible to be certain, but it is quite likely that the idea began to form in his mind during his holiday at Ballure in September 1936. Lang would not have found such a conclusion easy to reach. He recorded that he spent this time giving close study to the coronation rite and perhaps this led to reflection about Edward VIII. Lang had probably heard of the king's cruise in the Adriatic with Mrs Simpson on the *Nahlin*. Edward VIII returned to Britain on 14 September and spent the last fortnight of the month at Balmoral. For the first time in twenty-five years, Lang was not invited. Lang is unlikely to have missed the widespread offence that Edward VIII caused across Scotland when he suddenly declined to open a new hospital wing in Aberdeen on 24 September on the grounds that he was in mourning and sent the duke of York in his place. The king was photographed at the same time meeting Mrs Simpson at Ballater railway station.[41]

The duke and duchess of York, realising that Lang would not be visiting Balmoral, invited him instead to visit them at Birkhall, Deeside, on 9–10 September. Lord Wigram, who had recently retired as the king's private secretary, and Hardinge, his successor, came to dinner. Lang recorded on 10 September:

I had a good talk with Clive Wigram, at Craig Gowan, up and down the problem of His Majesty . . . In the afternoon we went on to Balmoral. Went into the house [the king had not yet arrived], looking rather sadly desolate and through the gardens. Memories crowded around at every turn.[42]

Lang returned to tea at Birkhall and wrote: 'The children – Lilliebet [sic], Margaret Rose and Margaret Elphinstone – joined us. They sang some action-songs most charmingly. It was strange to think of the destiny which may be awaiting the little Elizabeth, at present second from the throne!'[43]

Was it at this point that Lang first began to think seriously of the duke of York and his family as alternative king and line of descent?

THE SIMPSON DIVORCE

Lang returned to Lambeth Palace on 1 October. On 15 October, it became known that Mrs Simpson was to sue her husband for divorce at the end of the month. Baldwin had been warned a day earlier by Hardinge that he would have to intervene. Parliamentary colleagues and others also began to exert pressure on Baldwin to act.[44] The prime minister was invited to spend the weekend of 16–18 October at Cumberland Lodge in Windsor Great Park with Lord FitzAlan, a Roman Catholic former Conservative chief whip and viceroy of Ireland, the duke of Norfolk, Lord Salisbury, and Lord Kemsley, a press magnate. According to Middlemass and Barnes, the weekend had 'almost certainly' been arranged by FitzAlan to discuss the Simpson divorce and the reports in the American press, and Baldwin 'was quickly made to feel how urgent the others believed the crisis to be'. Hardinge drove over on 17 October and added his voice to the pressure on Baldwin to intervene to try to prevent the divorce and to advise the king not to flaunt his association with Mrs Simpson.[45]

Queen Mary, too, was alarmed. According to Pope-Hennessy, she 'consulted one or two extraneous persons in her anxiety and she had even urged the Cabinet to take some sort of "action".'[46]

The result of all this pressure was that Baldwin sought an audience with Edward VIII on 20 October. The prime minister was nervous and although he spoke of Mrs Simpson, he never mentioned the possibility of the king marrying her. The king said that he could not interfere in Mrs Simpson's divorce. He did not like Baldwin's suggestion that he conduct his affair with more discretion, nor his further suggestion that Mrs Simpson go abroad for a while. The audience ended with no clear decision or agreement, though the king told Baldwin, 'You and I must settle this matter together. I will not have anyone interfering.'[47]

Lang began to be directly involved the next day when Hardinge came to see him about Mrs Simpson's divorce. Lang wrote a secret memorandum:

> Saw Major Right Hon. Alexander Hardinge, Oct. 21, 1936. Mrs Simpson – divorce proceedings 23 or 24 October – if then – what? Prime Minister informed – realised situation – has seen His Majesty – hopes divorce proceedings stopped – in any case pleaded Mrs Simpson should not be given prominence in public, etc., etc. All this accounts for statements in even good American journals that His Majesty will retire, etc., etc. Prime Minister the right person to intervene as representing the nation. Alec Hardinge agrees not wise for me to intervene, at least at present.[48]

Lang, later made an undated addition to his secret notes on the abdication, elaborating the last point:

> I may add here that I had reason to know that His Majesty would not receive or listen to any advice (for which he did not himself ask) except from the Prime Minister who had a constitutional right to advise him. I was sorry for this; and afterwards there was much criticism that I had not apparently endeavoured to see His Majesty. But I knew that I would not be received and in any case there was nothing I could fitly and fruitfully say at that stage beyond what the Prime Minister had said to him.[49]

It was the job of king's private secretary to represent the king to the government and vice versa.[50] He was also supposed to know the mind of prominent people, and Hardinge's visit to Lambeth Palace might simply have been to ascertain Lang's views. Alternatively, Hardinge might have been seeking archiepiscopal support of some sort. Lang presumably felt that intervention at that early stage was inopportune and fraught with hidden dangers for himself and the Church of England. In fact, Hardinge was dismayed that Baldwin had neglected to ask the king if he intended to marry Mrs Simpson. Donaldson says that Hardinge discussed this point with some of the heads of the civil service and that in the week following Baldwin's audience a message from them was transmitted to Mrs Simpson via her solicitor warning her off marrying the king.[51]

In public, Lang carried on as though nothing was the matter. On 22 October, he discussed with the bishops the arrangements for Edward VIII's coronation.[52] He spent the following weekend at Hatfield House, seat of Lord Salisbury; Baldwin was also a guest. Lord Salisbury had previously been present at the meeting with Baldwin at Cumberland Lodge, and may have invited Lang and Baldwin together in the hope that they might find an opportunity to discuss Edward VIII and Mrs Simpson. In the event, Baldwin unburdened himself to the archbishop. Lang recorded:

> He told me he had an interview with the King on October 19 . . . This matter of a possible marriage with Mrs Simpson was one which did not only affect His Majesty personally but was of grave public importance and increasing public concern . . . The Prime Minister acknowledged His Majesty's desire for domestic happiness and companionship, but insisted that if Mrs Simpson was to supply this need she must be kept in the background and not given any place of her own in Court functions, etc . . . As to the possibility of His Majesty's marriage to Mrs Simpson, the Prime Minister said to me that he would find out exactly whether there was any constitutional bar to the King's unfettered choice, but that was a 'fence' which must be taken when it appeared . . . He realised my difficulty in intervening at present, and agreed it would be best to leave the matter in his hands at present. I said that possibly later when going over the Coronation Service with His Majesty I might be able to put in a word.[53]

Lang got the date wrong in his notes, as Baldwin saw the king on 20 October, not 19 October. Lang again shied away from intervening, although he did not preclude future action. Perhaps he felt that he could hardly support Baldwin's suggestion that the king retain Mrs Simpson for private domestic happiness and comfort. The significance of this meeting is that it broke the ice between Baldwin and Lang on a very delicate subject. Lang recorded, 'After my talk with the Prime Minister at Hatfield I kept in close touch with him and Hardinge.' In the six weeks before the abdication, Lang and Baldwin met seven times on 1, 19 and 26 November, 1, 3, 6 and 10 December. Baldwin telephoned Lang on 6 December and there may have been other telephone calls of which no record survives.[54] These conversations provided Lang with an opportunity both to support and to influence Baldwin.

On 27 October 1936, Mrs Simpson was awarded her divorce decree nisi, which would become absolute after six months. 'Meanwhile,' as Lang recorded, 'all sorts of newspapers from America kept pouring in, giving all sorts of rumours about Mrs Simpson and His Majesty.' Edward Fitzroy, the speaker of the House of Commons, Prebendary Percival, Major F.J. Ney from Canada, and Walter Runciman (later first Viscount Runciman) of the Board of Trade all expressed their anxieties to Don or Lang.[55]

Baldwin, too, was becoming increasingly troubled and the possibility of an abdication entered his mind. On 5 November, he confided in Tom Jones:

> I have grown to hate that woman [Mrs Simpson] . . . Walter Monckton sat next to her recently and came to the conclusion she was a hard-hearted bitch. I have turned on the lawyers and ascertained what our powers are. If he marries her she is automatically Queen of England. I would then hand in my resignation and I think my colleagues would agree to do so. Of course he may offer to abdicate. The best thing that could happen now would be for him to be received in silence in the streets, but outside London the facts are not widely known.[56]

Baldwin may have read the 1935 Special Branch report on Mrs Simpson, which revealed that at the same time she was seeing the prince of Wales, she appeared also to be engaged in an adulterous relationship with Guy Trundle, a Ford motor car salesman and the son of a clergyman from York.[57] It is not unreasonable to speculate that if Baldwin knew about Mrs Simpson and Trundle, he may have mentioned them to Lang, the former archbishop of York.

On 7 November 1936, Hardinge came to see Lang in confidence. On 11 November, Geoffrey Dawson, editor of *The Times*, asked to see Lang. The archbishop recorded, 'I had a long and very confidential talk with him in which he spoke to me about the possibility at some early date of *The Times* intervening in an article.' Lang gave Dawson the impression that he was 'sitting quite remote from the principal actors in the crisis, having made up his mind (wisely as I thought) that any intervention on his part would do more harm than good'. Dawson also saw Baldwin, who was very chary.[58] Lang wrote to Dawson on 12 November. The original letter does not survive in the Dawson Papers and the top part of the office copy at Lambeth Palace has been cut off, so that only the bottom six lines remain:

> I need not tell you how grateful I was to you for our confidential talk yesterday. Since I saw you I have talked to other responsible people and it becomes increasingly apparent that some decisive clearing of the air must be achieved within the shortest possible time. I only hope that the Prime Minister will now take some further definite step. I expect he would wish to do so before anything appeared in *The Times*.[59]

It is not clear which 'responsible people' Lang spoke with, but it is evident that he wished Baldwin to do more. Two days later, Hardinge, who had been in touch with Baldwin and Dawson, wrote to Edward VIII warning him that the press silence about Mrs Simpson could not last much longer and that the prime minister and senior members of the government were meeting to discuss what action should be taken over 'the serious situation that is developing'.[60] The king asked Baldwin to see him on 16 November and told him:

I want you to be the first to know that I have made up my mind and nothing will alter it. I have looked at it from all sides – and I mean to abdicate and marry Mrs Simpson.[61]

Edward VIII then asked him not to mention this 'except to two or three trusted privy councillors' until he gave him permission. Later that evening the king announced his intention to abdicate and marry Mrs Simpson to Queen Mary and Princess Mary, who secretly alerted her family about the king's decision. On 17 November, the king began a tour of South Wales and Baldwin went to Scotland.[62]

Lang, meanwhile, was facing the problem of the 'Recall to Religion', a nationwide evangelistic campaign which he had inaugurated to coincide with the coronation. On 17 November, he convoked a secret meeting of the bishops. No minutes were taken, but fortunately Henson wrote an account in his diary:

After the [Church Assembly] session had closed at 5 p.m., the Archbishop requested the Bishops to meet him in his room, a cloak room behind the platform, of which the windows were fast closed, and the atmosphere stifling.

His Grace explained that untoward circumstances had arisen, of which he doubted not the Bishops had general knowledge, and these did, in his judgement, render it unadvisable to carry out the plan which he had outlined at the Bishops' Meeting in October. It would not be edifying to stir up the nation to a religious preparation for the King's crowning when the King himself was making it apparent that he himself took anything but a religious view of the ceremony. It was becoming generally known that the King was behaving in an unseemly way with an American lady whose second divorce had been given publicity in the English papers, and who was openly described in the Press of America as Queen-designate of Great Britain! The English newspapers had exhibited a most commendable reticence, but of course, this could not be reasonably expected to continue. The King's constitutional advisers hoped to obtain from him some assurances which might alleviate, if not altogether remove, the suspicion that he intended to marry a twice-divorced American. But in the absence of such assurances, the Archbishop thought that we could not make the arrangements which had been designed. He ended by requesting the Bishops' advice.

The Bishop of London spoke shortly in support of the Archbishop's view: and then I spoke, explaining that I could not continue in the asphyxiating atmosphere of the room, but did not care to leave it before expressing my opinion. I said that I had been very doubtful of the wisdom of the action originally outlined by the Archbishop, but was quite certain that in the circumstances indicated by his Grace, that action could not be otherwise than in the highest degree unfitting and unedifying. We could but hope that, by the goodness of God, the King would give such assurances as would make it possible for them to attend the Coronation with a good conscience.[63]

Baldwin returned from Scotland on 19 November and had a long talk on the same day with Lang. Lang recorded:

> He said His Majesty had made up his mind to retire into private life with Mrs Simpson . . . The Prime Minister said that His Majesty was quite explicit in his statement of his determination and had communicated it to the Queen, to the Duke and Duchess of York and his brothers.[64]

Lang was afterwards very circumspect, even with Don, who noted: 'C.C. had a long talk with Mr Baldwin today – I know not what the upshot was, for C.C. is not very communicative.'[65]

Also on 19 November, Baldwin saw Dawson of *The Times*, and, 'to clear his own mind', discussed with him at what point the Cabinet could object to the king's marriage, and what might be the reaction in the country, concealing from him the news that Edward VIII had already decided to abdicate. Baldwin began to have a table of procedure for an abdication secretly drawn up later that day.[66]

On 19 November Edward VIII returned from South Wales, where he had received a warm welcome, and, as Lang put it, 'he seemed to waver'.[67]

In his absence from London, Esmond Harmsworth, son of the press magnate Lord Rothermere and editor of the *Daily Mail*, had suggested to Mrs Simpson that a solution might be found in a morganatic marriage between her and the king. Deriving from German Salic law, this meant that they would contract a marriage of unequals: Mrs Simpson would become Edward VIII's wife but would not become queen-consort and any children of their union would not inherit the throne. Middlemass and Barnes suggest that this proposal might have been part of a plan to 'spearhead' a 'King's party' in Parliament. Mrs Simpson suggested this compromise to the king on 21 November. After some initial distaste, Edward VIII came around to the idea, saying 'I'll try anything in the spot I'm in now.' He authorised Harmsworth to mention the possibility of a morganatic marriage to Baldwin on 23 November, but the prime minister was 'surprised, interested, and non-committal'. Baldwin ascertained that special legislation would be needed.[68] The prime minister was evidently anxious lest a 'King's party' should be formed in Parliament in support of Edward VIII, and to this end he secretly spoke with Clement Attlee and Sir Archibald Sinclair, the leaders of the Labour and Liberal parties, who pledged not to form an alternative government. Baldwin also spoke to Winston Churchill, a friend and supporter of the king, who promised to support the government.[69]

Having heard nothing from Baldwin about the proposal regarding a morganatic marriage, Edward VIII summoned him to an audience on 25 November.[70] Shortly before going to see the king, Baldwin received a letter from Lang marked 'Strictly Private'. Lang wrote by hand, so that no carbon copy existed and no secretary knew his private thoughts. The letter was delivered to Downing Street by hand for speed and to ensure that Baldwin received it before seeing Edward VIII. Lang omitted all mention of this letter in his notes on the abdication, but the original survives in the Baldwin Papers and reads thus:

> Forgive me if in this letter I seem to intrude unasked into your heavy responsibilities about The Affair.
>
> 1. I gather that it is becoming more and more difficult to prevent leakage into the press. If so, the leakage will soon become a

flood and burst the dam. This makes it most important that if any announcement is to be made of the kind you indicated to me it should be made as soon as possible. The announcement should appear as a free act.

2. I have reason to think that He does not fully realise that if the course indicated is to be taken, he must leave as soon as possible. It would be out of the question that he should remain until the decree is made absolute. It is needless to dwell on this necessity. I understand you are seeing him to-night; and doubtless you would make this plain.

Only the pressure of our common anxiety – and hope – can justify this letter. It is written shortly and hurriedly. Forgive it.[71]

It is evident that Lang possessed inside knowledge about the press, probably from Dawson. Whilst being cautious in his choice of words ('of the kind you indicated to me', etc.), he was pressurising Baldwin to act. An announcement of the king's abdication in order to marry Mrs Simpson should be made as soon as possible, presumably on the grounds that once this was done, the only thing that remained was for the king to leave. The abdication should appear as a free act. This would make good, long-term tactical sense, but Lang's sentence raises the question of whether Edward VIII had been manouevred – or whether Lang feared the king might subsequently *appear* to have been manoeuvred – into deciding to abdicate.

It is interesting that Lang wrote 'I have reason to think that He does not fully realise that if the course indicated is to be taken, he must leave as soon as possible.' Lang showed here that he had information about the king's thoughts and likely attitude. His source was probably Hardinge. Lang insisted that if Edward VIII had decided to abdicate and marry Mrs Simpson – 'the course indicated' – then the king 'must leave as soon as possible'. By 'leave' Lang probably meant abdicate the throne, though he might have also meant go into exile. In other words, the archbishop urged that it would be impossible for Edward VIII to decide to abdicate and then to hang on to his throne until Mrs Simpson received her decree absolute in May 1937. The prime minister must ('would make this plain') get the king to leave as soon as possible, for 'it is needless to dwell on this necessity.'

Finally, Lang referred to his and Baldwin's 'common anxiety and hope'. This presumably meant their common anxiety that Edward VIII would find some way of marrying Mrs Simpson and staying on the throne, and their common hope that the king would abdicate quickly. The letter paints a fascinating picture of the relationship which existed between Baldwin and Lang in late 1936. It shows that both men wished Edward VIII to abdicate, to the extent that Lang sought to nerve Baldwin to expedite this outcome.

Lang's letter was placed in the restricted royal papers of the Baldwin collection, where it was seen by H. Montgomery Hyde when researching his 1973 biography. Montgomery Hyde reproduced Lang's letter with the comment that this contradicted Lockhart's assertion that 'he never sought to influence the course of events during the constitutional crisis or impose a point of view on the Government,' and he suggested that Lang had apparently not heard of the morganatic marriage proposal when he wrote it.[72] In truth, it would be safer merely to observe that Lang did not mention the idea of a morganatic marriage. An upset Wigram had been to see him on 24 November, and perhaps Lang may have learnt from him of the proposal, but did not think it a realistic one and therefore considered it not worth mentioning to Baldwin.[73] A copy of Lang's letter was made at 10 Downing Street and is to be found in The National Archives, where it was read by Susan Williams when researching her book *The People's King: The True Story of the Abdication* (2003). She printed Lang's assertion that Edward VIII 'must leave as soon as possible' and his closing words, without comment.[74] Neither author seems to have appreciated how revealing or important is Lang's letter.

When the prime minister had his audience on the evening of 25 November, Edward VIII asked Baldwin formally to put the morganatic marriage proposal to the Cabinet and to the prime ministers of the Dominions. Edward VIII was constitutionally obliged to accept the advice of his ministers, and the consequence of consulting the Cabinet and the Dominion prime ministers was that if they said that a morganatic marriage was impossible, then the king was left with the choice of either abdicating or giving up Mrs Simpson.[75] Lang's concern that an abdication should appear as a 'free act' becomes explicable.

Baldwin and Lang met on the evening of 26 November.[76] According to Middlemass and Barnes, Baldwin appeared profoundly worried that day as he took stock of the situation. Baldwin also saw Geoffrey Dawson and Vincent Massey, the Canadian high commissioner, who told him that Canada would not accept the king's marriage to Mrs Simpson, but urged tact. At a Cabinet meeting on 27 November, Baldwin expressed his fears that the Cabinet might have to resign if the king refused their advice. Edward VIII, he reported, seemed to have been led to believe that Churchill might be prepared to form an alternative government. There was a risk of dividing the country.[77]

On Sunday 29 November, Geoffrey Dawson came to Lambeth, and Lang slipped away from entertaining bishops-designate to see him. Sargent recorded his belief that they had discussed the 'leader' that Dawson had ready to publish in *The Times*. Dawson made no mention of this in his brief note of their meeting. He found Lang 'very anxious, as he was bound to be', but again left Lambeth under the impression, from his conversation, that Lang 'was taking no hand in public affairs'. The following day Hardinge came to see Lang, but there is no record of their conversation.[78]

These days were very stressful for Queen Mary, who turned to Lang for support. On 28 November, Lang visited the queen at Marlborough House at her request. Lang also met Queen Mary secretly at lunch in a private house, and afterwards he told Sargent that it had been 'a most harassing interview'.[79] On 1 December, Lang again saw Queen Mary and the princess royal. They discussed the proposed morganatic marriage:

> She was wonderfully calm and clear, though of course greatly perturbed. She said His Majesty had come to tell her of his 'secret', that on the *rule nisi* becoming absolute, on or about April 27, he intended to marry Mrs Simpson making her Duchess of Lancaster or Cornwall or some other title but not making her Queen. The Queen was emphatic that to her this would be the worst possible

course, 'a Court within a Court' etc., and make her own position intolerable. She was clear that the only alternative was that if His Majesty determined to marry Mrs Simpson he must give up the crown. Princess Mary came in and joined the conversation. She fully agreed with her mother.[80]

After the audience, Lang went to see Baldwin, and, although there is no record of their conversation, it would be surprising if Lang did not pass on Queen Mary's views. Baldwin brought Lang up to date by saying that he had seen Edward VIII and told him that 'the suggested compromise would require special legislation – and that neither the Government nor the Opposition would introduce it; and that he must choose between Mrs Simpson and his throne.'[81]

The Bishop of Bradford's Speech

On 1 November 1936, Bishop Barnes of Birmingham preached what Don called a 'needlessly provocative' sermon in the Chapel Royal, advocating the de-sacramentalising of the coronation rite, the inclusion of Nonconformists and the removal of the Eucharist in order to involve the Salvation Army. Lang was annoyed, for he had previously told the bishops that there could be no role for Nonconformists. The Anglo-Catholic bishop of Bradford, Alfred Blunt, used the meeting of his diocesan conference on 1 December to talk about the forthcoming coronation and to defend the traditional, eucharistically centred coronation rite.[82] His speech was unexceptional, except for one section where he mentioned Edward VIII:

> The benefit of the King's Coronation depends under God, upon . . . the faith, prayer, and self-dedication of the King himself; and on that it would be improper for me to say anything except to commend him and ask you to commend him to God's grace, which he will so abundantly need, as we all need it – for the King is a man like ourselves – if he is to do his duty faithfully. We hope that he is aware of his need. Some of us wish that he gave more positive signs of such awareness.[83]

Blunt's speech was reported in the local press and from there it was taken up by the national press, who abandoned their previous restraint about the king. The duke of Windsor later described Blunt's address as a 'bombshell', and this was the point at which most ordinary people in Great Britain learnt of Mrs Simpson's existence. Mrs Simpson was smuggled to France.[84] Lang was horrified, as Sargent recorded:

> C.C. was furious with Bradford. 'Why can't he hold his tongue? If he only knew all that I know . . .' etc., etc. Don and I disagreed with him and argued quite forcibly, that it had to come out somehow, and that it was just as well that the occasion of the disclosure should be an address so thoughtful and dignified as the Bishop's.[85]

Lambeth Palace was contacted by the *Manchester Guardian*, *Platform*, the *Daily Mail* and journalists from other newspapers, but Lang refused to see them or to make any comment. The archbishop had all along sought to to avoid publicity for himself and the Church of England, and a story was fabricated to the effect that he had approved Blunt's address in advance.[86] Lang reproved Blunt on 7 December:

> Let me thank you . . . for the very clear and impressive description you gave of the real religious significance of the Coronation Service. As to the single sentence in which you made some criticism of the King, I myself at once imagined that they had reference mainly to his apparent neglect of attendance at Church, and I learn from you that you yourself in writing those words several weeks beforehand had no wish to refer to rumours which were so soon to monopolise the public attention. If you had consulted me beforehand I think I could have told you from my intimate knowledge that the time was imminent, had so to say almost arrived, when some intimation would be necessary of the problem which was concerning the King and Empire, and perhaps in view of this you might have modified your words. Moreover I am a little sorry that it could be represented that the initiative in the disclosure was taken by a Bishop because it seems to give

countenance in uninstructed quarters to the statement now being vigorously made that the Bishops held a secret meeting (alluding I suppose to our meeting at the time of the Church Assembly) and deputed you to initiate the controversy.[87]

On 3 December, Blunt was quoted in the press as saying that he had written his address six weeks earlier when he knew nothing of Mrs Simpson. He later repeated this point in a private account of the controversy, in which he said that Barnes had preached his controversial coronation sermon in June or July 1936. In fact, Barnes preached his sermon on 1 November, some two weeks after Blunt claimed to have written his address. Sargent noted that Blunt 'may have *written* his address before he knew much about her [Mrs Simpson], but he certainly knew the outlines of the story by the time he delivered it.' The truth leaked out in August 1937 when Blunt suffered a nervous breakdown. Reuters reported him as having said that his remarks had been deliberate: 'I took the risk because of the danger that silence was doing to the Crown and Empire.'[88]

On the evening of 2 December Baldwin had an audience with Edward VIII.[89] The next day, Baldwin saw Lang and gave him an account of their conversation:

It was necessarily somewhat painful and His Majesty was much agitated. The Prime Minister told him of the views of the Cabinet and Opposition. He told him frankly that he had been in communication with the Governments of the Dominions. They had one and all (except De Valera who had difficulties of his own) stated that they would not support the legislation necessary for the [morganatic] compromise. There was a particularly strong telegram from the Prime Minister of the Commonwealth of Australia, stating that in his view His Majesty could not now re-establish his prestige or command confidence as King. Baldwin did not hesitate to show His Majesty this telegram. He told him there were only three alternatives. (1) Give up Mrs Simpson. This His Majesty said he would never do. (2) Marry her but not make her Queen – this was ruled out by the impossibility of getting the

necessary legislation in this country and the Dominions through.
(3) Abdication. He left His Majesty with this last course plainly
before him. His Majesty must now come to a decision.[90]

The difficulty, as Lord Zetland, the secretary of state for India,
informed Lord Linlithgow, the viceroy of India, was that the king would
not reach a decision.[91] He began instead to compose a radio appeal to the
nation, asking it to decide for him in some unspecified manner, but on
4 December Baldwin wrote to Edward VIII that he 'cannot advise that
the King should broadcast as proposed'.[92] Edward VIII was clearly under
great psychological strain and rumours circulated at Windsor Castle that
he had become mentally ill.[93] Churchill advised the king to temporise.[94]
The Beaverbrook–Rothermere press and in particular the *Daily Mail*
supported the king, and between 3 and 6 December there was continued
talk of the formation of a 'King's party'.[95] Sargent observed:

> There, to my mind, was the danger point of the whole situation
> – the complication of the King's decision by bringing in the false
> sentiment and anti-Baldwin partisanship of the cheap press. They
> might have divided the country, and every country in the Empire,
> into two bitterly opposed parties, and they might well have
> encouraged the King – when the morganatic proposal was rejected
> – to defy his Government and precipitate a general election fought
> on the Mrs Simpson issue.[96]

The danger was not lost on Lang. On 3 December, *The Times*
published a leader, which skirted around about the crisis and omitted
to mention Mrs Simpson by name.[97] Lang wrote to Dawson that day
(though no copy of his letter is included amongst the abdication papers
at Lambeth Palace Library):

> I thank you for your admirable leader in the *Times* this morning.
> I note that the *Daily Mail* has broken loose and ventilates the
> impossible compromise: also the *News Chronicle*. I do most
> earnestly hope that the Government will stand firm. The two
> essentials of the present situation are swiftness and decisiveness.[98]

Psychological Information About Edward VIII

At the end of the first week of December 1936, Lang received some unexpected information, which, if true, shed important light on Edward VIII's infatuation with Mrs Simpson. On 3 December, the Rev. Donald Rea, vicar of Eye in Suffolk, contacted Lambeth about a confidential matter. Encouraged by Don, he sent a letter accompanied by notes (now missing) that seem to have suggested that Edward VIII, when prince of Wales, had undergone treatment for alcohol addiction at the hands of Dr Alexander Cannon of Welbeck Street, London, whose methods might be dangerous. Lang took the information seriously enough to write to Dr William Brown, another doctor whom Rea had mentioned. Brown replied that he was not acquainted with Cannon except through his writings, but he had been consulted about a patient who appeared to have been treated by Cannon for alcoholism using a hypnotic procedure, 'but not one that I, as a medical psychologist, would use at the present day or consider really useful – addiction to alcohol, treated with hypnotism, may be replaced by addiction to something else (varying in different cases)'.[99] Brown added that he had seen Lord Dawson of Penn and given him an account. Despite Donaldson's assertion to the contrary, there is clear evidence that the prince of Wales drank too much. On one occasion, a quick-thinking royal policeman, Frank Proud, had to recruit a passing civil servant, William Walmsley, to help him carry the prince of Wales, who was drunk and incapable, into St James's Palace via the servants' entrance, before he was spotted by passers-by. The prince was also once seen inebriated, weaving his way into a ladies' lavatory by mistake.[100] Perhaps Lang speculated that an addiction to alcohol had been replaced by an addiction to Mrs Simpson. Lang sent Rea's notes to Lord Dawson for him to write down his impressions.[101]

Baldwin, too, received psychological information about the king at the beginning of the following week. On 6 December, Dr Bernard Armitage, a sexual psychologist, sent Baldwin a letter marked 'Secret and Confidential' about Edward VIII's relationship with Mrs Simpson.[102] Armitage's diagnosis was that the king had experienced social and sexual inadequacy in his youth, and that he had 'overcompensated'. He added,

I had always foretold to myself (these being matters not to speak about to others out of respect) that when once he *did* find a woman who would in all respects satisfy him, he would prove to be singularly and persistently obstinate in attaching himself to her – all the more emphatically because he would think (as he does think, consciously or unconsciously) that he was turning himself *away* from being what would be regarded as an unsatisfactory man, into being a thoroughly satisfactory man, acceptable to the general opinion of the nation. The stage was set for disaster.[103]

What was the impact upon Lang and Baldwin at this juncture of these letters about Edward VIII? Lang evidently took Rea's information seriously and discussed it with Baldwin, who, after the king had abdicated, asked to see the correspondence and Lord Dawson's comments. Rea's notes and Dawson's comments were never returned to Lambeth and perhaps they were so sensitive that they were destroyed. Baldwin, however, carefully preserved Armitage's letter, despite his request that it be burnt.[104] The prime minister may have done so in order to protect himself in the future. In all likelihood, the letters from Rea and Armitage did not alter events to any great extent, for Baldwin and Lang had already decided that Edward VIII would have to go. Their probable effect was to steel the nerves of the prime minister and archbishop and to reinforce their conviction that abdication was the only desirable outcome. Rea's letter may also have helped to spur Lang's intervention.

In 2012 a Channel 4 television programme *Edward VIII: The Plot to Topple a King*, quoted a letter sent to Geoffrey Dawson on 6 December 1936 and signed by 'A.C.D.' of the Cloisters, Windsor Castle.[105] 'A.C.D.' reported that, according to Lord Wigram, Edward VIII was suffering from psychological problems:

He strongly confirmed what I heard from another trustworthy source - that H.M. is mentally ill, and that his obsession is due not to mere obstinacy but to a deranged mind. More than once in the past he's shown symptoms of persecution mania. This, even apart from the present matter, would lead to recurring quarrels with his ministers if he remained on the throne. It is an odd and tragic throw-back to George III, with Winston [Churchill] playing for leadership of the 'King's friends'.[106]

Edward VIII: The Plot to Topple a King claimed that 'A.C.D.' was Alan Campbell Don, Lang's chaplain, and alleged that Don had written at Lang's behest to the editor of *The Times* to smear the king's reputation. In truth, the letter was sent to Dawson by Anthony Charles Deane, a canon of St George's Chapel, Windsor, and almost certainly without Lang's foreknowledge.

LANG'S INTERVENTION

By 4 December, the day he received Rea's letter, Lang seems to have decided to try to influence events. He did so in two ways, with great discretion.

> That afternoon I saw the Moderator (Aubrey) and the Secretary (Berry) of the Federal Council of Evangelical Free Churches, and gave them as much information as to the position as I thought it was possible to give. I discussed with them the reactions of public opinion. They believed the mass of the people would support the Government but acknowledged that a large proportion of the young to whom the King was a popular hero and who knew little of the real circumstances felt a strong sympathy with him. 'He is doing the honourable thing. He wants to marry the woman he loves. Why shouldn't he?' etc. I suppose that those who like myself have known the whole business for two years can scarcely realise the effect of this sudden crisis on minds wholly unprepared for it, and ignorant of all that had led to it.[107]

Why should Lang decide to discuss something so sensitive with Nonconformists? It was not his usual mode of behaviour. Why should he seek their views about the reactions of public opinion when he had many other, closer channels of information? One possible explanation is that he was trying to ensure that they, with their different marriage discipline to the Church of England, did not publicly support the king and the idea of a 'King's party'. Lang was in a strong position, for Aubrey was very grateful to him for suggesting that Nonconformist representatives be included in the coronation procession.[108]

Lang then turned his attention to the Church of England:

> That evening I issued through the Broadcast service and the Press a plea that on the following Sunday those who spoke from the pulpit or otherwise should refrain from speaking directly on the King's matter, but that everywhere prayer should be offered for him and his Ministers.[109]

Lang was probably concerned to protect the reputation of the Church of England, and his plea might have been an attempt to avoid unseemly sermons which would be reported in the press and damage the Church. But if Lang's plea prevented attacks upon Edward VIII, it also prevented sermons being preached in support of the king's marriage to Mrs Simpson, which might be reported in Monday's newspapers and thus prolong the crisis. By specifically mentioning the king's ministers, Lang portrayed the situation not as merely a romantic love story, but as a constitutional crisis between the king and his ministers. In Durham, Henson read between the lines:

> The Archbishop of Canterbury counsels us to pray for the King, and say nothing about him. But what must we pray for in his behalf? If Mrs Simpson is his mistress (as is commonly thought), that he should cast her off? If she is not, that he should withdraw his offer of marriage, and, having deprived her of her second husband, bid her seek elsewhere for a third? That he should abdicate? It is probable that the last would be best for the country.[110]

THE ABDICATION OF EDWARD VIII

On Saturday 5 December, Edward VIII finally decided to abdicate and sent a message to Baldwin. Not knowing this, Lang went down to Canterbury to spend the weekend as usual in his diocese.[111] The following morning, Baldwin telephoned and asked Lang to return to London and see him at 3.30 p.m. Baldwin told Lang that Edward VIII was anxious lest Mrs Simpson's decree nisi divorce was not made absolute in four months' time, and he lost both his crown and his bride. The suggestion had been made that the government might introduce a Bill alongside the Abdication Bill, giving immediate effect to Mrs Simpson's divorce. Lang wrote:

> The Prime Minister in his anxiety to get the whole matter settled quickly in the only possible way was at first ready to fall in with this new proposal, and thought he could justify it to Parliament for reasons of State and personal considerateness to the King. But his colleagues who had met that morning were against it and were to meet again at 5.30 for final decision. It was this interval that he wanted my advice about. After much talk, I said that as he talked my mind went through three reactions – first surprise and dislike – then appreciation of the plan as securing once and for all the King's voluntary abdication in the interests of the country and Empire – then finally grave doubts. It seemed to me a very dangerous constitutional precedent that the legislature for the sake of one individual even a King should directly interfere with the course of justice in the Courts; and also that the plan would look very much like an attempt, so to say, to whitewash what there was a chance of proving to have been a collusive suit. But I pressed strongly upon him that he would have a strong case if he tried to show the King that this course would really not be in his own interest – that if he chose to abdicate rather than renounce his marriage for the sake of the country and Empire he would secure a great wave of sympathy which would be of immense value to him in the future – but that this would be greatly lessened if his going were mixed up with a discussion about Mrs Simpson's divorce. The Prime Minister seemed to be impressed by these considerations, and thanked me cordially. He described himself as like a dog in a sheep-dog trials who has to induce a single sheep into a narrow gate. As I write the decision of the Cabinet is being made.[112]

By saying that this plan would not be in Edward VIII's best interest, Lang was providing an argument for Baldwin to use with the king.

Lang's advice to Baldwin was in line with his letter of 25 November. Baldwin's remark about being like a sheep-dog inducing a single sheep into a narrow gate is of particular significance, for he here made it clear that he not only wished the king to go, but that he was actively working to realise that end. It also reveals that Baldwin had been a little disingenuous when he told the Cabinet the day before that 'if he had been trying to put pressure on the King to leave the Throne it would be a different matter, but that all his efforts were being directed towards an act of free will by the King.' At 5.30 p.m. the Cabinet met and rejected the suggestion of a Bill to expedite Mrs Simpson's divorce.[113]

By Monday 7 December, Lang felt that public opinion had hardened against the king.[114] On 8 December, Baldwin went to Fort Belvedere to ask Edward VIII to 'wrestle with himself' and reconsider, but the king said his mind was made up. Was Baldwin having doubts about inducing the sheep through the narrow gate? Was he salving his conscience? On 9 December the Cabinet sent Edward VIII a last request for reconsideration, which met with the same result. Sir Samuel Hoare, First Lord of the Admiralty, believed that 'Baldwin would have destroyed himself . . . had the Cabinet not sent this last request for reconsideration.'[115] Perhaps Baldwin's visit to the king the day before was motivated by political expediency.

Queen Mary appealed to Edward VIII to give up Mrs Simpson when they met on 8 December. Prebendary Percival again reported to Don that 'there had been the most painful scenes at Marlborough House' and the king 'had stormed and raged and shouted like a man demented'. Hardinge came to Lambeth Palace on the evening of 8 December and Lang asked if he should appeal to the king to give up Mrs Simpson. Hardinge replied that it was too late. Sargent noticed that Lang was very cheerful after Hardinge had left, 'and his cheerfulness was one of the signs that guided us'. Lang and Baldwin met again on 10 December, though there is again no record of their conversation.[116] Later that day, Edward VIII signed the instrument of abdication. The king's abdication was announced in Parliament in the afternoon. Lang spoke in the House of Lords:

> This is an occasion when our thoughts lie too deep for tears, certainly too deep for words. No such tragedy of a pathos so

profound has ever been enacted on the stage of our national life
. . . Of the motive which compelled that renunciation we dare not
speak. It takes us into the region of the inner mysteries of human
life and human nature. The heart knoweth its own bitterness, yet
even we can understand in some measure the ordeal through which
His Majesty has been passing and the cost of his renunciation.
We can only offer him the profound sympathy of our hearts and
accept with infinite sorrow the decision he has made. Was there
not, my Lords, something like a stab in our hearts when we heard
the words in which His Majesty took leave of his subjects?[117]

In the rest of his speech, Lang paid tribute to the past service of Edward
VIII and expressed sympathy and loyalty to George VI and Queen
Elizabeth and to Queen Mary.[118] It was a dignified speech, intended for
public consumption, and one which certainly did not reflect his true
opinion of Edward VIII.

Lang wrote the following day:

At 1.52 the Clerk of the Parliaments said 'Le Roy le veult,' and the
reign of King Edward came to a pathetic and inglorious end . . .
That evening the late King, on his own responsibility broadcast
a message from Windsor Castle. It was well done – his voice was
under good control. It had some real pathos; but there was one
passage that jarred: it was when he said that he had been 'denied'
the happiness of his brother in having his wife and children – as
though he might not at any time have possessed this happiness if
he had chosen.[119]

LANG'S RADIO BROADCAST

Lang observed that for a few days after Edward VIII's abdication, public
opinion was 'bewildered'.[120] Dr A.C. Bouquet, who was leading a mission
in a working-class parish, wrote to Don on 11 December:

I am convinced that the working folk are now expecting that His
Grace will speak with a little more feeling, and in the name of

Christian public opinion express his austere disapproval of the
influences which have in recent times polluted our Court life,
and have misled a most promising ruler, and also his disapproval
of the whole miserable business of collusive divorce proceedings
and sinful disregard of the principles of Christian marriage which
unless the King's Proctor intervenes look like taking their course
to the finish.[121]

Bishop Haigh of Coventry wrote to Don the following day:

Working and middle class opinion [in the Midlands] is dead
against our former King. Once it was learnt that he wished to
marry a woman like Mrs Simpson, his good qualities virtually
went for nothing. People felt simply that 'he had let the show
down.' So far from being necessary to try and disarm popular
feeling for Edward which might have made light of moral failings,
etc., it has been necessary rather to try to qualify indignation by
more sympathy . . . People refused to sing 'God Save The King' in
cinemas during the last few days and shouted 'Throne'. . . Anyway
– writing in great haste – I send this word in case by its influence
on a word or a comma it may help his Grace.[122]

Don showed these letters to Lang, who was thus 'emboldened to speak
out with regard to the circle of friends which King Edward had gathered
around him'.[123] Lang did not question the advice of Haigh and Bouquet,
which led him to make arguably the worst mistake of his primacy.

There are said to be two golden rules for preaching. Firstly, *how* a
sermon is delivered is often just as important as what is said. Secondly,
the preacher must have a clear message, which his hearers can quickly
understand and absorb. Lang broke both of these rules in his abdication
broadcast on the BBC (see Appendix 2). His address was preceded by a
rather lugubrious service, which probably did not help. Even allowing
for the primitive sound-recording equipment of the 1930s and the
distortions of time, Lang's voice sounds nervous in comparison with
other recordings. It really only comes to life in the second and third
paragraphs: the rest sounds surprisingly boring.[124]

One of the difficulties with Lang's broadcast was that he tried to say too much in one address. He began by acknowledging that there had been 'no confusion, no strife, no clash of parties . . . truly it has been a wonderful proof of the strength and stability of the Throne.' There was, for a few weeks at least, considerable lingering support for Edward VIII amongst people whose minds, to quote Lang's earlier words, 'were wholly unprepared for it [the abdication], and ignorant of all that had led to it'.[125] Perhaps by mentioning the stability of the throne, and by his similar expressions in the House of Lords on 10 December, Lang hoped to help the new king.

Lang went on to compare the departure of Edward VIII with the flight of James II in 1688: hardly a flattering comparison. Lang mentioned Edward VIII's 'high and sacred trust' from God of the monarchy, and lamented the 'surrender' – an emotive word for all who had lived through the Great War – of that trust. He said it was 'strange and sad' that Edward VIII sought happiness in a manner 'inconsistent with the Christian principles of marriage', and he vaguely rebuked the social circle 'whose standards and ways of life are alien to all the best instincts and traditions of his people'. He went on to express sorrow and disappointment, recalling Edward VIII's 'high hopes and promise', adding, 'It is the remembrance of those things that wrings from our hearts the cry – "The pity of it. O the pity of it!"' 'Pitiable' was a word Lang used elsewhere to express sadness.[126]

Lang paid a rather laboured tribute to Queen Mary and rather cheekily quoted her message to the nation, which he had himself written, as evidence that she knew of the nation's respectful sympathy.[127] He went on to pay tribute to Baldwin for steering 'the ship of state . . . into the harbour where it now safely rests'. He mentioned that the prime minister had given him his whole confidence 'throughout these anxieties', which would appear to be a claim to have been at the centre of things.

Lang spoke next of the new morning that had dawned with the accession of George VI, and spoke of sympathy turning into loyalty, 'which with one mind and voice the peoples of this Realm and Empire offer him today'. He claimed a personal connection of friendship with the new monarch, and then unhelpfully drew attention to his stutter. He spoke warmly of Queen Elizabeth, and said he remembered her childhood, again claiming a connection with her. He concluded with a message about the forthcoming 'Recall to Religion', in which he sought a new consecration of the king's people to the service of God.

The main themes of Lang's broadcast were sorrow at Edward VIII's waste of his gifts, dismay at those who had led him astray, a concern to stir up loyalty to the throne, and his claim of a close personal connection with the new monarchs. One may wonder whether Lang was not also trying to re-echo the conservative judgements about the former king which reached him from around the country. If he was, then Lang's words backfired upon him. The only parts of his address which seem to have registered with many listeners were the second and third paragraphs, in which he spoke of Edward VIII and rebuked his friends.

After the broadcast, Don wrote that he regretted that Lang had not shown his text to his chaplains first. In fact, Lang had shown it to Sargent, who had persuaded him to delete a reference to Edward VIII going out 'into the night', which was too reminiscent of Judas Iscariot. Sargent had found Lang kneeling in prayer beside his desk before he left for Broadcasting House, and a short while later he wrote, 'I am a little apprehensive about it [the address], for I think it may have the effect of confirming the suspicion (though perhaps after all it is not widely believed) that he had engineered the whole thing.'[128]

Why did Lang speak in this way? He had, after all, spent the past six weeks avoiding the limelight. His speech in the Lords was dignified, and if he had said no more, people would have thought highly of him. The answer is hard to find. Lang may have been moved by Lord Salisbury's description to the Lords of the abdication as a disastrous, mutilating wound in the body politic. Don speculated that it may have been because Queen Mary had told Lang of Edward VIII's behaviour when she had appealed to him to give up Mrs Simpson.[129] The letters from Haigh and Bouquet prodded Lang into an unusually unwise and unreflective action. Lang was possibly over-tired, suffering a reaction to the accumulated tension of the past year and to the events of the past six weeks, and anxious about the new reign.

The response to Lang's speech was immediate. Baldwin wrote the next day:

You said just what was wanted and, if I may say so, just what you ought to have said. I know how difficult a task you had, but you triumphed over all difficulties and you were indeed the voice of Christian England. Thank you.[130]

Lang's view of Edward VIII's behaviour was shared by Temple. Princess Mary told Lang that she had listened to his broadcast with Queen Mary and thought it admirable. Lords Astor, Blendisloe, Dickinson, Halifax and Selborne wrote to congratulate Lang, as did Edward Fitzroy, the speaker, Admiral Halsey, John Reith of the BBC, the dean of York, and many members of the public. However, far more letters arrived attacking Lang's address. It was widely felt that Lang had kicked a man when he was down. Don recorded on 15 December: 'A perfect deluge of letters about C.C.'s broadcast about two hundred and fifty have arrived during the last twenty-four hours – many highly appreciative . . . but the majority abusive and even vituperative.'[131] The press helped stoke the controversy. Don noted:

> The 'popular' Press has excelled itself and has talked an appalling amount of nonsense, interspersed with deliberate misrepresentation and lying – and much sheer fabrication. Things have been even worse in America . . . The vulgarity of it makes one positively sick.[132]

There were still masses of letters on 4 January 1937.[133] Only thereafter do things appear to have tailed off. Lang put a brave face on the controversy in his notes on the abdication:

> It was a difficult task. I felt that I could not in honesty and sincerity *merely* say kind, and of course true, things about the late King's charm and manifold services: that in my position I was bound to say something about the surrender of a great trust from the motive of private happiness . . . But I added some words, most sincerely, about that charm, about those services, etc . . . The address must have been listened to by millions at home and overseas. It was next day published in full in the leading newspapers, and more

or less fully in all the others. As I fully expected, my words about the King let loose a torrent of abuse from the less reputable Press and from a multitude of correspondents. On the other hand there were just as many letters of gratitude. The one which for me was sufficient was a letter which the next day the Prime Minister sent, written in his own hand . . . I had reason to believe that my address was not disapproved by the King and Queen or by Queen Mary.[134]

There is no corroborative evidence that Lang 'fully expected' a 'torrent of abuse'. His notes on the abdication were completed in late December 1936 or in the early part of 1937 and perhaps he thought he was writing for posterity. However, Lang appears to have admitted to Nancy Crawley on 27 December that his broadcast had been a failure.[135]

One explanation for the furore surrounding Lang's broadcast is that until 2 December 1936 most people were ignorant of Mrs Simpson. Edward VIII was their matinée idol monarch. Over the course of a few days, that image crumbled before their eyes. They were upset by Lang's unneccessary raking-over of the embers. This was also probably the first time that the new medium of radio had been used to voice disapproval of a member of the royal family.

THE MARRIAGE OF THE DUKE OF WINDSOR

After his abdication, Edward VIII was created the duke of Windsor by George VI. He travelled to Austria to wait until he could marry Mrs Simpson after her divorce decree absolute was granted in May 1937.[136] On 26 February 1937, Professor Berriedale Keith of the University of Edinburgh sent Lang a memorandum raising doubts about the legality of their forthcoming marriage. His case was based on Mrs Simpson's first divorce from Commander Spencer in 1927:

The matter at issue is . . . the divorce granted to Mrs Simpson in 1927 at Warrenton, Virginia . . . in respect of its effect in English law in conferring on her the status of an unmarried woman . . .

English Law recognizes the validity of a divorce granted outside England only in two cases. (1) It recognizes a divorce granted by the Court of the State in which the husband is domiciled at the time of the commencement of the proceedings for divorce . . . (2) It recognizes a divorce granted by the Court of a State in which the husband is not domiciled if that divorce would be held valid by the Courts of the State where he was domiciled at the time when the proceedings were taken . . .

Turning, therefore, to the known facts it seems clear that the divorce obtained by Mrs Simpson at Warrenton, Virginia, in 1927 was not granted by a court of her then husband's domicil. Her first husband Mr Spencer seems to have been of Chicago, and to have met his wife in Florida, later being sent to California. Mrs Simpson appears to have established legal residence in Warrenton, Virginia, in 1925 and to have obtained an undefended divorce from her husband in 1927 . . . There seems to be no possible reason to ascribe to Mr Spencer a Virginian domicil, and the divorce seems wholly incapable of being sustained as valid in England under the head (1) above.

The question then arises whether the Courts of the State of Mr Spencer's domicil would hold valid a divorce granted by the Virginian court. To express any opinion on this issue would require exact knowledge of (1) Mr Spencer's domicil in 1927 and (2) authoritative information of the view of the Courts of the State in which he was then domiciled as to the validity of the 1927 divorce. Neither part can be dealt with on the information available to me . . .

It seems, therefore, *prima facie* clear, on the information available to the public that in English law Mrs Simpson may still be the wife of Mr Spencer, and incapable of legal marriage to H.R.H. the Duke of Windsor.[137]

Keith's proposed solution was that the Privy Council should enquire into Mrs Simpson's 1927 divorce and if necessary legislate to render her capable of marriage to the duke of Windsor. Lang replied to Keith on 22 March, but the copy of his reply is missing from the file at Lambeth. Lang appears, unusually, to have written again the following day, but a copy this letter is likewise missing. Keith wrote to Lang on 23 March enclosing copies of letters he had sent on the subject to Baldwin and the *Scotsman*. Lang was unwilling to commit himself, and replied on 27 March that, 'while I am grateful to you for putting these problems with so much clearness before me, I think you will agree with me that it would be needless to continue our correspondence about them.'[138]

It is hard to imagine that Lang did not discuss this correspondence with Baldwin or Wigram, but no trace remains at Lambeth, and the absence of copies of two of his letters to Keith may indicate that he had passed them on to someone. It was not in the interests of George VI, Baldwin or Lang to stir up controversy over Mrs Simpson's 1927 divorce. It would not have suited them for the duke of Windsor to be forced to delay or abandon his marriage to Mrs Simpson, and then to return to London amidst a wave of sympathy.

A Religious Ceremony

On 2 January 1937, Bishop Staunton Batty of Fulham informed Lang that the duke of Windsor had read a lesson at a Christmas service in the Anglican church in Vienna. Batty feared that the duke might ask to be married there to Mrs Simpson. Lang saw the bishops of Fulham and of Gibraltar, who were responsible for continental chaplaincies, and told them that no public religious ceremony of marriage could be permitted in the Anglican church in Vienna or elsewhere. According to Ziegler, 'it is difficult to overestimate the significance he [the duke of Windsor] attached to the [wedding] ceremony.'[139] The duke's friend and legal adviser, Walter Monckton, sought an Anglican clergyman prepared to officiate. In April, he found Canon L.M. Andrews, who seemed especially suitable because he was a royal chaplain. Monckton told Don, who replied that Lang would be unable to approve and that 'there would be a regular hullabaloo in Church circles if an Anglican priest was imported for the occasion.' Monckton said he would try to persuade the couple to content themselves with a civil marriage.[140]

Wigram told Lang that he was furious when he discovered that the duke of Windsor was seeking a religious marriage.[141] Lang replied:

> I need scarcely say that I agree with all you say . . . It would be
> unfair to me and to the Bishops of Gibraltar and Fulham to bring

us in as formally disapproving of any such ceremony. It would be most undignified for the Duke of Windsor to hawk about for some priest who might be tempted to accede to his wishes. I am sure you are right in advising that no member of the Royal family ought to be present at the Civil Ceremony or at any subsequent religious ceremony that might be held. Moreover, even if any such ceremony were to take place privately in some house, as for example an Embassy, it would certainly be presented publicly as a religious celebration of the marriage which would be most undesirable.[142]

After the controversy that greeted his abdication broadcast, Lang was clearly anxious not to court further trouble by being brought in as 'formally disapproving' a religious ceremony, though that was clearly his attitude. His fear that a religious ceremony might be represented as a religious celebration of the marriage probably stemmed from his desire to protect the Church of England and uphold its teaching about the indissolubility of marriage. Wigram wrote to Lang on 8 April to inform him that Monckton had seen George VI and that the duke of Windsor was to be 'told definitely that none of his family can be present at the wedding and that one of His Majesty's chaplains cannot officiate'.[143]

At this point the Rev. R.A. Jardine, vicar of St Paul's, Darlington, wrote offering his services to the duke. According to the sister of his churchwarden, Jardine was a failure in his parish, where it was widely believed that he had offered his services because he was in financial difficulties. Monckton smelt a rat and warned the duke about Jardine.[144] Don recorded the reaction at Lambeth when the news broke on 2 June:

It was announced today that a Kensitite clergyman of the name of Jardine was going to take a religious service immediately after the civil marriage of the Duke and 'Mrs Warfield.' This is rather a bombshell as we had all hoped that Monckton had persuaded the parties to avoid this further complication. Of course Jardine (an entirely insignificant Vicar in Darlington) has acted without ecclesiastical authority and in defiance of what he knows to be the mind of the Church of which he is an accredited Minister. He is presumably a notoriety-seeker who has volunteered his services.

It so happened that the Bishop of Fulham came here at 2.15 to consult with C.C. about the offer of the vicarage of Halifax which he has received. He and C.C. naturally conferred on this different development and as a result I was authorized to inform Press Enquirers as follows:

> If if be true that the Rev. R.A. Jardine has undertaken to perform a religious ceremony in connection with the marriage of the Duke of Windsor, the Bishop of Fulham wishes it to be understood that this action on the part of this clergyman has been taken without his consent or even his knowledge.'[145]

Lambeth Palace 'was plagued all afternoon by telephone calls'.[146] Don regretted that the press had discovered that the bishop of Fulham had seen Lang and feared adverse publicity. He noted on 3 June: 'The Duke of Windsor married "Mrs Wallis Warfield" at 11.30 a.m. – Jardine recited the Church of England marriage service and the Hymn *O perfect love* was played. So that's that!'[147]

It would seem that the duke of Windsor attempted to settle a few old scores after his wedding, using Jardine. On 13 June 1937, Jardine resigned his parish and anounced he was going on a lecture tour of the United States of America. Percival told Don of Wigram's discovery that 'Jardine's iniquitous lecturing tour in the USA was being supported by the Duke of Windsor who has turned against his brother.' Jardine proved an unreliable agent. In Baltimore he referred to Lang as an 'ecclesiastical cad' and to Baldwin as 'a grandmotherly old woman', and was inhibited by some American bishops.[148]

Later in 1937, a book entitled *Why Edward Went: Crown, Clique and Church* by W.B. Wells was published in New York. It attacked Lang, portrayed him as manipulative during the abdication crisis, and asserted that Edward VIII was 'eased out' by a clique of politicians and unelected influential people. It criticised George VI, whom it claimed was weak.[149] *Why Edward Went* exaggerates details, but Wells broadly grasped the outline of much that had happened in December 1936. The conclusion is inescapable that either Wells made some very good guesses, or someone in the know helped him. The book's Erastianism, low church prejudices and its details of the duke's wedding suggest Jardine as a source. Were Wells and Jardine the duke's mouthpiece? In January 1938, Don recorded that '[the duke] is suffering from a kind of persecution mania – he goes about telling people that he was thrown out as a result of a conspiracy headed by Queen Mary, the present King, Baldwin and C.C.'[150]

SUPPORTING KING GEORGE VI AND QUEEN ELIZABETH

According to Queen Mary, George VI was appalled and wept when he succeeded to the throne.[151] Perhaps Lang knew of this. On the first day of the new king's reign, he wrote to Queen Elizabeth. The queen replied immediately, using her royal signature for the first time, which Lang would probably have felt a signal honour:

> I cannot tell you how touched I am at receiving your most kind and helpful letter today. I can hardly now believe that we have been called to this most tremendous task, and, (I am writing to you quite intimately) the curious thing is that we are not afraid. I feel that God has enabled us to face the situation calmly, and although I at least feel most inadequate, we have been sustained during these last terrible days by many good friends. I know that we may count you among them and it means a great deal to us to know this. When we spoke together at Birkhall only three months ago, how little did I think that such drama and unhappiness was in store for our dear country. Thank you from my heart for your unfailing sympathy and good advice.
>
> I would love to see you soon, there are so many things to talk over, and for many years now you have been so kind and wise about our troubles and joys that I fear you cannot escape this time. We both feel our responsibilities very deeply, and though quite prepared for a difficult time, are determined to do our best.
>
> Your dear kind letter has helped us more than I can say. We were so unhappy over the loss of a dear brother – because one can only feel that exile from this country is death indeed. We were miserable, as you know, over his change of heart and character during the last few years, and it is alarming how little in touch he

was, with ordinary human feeling. Alas! He had lost the 'common touch'. I thank you again from my heart for your wishes and prayers for our future, we pray most sincerely that we shall not fail our country, & I sign myself for the first time, & with great affection

Elizabeth R.[152]

The queen's letter reveals that she and the king had previously told Lang how miserable they had been over Edward VIII's behaviour, and it is interesting that from the first day of George VI's reign Queen Elizabeth saw that the duke of Windsor would have to go into exile. On 21 December, Lang visited the king and queen and found them very friendly:

The king was in good spirit; and for an hour we talked together with the utmost ease about 'the crisis', about the poor Duke of Windsor, and then about the arrangements for the coronation. What a relief it was after the strained and wilful ways of the late king to be in this atmosphere of intimate friendship, and instead of looking forward to the Coronation as a sort of nightmare, to realise that (as I had said in the House of Lords) I was sure that to the solemn words of the Coronation there would be a sincere response.[153]

George VI's nerves were more frayed than Lang realised, and on 22 December he became agitated by Temple's rebuke of the duke of Windsor in his diocesan newsletter. Wigram telephoned Lambeth Palace at 11 p.m. to ask for 'reticence', so that things could die down. Lang wrote to all the bishops the following day, asking them 'to refrain from further public direct criticism of his [the duke of Windsor's] conduct or allusion to the unhappy circumstances of his abdication'. Henson noted: '"Tuning pulpits" was an Elizabethan procedure which had been prematurely thought to have ceased. It is difficult not to perceive that his Grace has received what is commonly called a "wigging" from our new Defender of the Faith.'[154]

George VI wrote to Lang from Sandringham on 29 December:

I am sending you our Christmas card with all good wishes to you for the New Year 1937, and let us hope it will be a happier one for us all than this last one. It was so kind of you to have come and seen us the other day to explain the Coronation Service. We must meet again nearer the time, to hold rehearsals of the Service, so as to be well acquainted with what we have to do.

I am gradually getting over the trying and tragic days through which we have all passed, and am beginning to learn something of the gigantic task which lies before me. Coming down here will do me a great deal of good, as I do need a rest, and the only one I shall get before summer.

I have heard several times from my brother on the telephone. He is much quieter and calmer than he was, and I am glad that at last the Press are leaving him alone. I am afraid you must have had a tremendous amount of correspondence after your broadcast, which I hope is now diminishing.[155]

Although the king signed himself 'with renewed good wishes', was there perhaps a slight barb in his final paragraph? If so, it was lost on the usually sensitive Lang, who wrote: 'At Christmas the King wrote to me most kindly, and I noted that it would be difficult to see in his handwriting and especially his signature "George R.I." any difference from that of his father. *Prosit omen.*'[156]

The duke of Windsor, however, remained an anxiety for the king and queen. In September 1937, the duke announced that he would shortly visit Germany and the United States to inspect workers' conditions. The king feared that this presaged an attempted 'come-back' to public life by the duke.[157] Queen Elizabeth consulted Lang. He confided in Nancy Crawley:

Queen Elizabeth was more than cordial. She is really just an intimate friend. I had many talks with her about all that has happened – and about the Shadow in the background. But I urged that she should not think too much about it.[158]

Lang's advice proved sound, because although the duke was lionised by the Nazis in Germany, his visit to America was cancelled.[159]

The Coronation

It was decided to crown George VI and Queen Elizabeth on 12 May 1937, which was to have been Edward VIII's coronation day. The coronation added greatly to Lang's workload, for he was a member of both the Executive Committee, which issued general directions regarding the coronation, and also the Coronation Committee, which made detailed arrangements. Lang attended all coronation rehearsals and tended to take charge. The archbishop's desk at Lambeth became a sort of clearing house where many questions came to be resolved, including those relating to the Dominions, the coronation oath, the coronation rite and music. In the absence of any precedent, he assumed complete control over what might be broadcast, filmed or photographed.[160]

Lang was anxious lest George VI's stutter should cause the king difficulties during his coronation: a not unreasonable concern for an officiating archbishop of Canterbury. The king's stutter was the subject of the film *The King's Speech* (2010), which began with the disclaimer that some scenes were fictional. Many of the scenes involving Lang, played by the actor Derek Jacobi, fell into this category. In March 1937 Lord Dawson of Penn advised Lang that he had seen an alternative speech therapist, Raymond Wings, but felt it would be best to see how the king got on with Lionel Logue before suggesting anyone else. Lang had a full talk with Lord Wigram at Windsor on 25 April, but both men agreed that it would be undesirable to attempt to get the king to see anyone other than Logue. Lang took no further action, and George VI coped with the spoken parts of his coronation admirably.[161]

Lang was keen to proclaim the coronation's spiritual significance. On 27 December 1936, he inaugurated the planned evangelistic campaign, 'Recall to Religion', focused upon the coronation, with a radio address:

> Within five months, please God, our King will be consecrated to his high office and invested with it as a sacred trust from the Most High God by the solemn and sacramental rites which have been preserved for well nigh a thousand years. But let him not come alone to his hallowing. As the representative of the Nation he must bear his people with him. The august ceremony will be

bereft of its full meaning, it will be a mere splendid spectacle, unless the Nation with and through its King consecrates itself to the remembrance and service of God . . . At this time I am moved to make a somewhat special and solemn appeal to my fellow countrymen. I make it not primarily as the chief officer of the Church of England but rather, if I may presume to say so, as a representative of the Christian life of the Nation.[162]

Each diocese was encouraged to make its own arrangements. In the diocese of Chelmsford, for example, the evangelical Bishop Henry Wilson summoned special meetings of clergy and laity, issued a pastoral letter, encouraged laypeople to adopt a rule of life and asked for special prayers on coronation day. Lang issued three special forms of service for use in churches: one to be used on the Sunday before the coronation; a second to be used on the Sunday evening 'of a more popular character, leading up to that re-dedication of the national life for which the *Recall to Religion* had been preparing'; and a third to be used on coronation day, before listening to the coronation on the radio.[163]

Lang was also concerned to prepare the king and queen. He went through the coronation service with them at Easter 1937 'and found them most appreciative and fully conscious of its solemnity'. On the Sunday before the coronation the archbishop spent an hour and a quarter with the king and queen at Buckingham Palace. Lang's notes in preparation for this meeting survive, but unfortunately his handwriting is at its most indecipherable.[164] Enough is legible to see that Lang told the king and queen that the two most sacred times were the anointing, during which they would receive the gifts of the Holy Spirit, and the Communion, during which they would receive Christ himself.

Lang went from Buckingham Palace to Broadcasting House, where he took part in a special broadcast service. He again stressed the religious nature of the rite:

But the thought which I specially wish to impress upon your minds is that the Coronation is no mere historical pageant, however splendid and impressive. It is from beginning to end a most solemn religious act . . . I would remind you all that you will have a part in the Coronation of the King more personal, more responsible, than that of mere listeners or spectators. Let me repeat a sentence which I used in preaching at the Coronation of King George V of blessed memory – 'The King comes not alone to his Hallowing. He bears his people with him.' . . . Thus the full meaning of his Consecration will be missed unless it represents in some real sense the consecration of all his peoples in him and with him to the service of the King of Kings.[165]

Coronation Day

There were a few minor problems during the coronation, but thanks to Lang's attention to detail the service mostly went according to plan.[166] Lang sailed through, as Don recorded:

C.C. made full use of his unique opportunity and conducted the whole service with complete mastery of detail and due regard for the solemnity of occasion. His fine voice and dignity of manner made a profound impression upon all. He made the whole ceremony live and imparted to it a sense of reality, in keeping with all that he had said in his broadcast address last Sunday evening. It was his great day – the crowning act of his career – and he rose grandly to the occasion . . . When administering the Oath, C.C. raised his voice and turned slightly westwards towards the choir where many of the Dominion representatives were sitting and with great care and emphasis spoke the names of each of the King's dominions and territories overseas – bringing home the imperial significance of the King – 'King of each and all'.[167]

The coronation had a great impact upon the two central figures, the king and queen. George VI described his feelings in a letter to Lang:

I must write and tell you how much I appreciated all your help and kindness during that wonderful ceremony in the Abbey, and I can never thank you for those words of encouragement you gave me in the course of that very trying ordeal. An ordeal it was, but I felt I was being helped all the time by Someone Else as you said I would when you came to see me on Sunday. I have never felt that feeling of real calm before, as I was very nervous before I came into the Abbey . . . You, my dear Archbishop, were quite marvellous in carrying out your part in the long ceremony.[168]

Queen Elizabeth, too, was very affected by the coronation and described it to me in 2001:

[The coronation was] a great ordeal, because it is *for real*. And yet it was wonderful and there is a great sense of offering oneself. He [Lang] got the crown the wrong way round and he whispered 'I've got it the wrong way round,' but he sorted it out beautifully . . . [The coronation robes] were enormously heavy. I wore a white dress beneath them. You do have a little break half way through the coronation, behind the high altar in the Henry VII chapel. I remember sitting down and easing the robes from my shoulders, just for a minute . . . [The crown, too, was] *very* heavy . . . [and the coronation seemed] of inordinate length. As was The Queen's, and as will be the next one.[169]

The countess of Strathmore and Kinghorne, Queen Elizabeth's mother, told Lang, 'I think that nearly everyone felt the great *spirituality* of this Coronation,' and this view was shared by others. There are several reasons why George VI's coronation was perceived in such religious tones. Lang himself believed that the demeanour and piety of George VI and Queen Elizabeth were important. He also felt that the use of microphones made a difference. Temple believed that the way Lang officiated had been significant. The 'Recall to Religion' prepared the minds of at least some of the public to view the coronation in religious terms. There may have also been an undercurrent of relief that it was George VI and Queen Elizabeth being crowned. 'You were right,' Churchill is said to have whispered to his wife, 'I see now that the "other one" wouldn't have done.'[170]

Lang's Role in the Abdication Crisis

Lockhart's Account of Lang's Role in the Abdication

Lockhart's chapter on the abdication is only nine pages long. It gives a fair, though not very detailed overview. Two and a half pages are taken up with Lang's radio broadcast. Lockhart said nothing about the influence Lang exerted during the abdication crisis. He mentioned Lang's concern and recorded that he was kept fully informed (without saying by whom), but added that, 'except for one occasion, when the result was no longer in doubt and his opinion was asked on a contingent point [the suggested legislation to bring forward Mrs Simpson's decree absolute], he neither influenced, nor tried to influence, the course of events.'[171]

How did Lockhart reach this misleading conclusion? There are four principal explanations. Firstly, Lang took care to cover his tracks. His letter to Baldwin of 25 November was written by hand, so there was no carbon copy. His letter to Dawson of 12 November has had the top cut off. No copy was kept at Lambeth of his letter to Dawson of 3 December.[172]

Secondly, much material about the abdication in Lambeth Palace Library, the Bodleian Library, Oxford, Cambridge University Library and The National Archives, London, was not available to Lockhart and has only become available since the death of Queen Elizabeth The Queen Mother in 2002.

Thirdly, and perhaps most importantly, Don's influence is discernible. Don was Lang's chosen biographer and had to abandon his work when he became dean of Westminster in 1946. Lockhart was selected to continue the project. It is clear from the footnote on page 404 that Lockhart discussed the abdication with someone close to Lang, and in all probability this was either Don or Sargent. Neither chaplain believed that Lang had been involved in a plot to topple Edward VIII. Yet both recorded that Lang had been very discreet and had not discussed the king, or his conversations with Baldwin with them. Sargent wrote that 'the Archbishop simply came in as a private consultant, leaving all the initiation to the Prime Minister.'[173] This is true, in so far as it goes, but Sargent failed to appreciate that Baldwin did not think of himself as consulting a private spiritual director, but the primate of all England.

Evidently the chaplains only knew a little of what Lang was doing. Neither chaplain appears to have known of his letter to Baldwin of 25 November. Don was dismayed by the vehement reaction to Lang's broadcast.[174] It is not too much of a leap of the imagination to see that Don – who had only partial knowledge, who believed Lang was not involved in a plot, and who was perhaps anxious to avoid a recrudescence of the controversy surrounding Lang's broadcast – tended to play down Lang's role in the abdication. Lockhart, assured by someone close to Lang that there was no plot, does not seem to have questioned Don's or Sargent's version of events.

Lockhart was granted access to Lang's secret account of the abdication, probably by Don, who had charge of Lang's papers, and he used parts of it for his book.[175] The rest of Lang's papers connected with the abdication were then loose and uncatalogued, and there is no evidence that Lockhart ever saw them.

Lang wrote his account of the abdication in pencil in a notebook, and it is an odd and unpolished work. The archbishop wrote part as events were unfolding and the outcome was uncertain, but the last eight and a half pages, including many of his kindly remarks about the exiled duke of Windsor, appear to have been written after the abdication, and, more importantly, after Lang's broadcast.[176] Lockhart does not seem to have asked himself whether the controversy had any bearing upon what Lang wrote. He did not see any deeper significance to Lang's conversations with the Nonconformists Aubrey and Berry and his message to the clergy on 4 December.

Fourthly, Lockhart interviewed Baldwin a few weeks before his death in 1947:

> he told the present writer [Lockhart] that the Archbishop had made no attempt to force an issue, or even to press his point of view, and that the decisive factor was the uncompromising stand of the Dominion Premiers, and especially of the Premier of Australia.[177]

Baldwin's memory, to say the least, must have been misleading him. It is worth asking whether any twentieth-century prime minister would publicly admit to having been influenced by an archbishop. Furthermore, by 1947 it was in no one's interests to stir up the abdication controversy afresh. George VI had proved himself to be a popular and much-respected wartime monarch, and the Windsors were out of sight and out of mind in Paris. It was convenient for Baldwin to lay the responsibility at the feet of the Dominion prime ministers: it would not have suited for it to be shown too clearly that, although there was no overt plot, Edward VIII had been helped into painting himself into a corner, and left with a choice between abdication and abandoning Mrs Simpson.

A New Assessment of Lang's Role

It is clear that, throughout the abdication crisis, Lang did not lift a finger to help Edward VIII. If he had been involved in no other way, this fact alone would still be significant. In retirement, this point seemed to bother Lang. In December 1942, he added some further lines to his confidential account of the abdication:

> On looking through these notes among my papers I am disposed to think that I might have written to Edward VIII if only to liberate my conscience. Yet most certainly this would have invoked, even if any reply had been given, the sort of slight which *I* personally might have understood but to which the Archbishop of Canterbury ought not to be exposed.[178]

This is a rather odd thing to have written. Ought not an archbishop be prepared to accept slights in the furtherance of pastoral care? Was the archbishop motivated solely by concern for his great office, or by anxiety about breaking the bonds linking it with the Establishment? His explanation does not entirely ring true. It is unlikely that he refused to intervene because of fear, for Lang was no coward, and he might have known that Davidson had spoken to Edward VII about his personal conduct in 1902.[179]

There are two other more likely explanations for Lang's behaviour. Firstly, throughout the abdication crisis, Lang was anxious to avoid the limelight. His summoning of a confidential meeting of bishops in a cloakroom took this anxiety to almost comical proportions. He probably realised that an unsuccessful intervention could damage the Church of England. When Lang said that he would look for an opportunity to talk to the king, he may have meant precisely that.[180] The right opportunity never presented itself. Perhaps Lang did not look too hard for it for another reason. By the late summer or early autumn of 1936, it had become clear to Lang that Edward VIII was unfit to be king. Lang would have had little incentive to intervene to save an unsuitable king who was intent – as he would see it – upon damaging the throne by an un-Christian marriage to a double divorcee.

Lang, however, did more than simply omit to help the king. He was closely involved in the chain of events which led to Edward VIII's abdication and exile. For a start, he was well informed about the king and Mrs Simpson.[181]

There is no evidence of a plot to get rid of Edward VIII, if by 'plot' something like the 1605 Gunpowder Plot is meant. A handful of people, especially Wigram, Hardinge and Geoffrey Dawson, were concerned about Edward VIII. The king's conduct provoked a few conversations about what might be done in the face of his growing infatuation with Mrs Simpson, such as the weekend meeting at Cumberland Lodge.[182] Lang may have heard gossip about these conversations, but there is no evidence that he participated in them, although he spoke with a few anxious individuals who called upon him at Lambeth.

The central figure in the events leading up to the abdication was the prime minister, Baldwin. Edward VIII would only discuss Mrs Simpson with him. Baldwin came under pressure to take action, initially much against his will. He had very limited ability to manoeuvre. The king took the initiative, and his avowed wish was to marry Mrs Simpson and to have her crowned queen: 'the whole bag of tricks'. To begin with, Baldwin's role was to react to the king's initiatives, and, in so doing, to nudge him along. His concern as prime minister was that Edward VIII's marriage to Mrs Simpson would undermine national and imperial unity. Hastings has claimed that 'there was no doubt that this [the abdication] was a political not a religious decision.'[183] This is an unhelpful over-simplification. In the end, Mrs Simpson was unfit to become queen because of a religious reason, namely, that she was divorced and had both previous husbands still living. Had Lieutenant Spencer and Mr Simpson both died after their divorces, Mrs Simpson would have been free to marry Edward VIII and become queen. The fact that large numbers of people would have regarded her marriage to Edward VIII as adulterous whilst Spencer and Simpson lived would have damaged the monarchy and divided the country and empire. Baldwin could not take that risk. Thus the abdication was a political decision, stemming from religious concerns.

Lang became involved after Baldwin had unburdened himself at Hatfield House. Baldwin disliked clerical and episcopal 'interference' in politics. Lang, ever the careful judge of men, engineered a close relationship with Baldwin during the closing months of 1936; they had not been especially intimate before Edward VIII's accession, nor were they after his abdication, but the abdication crisis took its toll on Baldwin. Geoffrey Dawson met Baldwin on 3 December 1936 and noted: 'He seemed to be nearly at the end of his tether and sat with his head in his hands on the table, probably just glad to have someone with him till the time that his interview [with the king] came.' Even the self-absorbed Edward VIII realised the strain Baldwin had been under. It is likely that Lang offered Baldwin a degree of pastoral care and support during their seven meetings. It would be surprising if Lang had not used his meetings with Baldwin to ascertain the state of the prime minister's mind and to guide his thoughts. Certainly, by the time Lang wrote to Baldwin on 25 November he could refer to 'the pressure of our common anxiety – and hope'. This letter was clearly an attempt to ginger up Baldwin. Lang's letters to Geoffrey Dawson of 12 November advocating a decisive clearing of the air, and of 3 December saying that the government must be firm and advocating swiftness and decisiveness may also have been attempts to pressurise Baldwin through *The Times*.[184] Alternatively, it has sometimes suited prime ministers to test public reaction by airing things unofficially in the press, and although there is no evidence to support it, the possibility that Lang may have written to Dawson with the foreknowledge of Baldwin cannot be ruled out.

From about the time that a morganatic marriage was mooted, Baldwin did more than simply react to Edward VIII's initiatives. He found the idea distasteful, telling Tom Jones, 'If I have to go out, as go I must, then I'd be quite happy to go out on this.' On 4 December, a day after seeing Lang, Baldwin told the Commons that there was no such thing as morganatic marriage in British law and that the government was not prepared to introduce legislation to permit it.[185] By leaving Edward VIII with the alternatives of either staying on the throne without Mrs Simpson, or of abdicating and marrying her, Baldwin led the king in the direction of abdication.

If we are to believe Lang's remark about their common hopes and Baldwin's description of himself on 5 December 1936 as 'like a dog in sheep-dog trials who had to induce a single sheep into a narrow gate' – and there is no good reason to doubt Lang's veracity – then they are the clearest evidence so far that Baldwin was actively working to bring about Edward VIII's abdication, rather than allowing events to drift in that direction and merely guiding them a bit. The assertion by Middlemas and Barnes that it was only on 3 December 1936 that Baldwin broke the news to Lang that the king might abdicate, 'whom up till then he had excluded, fearing an ill-judged ecclesiastical intervention', cannot be sustained.[186]

Lang's secret briefing of the bishops on 17 November was firstly concerned with the future of the 'Recall to Religion' campaign, but may also have been an attempt to stop an episcopal maverick such as Barnes from supporting the king's marriage to Mrs Simpson. His briefing on 4 December of the Nonconformists Aubrey and Berry was almost certainly an attempt to influence them. His plea issued the same day, that Anglican preachers should not mention the king, was an attempt to prevent controversial sermons, some of which might favour the king's marriage to Mrs Simpson, and be reported in the press.

Thus, Lang sought to influence events. Were Baldwin and Lang pushing at an open door? Edward VIII complained about his life when prince of Wales and there were rumours that he would renounce his right of succession, but once he acceded to the throne he enjoyed his popularity and aspects of being the king. Moreover, there is evidence that Edward VIII genuinely thought he could marry Mrs Simpson and remain on the throne. Duff Cooper advised Edward VIII to delay marriage with Mrs Simpson until after his coronation. Lang's insistence to Baldwin that 'if the course indicated is to be taken, he [the king] must leave as soon as possible' was probably because Lang realised that delay would only worsen matters.[187] It might have proven harder to dislodge Edward VIII after a coronation, and he would have toppled from a higher pedestal. The country and empire could have been left divided, with a tarnished monarchy. A delayed controversy of longer duration might also have proved more damaging for the Church of England.

1. The arms of
Cosmo Gordon Lang,
Archbishop of Canterbury 1928–42

2. The Rev. Dr John
Marshall Lang, father of
Cosmo Gordon Lang

3. The Manse, Fyvie, Aberdeenshire, where Lang was born in 1864

4. 5 Woodlands Terrace, Glasgow, where Lang grew up

5. Tav-an-Taggart, at Tay-in-Loan, Argyll, the house built for Lang by John Morton Macdonald

6. The exterior of Ballure, Tay-in-Loan

7. The 'Cell', Lang's oratory at Ballure

8. Norah Dawnay, to whom Lang twice unsuccessfully proposed marriage, with her father Hugh Dawnay, eighth Viscount Downe

9. Ann Todd, the actress with whom Lang said he fell in love in 1933

10. Lang with King George V and Queen Mary
during the royal tour of the north of England, 1912

11. Lang in procession at the creation of the Province of Wales, 1920

12. Lang presiding at the conclusion of the thirteen-hundredth anniversary of York Minster

13. The bishops discussing the Revised Prayer Book at Lambeth Palace

14. Watercolour of Lang by Angus Malcolm, shortly after his appointment to Canterbury, 1928

15. Lang in January 1931 at Lovell Hill, Windsor Forest, recuperating from illness with Lumley Green-Wilkinson, his 'Comptroller'

16. A fairly typical photograph of Lang when Archbishop of Canterbury

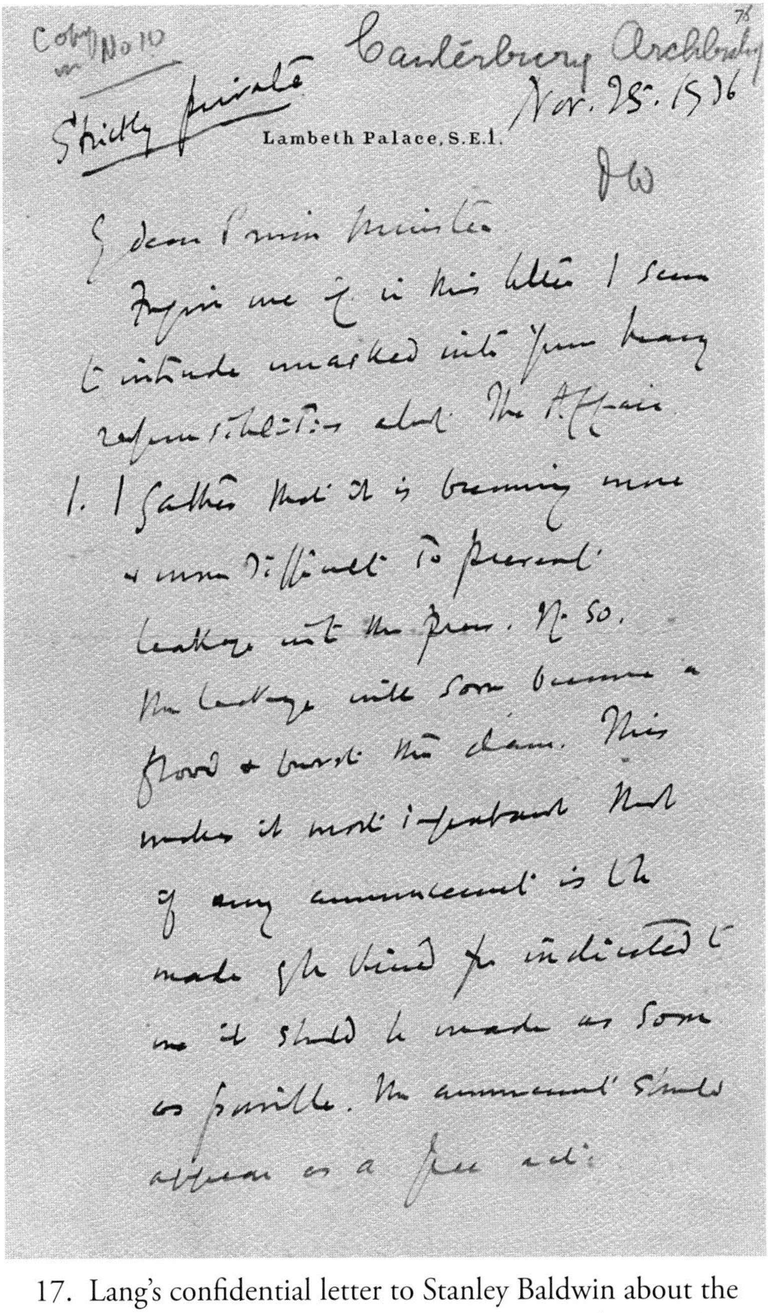

Copy No 10

Strictly private

Canterbury Archbishop
Nov. 25. 1936

78

Lambeth Palace, S.E.1.

My dear Prime Minister

Forgive me if in this letter I seem to intrude unasked into your heavy responsibilities about the Affair.

1. I gather that it is becoming more & more difficult to prevent leakage into the Press. If so, the leakage will soon become a flood & burst the dam. This makes it most important that if any announcement is to be made of the kind you indicated to me it should be made as soon as possible. The announcement should appear as a free act

17. Lang's confidential letter to Stanley Baldwin about the abdication of King Edward VIII, 25 November 1936

2. I have reason to think that
He does not fully realise that
if the course indicated is to be
Taken, he must leave as
soon as possible. It would be not
if the question that he should
remain until the decree is
made absolute. It is needless
to dwell on this necessity.
I understand you are seeing him
To-night: & doubtless you
would make this plain.
Only the pressure of our common
anxiety and hope — can
justify this letter. It is written

shortly & hurriedly. Forgive it.
by
yours very truly
[signature]

18. Lang with his chaplains at the coronation of King George VI and Queen Elizabeth, 12 May 1937. From left to right: Alexander Sargent, Cosmo Lang, Alan Don, Lumley Green-Wilkinson

Lambeth Palace, S.E.1.   3rd July 1940.

Dear Marjorie

I must send you a word of thanks for your letter.
It went to my heart. I need not tell you how fully I
understand and sympathise with everything you write, but at
least it is good to know that Rupert's life has been spared
and that he is well and, so far, well treated. I am sure
that his resources of mind and spirit will enable him to
endure the sad privation of liberty and he will always know
that at a critical moment he was able to render valiant
service to his country. It is hard for you to have to make
all your arrangements about family, house, etc., without his
help and guidance but I know you will rise to the need.
I do hope that you may be able to get some time with your
Mother at Balderstone. Meanwhile keep your faith, however
much it may be tried,for at a time like this when we are
beseiged by so many distresses and doubts the one thing
necessary is to keep one's faith as men in the beseiged
fortress keep the well.   May God help you and strengthen
both you and Rupert.

Yours aff.
Cosmo Cantuar:

19. Wartime pastoral care: a letter from Lang to Mrs Marjorie Holland, whose husband was a prisoner-of-war of the Germans, 3 July 1940

20. The Library of Lambeth Palace showing bomb damage during the Blitz, 1940

21. Lang photographed after preaching for the troops
at Addington Church, 1942

22. The burial place of Lang's ashes, Canterbury Cathedral

6

Lang and the Revised Prayer Book, 1928–1942

'HE COMES TO HIS THRONE in an evil time,' wrote Henson in July 1928 upon learning of Lang's appointment as archbishop of Canterbury, adding, 'since Cranmer's accession was there ever a darker outlook for the Church of England?'[1] The evil time of which Henson wrote was the crisis occasioned by the House of Commons' rejection for the second time in 1928 of the Church of England's Revised Prayer Book.

Nearly two decades later, in 1947, when Lockhart was working on his biography of Lang, George Bell sent him some reminiscences of Lang and Davidson. Having paid tribute to Lang's diligence and gifts, Bell went on to criticise his handling of the 1928 Prayer Book crisis:

> The great disappointment of the whole Church Reform movement has been that on fundamental issues, ever since, there has been either No Action or Defeat. And I do myself find it hard to aquit Lang of a heavy responsibility here . . . Where Lang failed in my opinion was after the rejection of 1928. Many brave words were spoken in the Assembly debate. An Archbishops' Commission was appointed and reported – but from 1919 to 1947 no effective steps whatever have been taken to enable the Church of England to revise its forms of worship, to frame its laws on spiritual matters, to exercise its discipline through proper Church courts, to have an effective voice in the election of its Bishops.

Lang was a great speaker and preacher: a superb draftsman in so many ways, and a most diligent administrator; but he was not a reformer. And it was a reformer with a policy, wise, patient, conciliatory but determined and inflexible, that the Church of England even more urgently required.[2]

Lockhart reproduced part of Bell's criticism and from there it entered history as accepted fact. Adrian Hastings, for example, described Lang as 'neither the man to enforce the decision of Parliament, nor to challenge it', and commented that the Church of England 'could not but suffer from such a state of affairs'.[3]

There can be no doubt that by the time of the outbreak of the Second World War in 1939, nearly thirty years of Prayer Book revision had largely fizzled out. Lang must shoulder his fair share of the blame for this failure; but not all the responsibility was his, and some of the reasons for failure lay elsewhere. Material in the Lang Papers, previously unavailable to Bell, shows that Lang made repeated attempts throughout the 1930s to overcome the Church of England's liturgical log-jam, though his efforts ultimately met with only partial success. It should be borne in mind that Lang was hampered for much of this time by illness, for on 20 December 1928 a blood clot passed through his heart. He was gravely ill during 1929 and suffered periodic debilitating illness until the mid-1930s.[4]

THE BACKGROUND

Anglican Churchmanship

From the Elizabethan Settlement onwards, the Church of England had contained a range of theologies, including a diversity of beliefs about the relationship of God's gift to the elements of bread and wine of the Eucharist.[5] Some Anglicans held a *virtualist* view of the sacrament. They believed that bread and wine were solemnly set apart in the prayer of consecration, and while not changed physically into Christ's body and blood, became so in virtue, power and effect. Other Anglicans held a *receptionist* view and believed that when the congregation received the consecrated bread and wine with faith, they received the body and blood of Christ in their hearts.[6] Virtualism and receptionism were the most widely held views of the sacrament in the Church of England between the seventeenth and nineteenth centuries, though a minority of Anglicans maintained a belief in the objective Real Presence of Christ in the bread and wine upon the altar once they had been consecrated by the priest.[7] The 1662 Book of Common Prayer was used by Anglicans of all churchmanships, and was capable of being interpreted by each to suit their own theology and spirituality. A celebration of the Eucharist would have looked much the same in most parish churches, whatever the theology of the celebrant.

After 1833, the Oxford Movement and the Catholic Revival that succeeded it altered the balance of views of the Eucharist. Anglo-Catholics, as they came to be known, increasingly taught the doctrine of the objective Real Presence; indeed, the Confraternity of the Blessed Sacrament was founded in 1862 precisely to propagate this doctrine. Anglo-Catholics began celebrating the Eucharist more often and with greater ritual. Many low churchmen and evangelicals opposed such Anglo-Catholic liturgical changes, fearing that they were a betrayal of the 1562 Thirty-Nine Articles and the reintroduction of Popery via the vestry door.[8] The nineteenth century saw frequent hostility between evangelicals and Anglo-Catholics. From an evangelical perspective, one of the problems with Anglo-Catholics was that they demanded ever more changes, and, to use a modern cliché, constantly pushed the boundaries as they sought to give liturgical expression to their beliefs about the Eucharist: first candles on the altar, then changes of vesture, the eastward position, elevation and genuflection, incense, Reservation, and so on.

By the time Lang became archbishop of Canterbury, many Anglicans, if asked to describe the range of churchmanships contained within their Church, would probably have pictured the Church of England as something like a candle, with Anglo-Catholics at the top, evangelicals at the bottom, and liberals or modernists in the middle. The expression 'going up the candle' was coined amongst Anglicans in the twentieth century to refer to increasing levels of ritual.

This popular image was confused by the tendency of some people to talk about 'high church' and 'low church'. By the 1920s and 1930s, these expressions were not really synonymous with Anglo-Catholicism and evangelicalism, but merely referred to a taste for elaboration or plainness in worship; thus someone such as Garbett could probably have been described as a bit high church, but certainly was not an Anglo-Catholic. The twentieth century also saw the development of high- and low-church expressions of liberalism; thus Dean Hewlett Johnson of Canterbury may be seen as a high church liberal. Further complexity is provided by the existence of a strand of churchmanship variously described as 'middle of the road', 'central', 'moderate' or 'plain C of E', which should not be confused with liberalism. This is perhaps the hardest to define because it essentially identified itself by what it was *not*: neither Anglo-Catholic, nor evangelical, nor liberal. It should also be borne in mind that there were many subtle variations within Anglo-Catholicism, evangelicalism and liberalism. All three depended upon the imagination of their members and sometimes were in thrall to dominant personalities.

This image of the Church of England as a candle with different churchmanships ranged up it, although widely held, is misleading. It would be better to picture the Church in the 1920s and 1930s as a dynamic and moving triangle, with Anglo-Catholics, evangelicals and liberals in the three corners. The various intermediate churchmanships might be pictured as ranged along the three sides of the triangle. Each corner of the Anglican triangle tugged in a different direction and tussled for the identity of the Church of England. Broadly speaking, the Anglo-Catholics stressed the Church of England's Catholic heritage, increasingly expressed interest in Eastern Orthodoxy and contemporary Roman Catholicism, and sought to enrich their worship in a more Catholic and frequently Roman direction. The evangelicals saw themselves as children of the Reformation, the influence of which they sought both to promote and also to protect from watering-down by Anglicans of other hues. Liturgically speaking, they wanted nothing other than the 1662 Prayer Book, which they interpreted in a Protestant manner. The liberals wished to remodel or 'modernise' Christianity to accommodate their own interpretations of modern thought.

Prayer Book Revision

'There is no book, with the exception of the Bible itself, to which Englishmen are so warmly attached as the Book of Common Prayer,' observed Evan Daniel in 1894. No liturgy is perfect, and after two and a half centuries the 1662 Prayer Book not unreasonably needed revising to meet altered conditions and expectations. During the second half of the nineteenth century, Anglo-Catholics increasingly augmented the Communion rite with additional material, often from the Roman Missal, and this led to increased friction with evangelicals. Further controversy was sparked from a different quarter in the early years of the twentieth century, when several modernist theologians advocated the revision of the liturgy in a liberal direction, by, for example, abolishing the Athanasian Creed.[9]

Part of the difficulty was that the Church of England had replaced several pre-Reformation rites with a single Book of Common Prayer; and the concept of *common* prayer, expressed in one service book used by all Anglicans, had become part of Anglican self-identity. In 1906, a Royal Commission on Ritual had recommended that the Convocations should revise the law relating to worship 'as may tend to secure the greater elasticity which a reasonable recognition of the comprehensiveness of the Church of England and of its present needs seems to demand'. The task proved larger than expected, and by 1922 it had become evident that what was needed was not a tinkering with the 1662 Prayer Book but a newly revised Prayer Book. This process of Prayer Book revision suffered from a serious ambiguity in that it was not clear whether it was intended as a means of providing an enriched liturgy which might be used by Anglicans of all churchmanships, or of applying a brake to what were regarded by some as extreme Anglo-Catholic practices, or a bit of both.[10]

The Church Assembly

The nineteenth century saw the revival of the Convocations of Canterbury and York, which, by the start of the twentieth century, sat with a House of Laymen as a Representative Church Assembly.[11] In 1919, this entity was transformed by the Enabling Act into the National Assembly of the Church of England, usually known as the Church Assembly, consisting of bishops and representatives of the clergy and laity. The Assembly was given power to run the pastoral machinery of the Church of England. It passed Measures, which were submitted to Parliament. Parliament could approve or veto these Measures, but no provision was made for Parliament to amend them or to ask the Church Assembly to amend them. According to Chadwick, the creators of the Church Assembly never expected Parliament to use its veto.[12] This expectation, together with the Assembly's 'take it or leave it' approach to Parliament, was a major weakness.

THE 1927 AND 1928 REVISED PRAYER BOOKS

By the mid-1920s, work on a Revised Prayer Book by a committee of the Convocations of Canterbury and York was progressing, but was proving highly controversial.[13] The Anglo-Catholics sought a liturgy which gave full expression to their beliefs about the Eucharist and in particular to the doctrine of the Real Presence and the eucharistic sacrifice. The evangelicals saw this as an attack on the Reformation and opposed it bitterly. Part of the background was furnished by the growth of Anglo-Catholicism. By the 1920s, Anglo-Catholics had become fairly respectable and were starting to occupy positions of importance and influence in the Church.[14] As mentioned earlier, Cosmo Lang is a good example of this development. Another part of the context was the 1922–26 Malines Conversations. These were talks about Church unity, held unofficially but with the foreknowledge of Davidson and Lang, between a group of predominantly Anglo-Catholic Anglicans and some Roman Catholics led by Cardinal Mercier of Malines. There was a storm of controversy when it became known that they had taken place, and Davidson and Lang were attacked for betraying the Church of England's Reformation inheritance.[15] It is worth remembering that in inter-war Britain, one was more likely to encounter anti-Catholicism than anti-Semitism.

By 1927, the Church was ready to submit a Measure to Parliament sanctioning a Revised Prayer Book. Many of the changes were entirely unexceptional, but two areas proved contentious. An alternative Communion rite contained a longer canon, intended to meet Anglo-Catholic complaints that the 1662 consecration was mangled and ended abruptly after the words of institution. The 1927 canon, however, proved unacceptable to many Anglo-Catholics because it contained an *epiclesis*, or invocation of the Holy Spirit, in the Eastern Orthodox position *after* the words of institution, rather than in the Western Catholic position prior to them.[16] The significance was that in the Western Catholic tradition, to which many Anglo-Catholics looked for an example, the moment of consecration was believed to occur during the words of institution, for which the *epiclesis* had been said preparatory. This contrasted with the Eastern Orthodox liturgy, where the process was reversed and the words of institution prepared the way for the moment of consecration during the *epiclesis*. Much sweat and ink were spilt over this difference, except by the evangelicals, who did not believe in a moment of consecration and consequently required only the 1662 rite.[17]

A second sticking point was permanent Reservation of the Sacrament of the Eucharist, in order to be able to give Holy Communion quickly and simply to the sick and dying. The 1927 Revised Prayer Book contained a rubric permitting Reservation for the sick, subject to episcopal licence. This provision irritated Anglo-Catholics, who wished to communicate the whole as well as the sick using the Reserved Sacrament. They also desired sometimes to use the Reserved Sacrament as an aid to prayer, and to hold services in connection with the Reserved Sacrament such as Benediction of the Blessed Sacrament. It also displeased many evangelicals, who feared that Reservation would lead to an idolatrous view of the sacrament.

Thus, in a nutshell, the 1927 Revised Prayer Book was unacceptable to Anglo-Catholics because it was not Catholic enough, and unacceptable to evangelicals because it was too Catholic. The Anglo-Catholics and evangelicals marshalled their respective forces, held meetings, publicly criticised the proposed new liturgy, and sent letters and petitions to their MPs. For their part, Anglican evangelicals enlisted support outside the Church of England from English Nonconformists and Scottish and Welsh Protestants. The 1927 Revised Prayer Book was overwhelmingly approved by the Church Assembly and was passed by a majority of 155 in the House of Lords. To the surprise of many, it was rejected by the House of Commons on 15 December 1927, by 238 votes to 205, largely because of evangelical pressure, but also because the proponents of the

1927 Prayer Book failed to make a good case for the Prayer Book during the debate.[18]

The bishops, led largely by Lang, believed that this outcome was because of 'misunderstandings' and responded by modifying the Revised Prayer Book in 1928 in the hope of making it more acceptable to evangelicals and critics in Parliament.[19] The *epiclesis* was retained in the Eastern Orthodox position after the words of institution. Reservation was still permitted, but as the exception rather than the rule. These changes failed to appease evangelicals and were resented by Anglo-Catholics, who thought the result a much worse Prayer Book. The protest meetings, letters and petitions continued, and on 13 June 1928 the Commons again rejected the modified Prayer Book by 268 votes to 222. Davidson was profoundly shaken. On 17 June, he noted that he had 'never known a situation which was so perplexing – every pathway in every direction seems to lead into a morass'. On 25 July, he announced his resignation and was succeeded by Lang in December 1928.[20]

THE PRAYER BOOK CRISIS CONFRONTING ARCHBISHOP LANG

Lang was immediately confronted by a skein of interwoven problems. To begin with, the controversy about the Revised Prayer Books had seen much dirty linen washed in public. Disagreements about churchmanship had been exacerbated. Many Anglicans felt hurt by the Commons' rejection of twenty years of liturgical revision. Others, though not greatly enthusiastic towards the Revised Prayer Books or even very interested in liturgy, were dismayed and dispirited by the Commons' action and by some of the things said by MPs during the debates. Michael Ramsey, then an ordinand at Cuddesdon and later archbishop of Canterbury, found the rejection of the Revised Prayer Books a searing experience which he remembered all his life. Support for at least parts of the 1928 Prayer Book remained high. There was also the lurking fear of Anglo-Catholic secessions, which, according to Davidson, would lose the Church 'men of the intensest devotion, greatest pastoral effectiveness, and deep piety'.[21]

Moreover, the Church's relationship with Parliament was left unclear. The 1919 Enabling Act had given a degree of responsibility to the Church Assembly, and yet Parliament appeared to have ridden roughshod over this.[22]

Finally, the revision of the liturgy, and the issue of Reservation, remained unresolved.

Numbers

Davidson received some 800 letters and petitions about the Revised Prayer Book. The largest petition submitted against it is said to have attracted 308,000 signatures.[23] These would have represented a cross-section of the Church of England, ranging from those deeply opposed to change in the Communion rite, to parishioners who only signed because the vicar asked them to do so. It is probable that some signatories were Nonconformists and irregular-churchgoing, cultural Protestants. A very few may have been Anglo-Catholics, using any tactical means to attack the Revised Prayer Book, though Anglo-Catholic commentators such as Dom Anselm Hughes OSB make no mention of this. If one takes this figure of 308,000 as a rough benchmark and then adds a similar number of irritated Anglo-Catholics, and for good measure throws in those Anglicans uncommitted to the Revised Prayer Book but troubled by the Commons' action, then one ends up with perhaps 700,000 or so annoyed or worried Anglican clergy and laity. This is an educated guess, but the disaffected on all sides would likewise have included a cross-section of Anglicans, including hard-working clergy and devoted laity, the less-committed, and those just looking for a reason to be angry.

I am familiar with early twentieth-century history of the parish churches of Colchester, Essex. By way of establishing a context – and not discounting the possibility of regional bias – I have examined parish magazines from Colchester from the mid-1920s until the mid-1930s, which reflect a range of churchmanships. Not all editions have survived, but of those which remain, none contain articles hostile to the Revised Prayer Books of 1927 and 1928. St Mary-at-the-Walls printed three articles which were broadly supportive of Prayer Book revision and were unwilling to accept the Commons' rejection of the 1927 and 1928 revisions as final. A new incumbent at St Botolph's made a solitary suggestion in 1931 that disestablishment was the ideal remedy, and the following year expressed the hope that the Commons' rejections had been the final fling of 'the protestant underworld'.[24] There were no other references to the controversy surrounding the 1927 and 1928 Prayer Books. Now, this might simply mean that the editors kept controversial items out of their magazines for fear of upsetting their congregations; but it might also mean that the parishioners of these different sorts of churches were not really very interested in the 1927 and 1928 Prayer Books and that they simply carried on with leading their lives, looking after their families, and going to church as usual. (It might have been different, of course, had a Revised Prayer Book been *imposed* upon them.)

The large number of people on all sides disaffected by Prayer Book revision would have concerned Lang. But Lang was a realist, and from his visits to parishes he would have known that there were many regular churchgoers, perhaps as many as two million, let alone a penumbra of occasional churchgoers, who were not overly concerned by the controversy.

KEEPING THE SHOW ON THE ROAD

Archbishop Rowan Williams has described the heavy burden of expectation that descended upon him when he became archbishop of Canterbury in 2002: almost that, *Deus ex machina*, he would right all wrongs and solve all problems.[25] It is probable that a similar weight descended upon Lang when he became archbishop in 1928, the first new archbishop of Canterbury since 1903. He became primate of a divided and irritated Church and it was necessary for him to apply some balm quickly. He made a start with his enthronement on 4 December 1928. He decided to wear convocation robes rather than a cope and mitre in order to avoid offending evangelicals.[26] Lang touched upon many things in his sermon, including the archbishopric itself, the continuity of Christian faith, the expansion of the Anglican Communion, the claims of a materialistic society, ecumenism, evangelism, the problems of unemployment and the problems confronting the Church of England in its relations with the state. He then turned his attention to the different churchmanships making up the Church of England:

We know, alas too well! Its weaknesses and failures; we know its lack of many gifts and graces which other Churches may possess. But we lift up our eyes above our complaints and quarrels unto the hills and see the ideal, and therefore the real, *Ecclesia Anglicana* shining in the light of God's purpose. We see there a Church of which we have no cause to be ashamed . . . Plainly it is in the actual life of the Church in England itself that this ideal must first be fulfilled. Three main movements of thought and experience are lodged within our household – Catholic, Evangelical and Liberal, so we call them. Is any one of them an intruder? Does not each stand for a spirit, an aspect of truth, without which the Church would be impoverished and its power to answer God's call would be hindered? Then why should they contend with one another? Let not each tolerate the others but learn from them.[27]

Lang offered an element of carrot and stick in this sermon: Anglo-Catholics would have been pleased with his emphasis on continuity with the past, evangelicals with his words on evangelism, and all with his words about Christian unity. Lang then set out to challenge: he asserted that there was a proper place within the Church of England for all churchmanships, and indeed Anglo-Catholics, evangelicals and liberals needed to listen and cooperate in order to carry out God's purpose. Lang did not mention schism, but he gave no comfort to evangelicals thinking that the Church would be better off without Anglo-Catholics or to Anglo-Catholics tempted to break away. Instead, he exhorted them to high ideals of service.

Lang's next move to sort out the muddle and to pacify the Church of England came during a meeting of the Canterbury Convocation on 10 July 1929. Lang began his address by asserting that the worship of God was a primary concern of the Church in every generation. It was, he claimed, impossible and undesirable to return to a strict interpretation of the 1662 Prayer Book. Church attempts to secure 'the statutory sanction which was desired and sought' for the 1928 Prayer Book having failed, the bishops 'were compelled in the present difficult situation to fulfill by administrative action their responsibility for the regulation of public worship'.[28] In other words, the bishops had decided to carry on as though Parliament *had* sanctioned the 1928 Prayer Book. Lord Woolmer and others had previously suggested that they might enact a canon authorising the 1928 Prayer Book, but this would have provoked a conflict with Parliament, which would have had to approve the canon.[29] The bishops evidently felt that the Commons had twice made a mistake, and they decided more or less to ignore them: a courageous decision on the part of men not previously accustomed to flout the legislature.

Lang announced that the bishops had resolved that, 'in the exercise of their administrative discretion', they would consider the needs of individual parishes and 'give counsel and direction'. They agreed to conform themselves to three principles: (1) the 1928 Book having been accepted by the Convocations and by the Church Assembly, its use would not be inconsistent with Church loyalty; (2) the bishops would be guided by the 1928 proposals and would seek to end liturgical practices inconsistent with 1662 and 1928; and (3) the use of 1928 material in a parish must have the goodwill of the people.[30]

Lang spent some time carefully handling dissentients in Convocation. The result was that his resolution was accepted by a large majority. The Rev. Dr Charles Harris, a member of Convocation, told Lang that he had reduced the opposition from fifty-four ('a formidable minority') to nineteen ('a veritable triumph for your Grace'). Harris thought Lang's proposal would enjoy the support of nine-tenths of Anglo-Catholics and the bulk of evangelicals.[31]

The 1929 Convocation resolution eased some of the tension in the Church of England. It bought time for Lang to address wider issues, and enabled the Church to retain a modicum of dignity. However, it contained two fatal flaws. Firstly, it sought to regulate worship by means of the 1662 Prayer Book, which Convocation admitted to be inadequate, augmented by the 1928 Prayer Book, which was unacceptable to those – principally Anglo-Catholics – whose liturgical needs it sought to address. Secondly, the resolution relied upon the bishops to take action in their dioceses, without laying down any common standards or benchmarks. The consequence was a wide variety of interpretation of the 1929 resolution across the dioceses. There was little Lang could do about these flaws, which came to bedevil his attempts to guide the Church.[32]

CHURCH AND STATE

Many reasons have been advanced for the Common's rejection of the Revised Prayer Book measures of 1927 and 1928. The Scottish Presbyterian MP Rosslyn Mitchell and others had raised the old cry of 'No-Popery'. Sir William Joynson Hicks, the evangelical home secretary, spoke effectively against the Revised Prayer Book, whilst the speeches in favour were lacklustre.[33] Perhaps the most telling reason was that many people not directly caught up in Church life failed to appreciate the reasons for reform of the 1662 Prayer Book. As Davidson put it, 'the average MP or County Councillor, or local squire, or man of business, says emphatically, "let it alone."'[34] Alarmed by the months of controversy stirred up by evangelicals and Anglo-Catholics alike, and not fully understanding liturgical reform, many MPs quite simply seem to have been unwilling to risk further disruption and to have decided to play safe by supporting the status quo.

THE NATURE OF THE CRISIS

F.A. Iremonger, William Temple's biographer, described the Commons' rejection of the 1928 Prayer Book as 'the gravest crisis affecting the relations of Church and State since the Reformation'. The Commons' rejection of the 1927 and 1928 Prayer Books seemed to some like a kick in the teeth for the Church of England and resulted in great shock and emotion.[35]

It is important, however, to qualify and to understand correctly the nature of the Church–state crisis which confronted Lang. This was not a Church–state crisis comparable to that which had divided France in 1905, or even to the crises which existed in contemporary Mexico or the USSR. Indeed, it is questionable whether it was truly a Church–state crisis. It was not government policy to oppose the Revised Prayer Books. The executive had no interest in a conflict with the Church. It was, rather, a clash between the Church of England and some of the MPs who at that time made up the lower house of the legislature.

It should be remembered that the Commons, both before and after the rejections of the 1927 and 1928 Prayer Books, routinely passed Measures submitted by the Church Assembly. From a constitutional point of view, they might just as well in 1927 and 1928 have been rejecting a Measure establishing a new archdeaconry or amending clerical pensions. The question therefore arises: was this truly a Church–state crisis, or rather a couple of severe (and, for the Church, painful and demoralising) hiccups as Parliament and the Church Assembly worked out their new roles and established a *modus vivendi*, based upon the imperfect 'take it or leave it' constitutional arrangement subsisting between them?

STANLEY BALDWIN

The prime minister, Stanley Baldwin, received a number of letters complaining about the 1928 Prayer Book, the bishops and their 1929 declaration that they would use their 'administrative discretion' to authorise the 1928 Prayer Book. Baldwin's private secretary, Sir Patrick Gower, spent some days during November 1928 examining the whole subject on behalf of his master.[36] If Baldwin's correspondents are any guide to the people who opposed the Revised Prayer Book in the early part of Lang's primacy, they were predominantly middle-aged or elderly. All saw themselves as children of the Reformation, which they regarded as national deliverance from Popish superstition. They seem to have believed the Church of England to be episcopally managed Protestantism: *managed* rather than governed, because they all had a low opinion of contemporary bishops and a high view of Parliament, which they believed to be the ultimate authority and the guarantor of their Protestant beliefs and their narrowly Protestant interpretation of British national identity and history. They saw Anglo-Catholics as dangerous interlopers, reintroducing erroneous Catholic beliefs and practices which had no place in a pure, reformed Church. If only Parliament would pressurise the bishops to discipline these errant clergymen, they would either leave the Church of England or fall into line as good Protestant churchmen, and all would be well. Engineer Rear-Admiral Emdim (retired) wished something like the Naval Discipline Act, which made provision for the discipline of officers and ratings in the Royal Navy, to be applied to the Established Church. W. Poynter Adams of the National Church League ('President: Sir W. Joynson Hicks, Home Secretary'), asserted that if only they could get rid of W.H. Frere CR, bishop of Truro, and about one hundred Anglo-Catholic priests, Cornwall would be ripe for 'Home Reunion' with Protestant Nonconformists.[37]

Gower reported back to Baldwin in November 1928. He evidently did not understand much about liturgy, but he pointed out that the 1927 and 1928 Prayer Books were submitted to Parliament by those responsible for ecclesiastical administration; they were a genuine and sincere attempt to improve that administration, and received the support of the archbishop and the whole body of bishops ('with one or two exceptions') and of the Church Assembly. He reminded Baldwin that the votes in the Commons had been free; that the proponents of the Revised Prayer Books could not reasonably be excluded from preferment; and that it was undesirable that 'a question of this kind' should become a subject of public political controversy. Baldwin consequently adopted the policy that the Prayer Book controversy was a spiritual issue, which 'far transcends Party Politics or the issues at a General Election' and expressed the hope that guidance might be given 'to those to whom responsibility falls'.[38]

There is no surviving correspondence to show that Baldwin told Lang that this would be his policy, but the two men might easily have had a word, and it is similarly possible that some Protestant-minded complainant, irritated at being fobbed off by Baldwin, might have said something, so that the news eventually got back to Lambeth Palace. Lang is unlikely to have been left in the dark for long, and would have been relieved not to have to confront the prime minister and government.

THE CHURCH–STATE COMMISSION

As early as June 1928, when he was still archbishop of York, Lang had told the bishops that he believed the Commons' action had troubled the consciences of many Anglicans and raised the whole question of whether the existing law of the relationship between Church and state was satisfactory and consistent with the fundamental rights of a Christian Church. In July 1929, he announced that a commission would be established to examine thoroughly the whole question of Church–state relations.[39]

The appointment of the members of the commission showed Lang at his best, as a good judge of character and with his finger on the pulse of the daily life of the Church of England. Although the commission was nominally appointed by both archbishops, Lang selected its members and then sought Temple's acquiescence. In May 1930, Lang appointed as chairman Viscount Cecil of Chelwood, parliamentary under-secretary at the Foreign Office and a member of the League of Nations and the Church Assembly. Lang was anxious, in choosing the rest of the commission, to secure representatives of all shades of churchmanship. He insisted that the commissioners should not already have definitely committed themselves to a policy of disestablishment, but should have an open mind. When the commission finally began work on 4 November 1930, it consisted, apart from Cecil and Temple, of the bishop of Carlisle, whom Lang had nominated because he thought he would take more pains than the bishop of Oxford; the bishop of Chichester, representing the younger bishops; G.A. Weekes, master of Sidney Sussex College, a Cambridge don and representative of Anglo-Catholicism; Canon Vernon Storr, representing the evangelicals; the earl of Selborne, chairman of the House of Laity in the Church Assembly; Lord David Balniel, MP, 'a thoughtful and able representative of the younger public men'; Sir Charles Grant Robertson, vice-chancellor of Birmingham University, a historian 'versed in public affairs'; Professor Ernest Jacob of Manchester University, 'a historian much interested in this particular problem'; Sir Lewis Dibdin, dean of the Arches; Sir Philip Wilbraham, chancellor of many dioceses, knowledgeable in ecclesiastical law and the workings of the Church Assembly; Caroline, Viscountess Bridgeman, chosen 'because she is a woman and there ought to be some woman on the commission and because she is well known in public life'; and Sir Ernest Bennett, a Labour MP and former Oxford don. H.B. Vaisey, a barrister, and the Rev. Edgar Hellins, representing the parochial clergy, were subsequently appointed.[40]

The commission met sixteen times and received evidence and submissions from interested parties.[41] It is surprising to discover that neither Lang nor any of his staff made a submission. He probably omitted to do so because the commission was acting in his name and would report to him and Temple; and yet a bird's eye view from Lambeth Palace, or an assessment of how the issues affected the primate might have been useful to the commissioners and a way could perhaps have been found to include them. Lang was not shown an advance copy of the commission's report and told Baldwin in 1935, 'I have carefully refrained in interfering in any way in the work of the Commission.' This statement was not completely true. On 9 September 1932, Viscount Cecil of Chelwood had written to ask Lang about Church courts.[42] Lang replied from Ballure:

> No doubt, as you say, your main task is to consider the situation created by Parliament through its rejection of the Prayer Book Measure and *to suggest some way of securing some reasonable autonomy on the part of the Church concerning doctrine and worship* [my italics].[43]

In other words, three years before the commission published its report, Lang and Cecil had hinted to one another what they thought would be a desirable outcome: greater autonomy for the Church of England, but not disestablishment.

The report was published in January 1936 in two volumes. The commission rejected disestablishment, claiming that the Church of England could only ask the state for disestablishment but not determine the terms upon which this would be granted. It also feared the unforeseen consequences, observing 'that if England, by Disestablishment, should seem to become neutral in the fight between faith and unfaith in Christianity, that would be a calamity for our own people and, indeed, for the whole world.'[44] The report recommended, firstly, that the archbishops should summon a round-table conference 'of representatives of every school of thought' to secure agreement on the permissible deviations from the 1662 Prayer Book and the use and limits of Reservation of the Sacrament. Secondly, it recommended that the Canterbury and York Convocations, with the agreement of the Church Assembly, should then formally frame and adopt a 'Synodical Declaration' about the meaning and limits of the words 'Lawful Authority' in the declaration of assent.[45]

Subject to these conditions, the report suggested that the Church Assembly should introduce a Bill to Parliament to secure the right to bypass Parliament entirely in some fields. Provided a Measure

contained no fundamental doctrinal changes and had been approved
by the convocations, Church Assembly and three-quarters of diocesan
conferences, the report suggested that it might be presented directly to
the king for the royal assent.[46]

The report was debated by the Church Assembly in February and
June 1936. The assembly was not asked to register an opinion, but merely
to commend the report to the attention of the Church. Several speakers
claimed that things had calmed down since the dramatic events of
1927–28 and questioned the necessity of further action. Here is a clue
to one significant aspect of the Church–state commission: it bought
time for the Church to quieten down. By 1936, the underlying problems
remained the same as in 1928, but they did not seem so threatening.
Lang brought the debate to a close by supporting the idea of a round-
table conference and stressing that it needed to deal with fundamental
principles before tackling liturgical details.[47]

The Round-Table Conference

The task of organising the round-table conference to consider a
synodical declaration on 'lawful authority', liturgy and Reservation of
the Sacrament fell to Lang. He consulted the bishops in January 1937
and asked Temple to be the chairman. Once again, he worked hard to
ensure a balanced membership. When the conference met on 18 March
1938, it comprised nine evangelicals, nine Anglo-Catholics, eleven 'more
Central' Anglicans, twelve laymen of unrecorded chuchmanship, seven
bishops representative of the range of churchmanships, E.C. Ratcliff
to advise on liturgy and Norman Sykes on history, and two women,
Viscountess Bridgeman and Lady Bates. One member of the conference,
Bishop Bell, kept Lang informed of its progress, frequently adding his
own observations and suggestions.[48]

On 1 February 1938, Lang repeated his opinion that the round-table
conference should first study 'lawful authority', before tackling liturgy
and Reservation.[49] This might have been an intellectually coherent
way of proceeding, but its unfortunate effect was to stifle any progress.
Temple reported that several members of the conference had said that
it was impossible for them 'to reach a judgement on the policy of the

[Synodical] Declaration unless they knew what kind of regulations would in the first instance be attached'.[50] Quite simply, the evangelicals were not going to support a declaration which might later be used to justify something like Benediction. Lang evidently still believed that liturgy should be based upon underlying principles, rather than that principles should be constructed to justify liturgical reality. He repeated his wish that the conference first resolve the issue of 'lawful authority'.[51]

Lang intervened in the work of the conference on only one occasion – when he saw Samuel Hoare, the home secretary, at Lambeth on 13 July 1938. Hoare had earlier told Bell that the Crown's law officers believed that 'lawful authority' meant the Crown, as advised by its ministers. Lang asserted the importance of a clear definition of *spiritual* authority, and Hoare did not demur.[52]

The round-table conference continued to meet, but achieved no significant progress because of its failure to define lawful authority. Lang noted that 'the old fact emerged that men were afraid of what they called "those with whom we are accustomed to associate" – in other words, that it is the tail that wags the dog, not the dog that wags the tail.'[53]

On 15 September 1939, Lang and Temple cancelled the next meeting because of the outbreak of war.[54] The conference never met again. Effectively, nine years of work simply fizzled out. This must surely be regarded as a failure on Lang's part and it is not easy to explain. Admittedly, he had many other problems to deal with as Europe slid into conflict; but he might have done a little more to help the round-table conference, given that the identity and intellectual coherence of his Church was at stake. The biggest failure was his insistence that the conference first resolve the question of 'lawful authority' before tackling liturgy. With hindsight, it might have been wiser to have adopted a two-pronged approach, examining lawful authority and liturgy in tandem. Discussion of each subject might have informed understanding of the other.

THE LITURGY AFTER 1929

The most intractable liturgical problem facing Lang was the eucharistic canon. Since 1559, the Church of England had contained people with differing eucharistic theologies and spiritualities. They used a common liturgy, but put their own glosses upon it. By the twentieth century, Anglo-Catholics were growing restive. 'There really is something very profane', commented Dom Gregory Dix OSB towards the end of Lang's primacy, 'about the idea that we can only come before God with circumlocutions which it has been agreed to misunderstand differently.' What they particularly sought was a 'second half' to the eucharistic prayer after the words of institution, which reflected upon the meaning of the eucharistic action. This, of course, meant having to state what happened in the eucharistic action, which was not easy, given the range of Anglican eucharistic beliefs.[55] The abortive 1928 Prayer Book contained a longer canon, but, as has been mentioned, it was unacceptable to many Anglo-Catholics. Which rite to use at the altar proved a big headache for many Anglo-Catholic clergy in the 1920s and 1930s. The consequence was that by the time Lang went to Canterbury, many Anglo-Catholic priests were 'enriching' the eucharistic rite, to use the jargon of the day, sometimes with material drawn from the Roman Missal. The 1930s saw the publication of a number of Anglo-Catholic missals containing material other than that in the 1662 and 1928 Prayer Books, of which the *Altar Book* (1930), the *English Missal* (1933), the *Anglican Missal* (1934) and the *English Sacramentary* (1934) may especially be mentioned. Bishops Garbett and Bell in particular were annoyed by the appearance of such unauthorised missals.[56] Anglo-Catholics, in consequence of all this, found themselves surrounded by liturgical chaos. Professor N.P. Williams commented in 1932:

> The Faithful, as they move from place to place, find themselves confronted with a bewildering variety of uses, while even in their home church a change of incumbency may mean a change not only of ceremonial but of rite. A priest saying Mass in a strange church has to enquire beforehand exactly what to do unless he is to bewilder the congregation by an unaccustomed method; and if he is to change his method, he must perforce abandon all hope of recollection in the desperate attempt to remember what he has to do next. The spiritual life of both clergy and laity suffers inevitably from such wide divergences.[57]

Even Dom Gregory Dix OSB, an Anglican Benedictine monk of Nashdom Abbey and a liturgical scholar, who might have been expected to be sympathetic to Anglo-Catholics seeking a better canon, believed that the resulting liturgical diversity was 'a trouble which we shall not easily end'.[58]

Lang made repeated attempts to reach an accommodation with Anglo-Catholics and to end the liturgical disorder in his Church. In 1930, Viscount Halifax, president of the English Church Union, suggested that the authorisation of the 1549 Prayer Book might remedy the situation. Lang's response to Halifax was cautious but not dismissive: he pointed out that 'these good Evangelicals regarded it [1549] as one of the documents which had been definitely discarded by the Church of England,' but he said that Halifax's suggestion was important, 'and when the time comes after this present most unsatisfactory interim period following the rejection of the Prayer Book proposals of 1928 for reconsidering our whole position with regard to a Liturgy, I shall keep it in mind.'[59] The significant thing about this reply is that Lang made it plain that he was thinking in terms of an 'interim period' and did not regard the 1929 Convocation resolution as final. Lang raised the idea of authorising the 1549 rite at two bishops' meetings in 1932 but none of the bishops was supportive.[60]

In 1934, Lang took advantage of disquiet amongst some prominent Anglo-Catholics about the range of liturgical usage to put out feelers to the Rev. Humphrey Whitby of St Mary's, Graham Terrace, Chelsea.[61] Whitby spent the summer consulting 'some friends of the more advanced Anglo-Catholic school' and reported in October that the consensus was a desire for:

> A form of Communion Office which is at once definitely Anglican in the sense that it includes the actual words in their entirety of the 1662 Office, and is at the same time structurally in keeping with the traditions of Western Liturgies. The general principle underlying this suggested re-arrangement of the 1662 Office may be expressed thus: 'The words of 1662 in the order of 1549'.[62]

This suggestion became known as the 'interim rite' and received powerful advocacy in 1932 from Professor N.P. Williams in a pamphlet,

For the Present Distress: A Suggestion for an Interim Rite. Some Anglo-Catholics seem to have thought not merely in terms of rearranging the 1662 rite, but also of inserting other material, such as the Kyries, Benedictus and Agnus Dei, and possibly some prayers from the Roman Missal. Episcopal reaction was mixed: Blunt encouraged further exploration of the interim rite, Bell condemned it and ordered his clergy to use the 1662 material in its original sequence, whilst the evangelical bishops of Exeter, Worcester, and St Edmundsbury and Ipswich told Lang that they objected to the whole idea. Lang privately consulted evangelicals, liberals and members of the liturgists' Alcuin Club, who were all uneasy about the proposal.[63]

Lang laid the proposal for an interim rite before the bishops on 21 January 1935. He said it had emanated from certain Anglo-Catholics who were anxious to restrain the current liturgical chaos, but he kept quiet about his own role. After a short discussion, the bishops asked for a special meeting to discuss the interim rite a fortnight later on 4 February. No bishops favoured the Interim Rite at that meeting.

At their meeting on 23 October 1935, Lang asked the bishops to discuss the idea of transferring the prayer of oblation, as a means of re-establishing order. This prayer, said after Communion in the 1662 rite, would be transferred to the end of the prayer of consecration, and could be interpreted by Anglo-Catholics as largely recreating the shape of the eucharistic canon. Temple said he thought that this would 'give a large measure of alleviation of the present discontent', and the bishops of St Albans and Wakefield suggested that many clergy who had supported the interim rite would be content with such a transfer. The bishop of Manchester undertook to consult liberal evangelicals in order to forestall criticism. The brief period of optimism generated by this meeting had dissipated by the time of the next bishops' meeting on 20 January 1936, when the transfer was rejected.[64]

Lang returned to this subject on 21 October 1936. Bell, who had previously opposed the transfer of the prayer of oblation, indicated that he was coming round to support it. Garbett, however, said that it was dangerous to depart from the 1929 'norm', and the bishops again rejected the transfer of the prayer by a large majority.[65] Lang expressed his frustration to Bell:

I feel increasingly that to permit this transfer would not only be justified in itself but would be welcomed by the growing number of Anglo-Catholics who want to live in peace and under authority. I cannot regard the matter as closed. I think it must be re-opened.[66]

At their meeting on 19 January 1937, Lang told the bishops that he was greatly dissatisfied with their discussion of the transfer of the prayer of oblation at their previous meeting. He said that the present position was unsatisfactory because what was tolerated in one diocese was forbidden in another and the chance to restrain disorder and promote unity, once lost, might never be regained. He was supported by Bell, but there was no discussion because the bishops were disinclined to reconsider the matter. The transfer of the prayer of oblation was raised at the very end of Lang's primacy, in January 1942, when the bishops discussed a point about procedure to enable them to consider the place of the prayer of oblation in Convocation, but nothing appears to have come of this initiative.[67]

Lang thus may be seen to have made three sustained efforts to end the liturgical chaos troubling the Church of England, involving the 1549 rite, the interim rite and the transfer of the prayer of oblation. Why was he constantly frustrated by the bishops? There are several possible explanations. The bishops repeatedly returned to the 1929 resolution that they would treat the 1928 Prayer Book as though it had received parliamentary sanction and would not tolerate anything other than the 1662 or 1928 Prayer Books, and most of them would not budge from this position. The 1929 resolution had been a brave step by the bishops, and they may have been nervous of doing anything further which might reopen old wounds.

The Church of England has never claimed a *magisterium* and was unable to agree upon its 'lawful authority.' In such a Church, a common liturgy such as the 1662 Prayer Book may have acted as an ecclesial glue, uniting different churchmanships and spiritualities in one body. The bishops had realised that the 1662 Prayer Book needed augmenting, and in 1929 they were prepared to make the best of a bad job and tolerate the 1928 Prayer Book. Perhaps the reason they were not prepared to go beyond this was their desire to bolster internal unity and to avoid further destabilising diversity. Apart from Frere of Truro and Blunt of Bradford, not many bishops appear to have been interested in liturgy. All busy men, they may have resented time spent dealing with liturgical matters. Lang had more of an understanding of the Anglo-Catholics' liturgical concerns than most bishops. He was impressed by the wish of some Anglo-Catholics to put their house in order and he sought to assist them. The result was a series of impasses between Lang and the bishops.

RESERVATION OF THE SACRAMENT

It was the guarded provision in the Revised Prayer Books for continuous Reservation of the Blessed Sacrament which more than anything else excited Protestant ire and led to the Commons' rejections of 1927 and 1928. Lord Stamfordham (formerly Sir Arthur Bigge), George V's private secretary, put his finger on the nub of the problem when he asked Lang in 1928 'why should churches in which there is daily Holy Communion insist upon perpetual reservation?'[68] The answer, as Stamfordham supposed, was that Anglo-Catholics desired Reservation for a variety of devotional reasons and not solely for extended communion of the sick. Anglo-Catholics believed in the objective Real Presence of Christ in the sacrament from the moment of its consecration. Moderate Anglo-Catholics, whilst practising Reservation for extended communion, often set apart the areas of their churches where the sacrament was reserved as places of private prayer, believing the presence of the sacrament brought an added stillness and sense of the numinous. Amongst advanced Anglo-Catholics there was a revival of a *cultus* of the reserved sacrament with extra-liturgical devotions, including Benediction.[69] Needless to say, this spirituality was not shared by the rest of the Church of England. The *cultus* of the sacrament made no sense to those whose eucharistic theology was receptionist or virtualist, it appeared to contradict Article 28 of the Thirty-Nine Articles, and it smacked of Romanism.

The rubrics governing Reservation had been tightened up in the 1928 Prayer Book by Garbett and Haigh, in an effort to get the book through Parliament, by insisting that Reservation was practised solely for the communion of the sick and aiming to preclude all extra-liturgical devotions.[70] When the Commons rejected the Revised Prayer Book for a second time, the Church of England found itself in a great muddle over Reservation. As Garbett had earlier pointed out, if the bishops omitted any provision for Reservation, they would drive moderate Anglo-Catholics into the hands of extremists and lose all moral authority, 'for we would lie open to the charge that we had really given up perpetual Reservation on account of a vote by the House of Commons.'[71] Yet the bishops themselves were divided. The evangelical Bishop Warman of Chelmsford declared:

> I may presently be asked to choose between permanent reservation and disestablishment. I value the establishment immensely; I value permanent reservation not at all. I dislike saying it, but I sometimes doubt the honesty of the demand for it.[72]

The bishops' 1929 resolution that they would tolerate the 1928 Prayer Book meant that they would be guided by Garbett and Haigh's restrictive 1928 rubrics governing Reservation. Two problems arose in consequence. Firstly, some Anglo-Catholic clergy and laity found it very painful to give up extra-liturgical practices which formed a large part of their spiritual lives, and their congregations dwindled. Winnington-Ingram passed on to Lang correspondence from one priest who said that the instruction to give up Benediction was almost more than he could endure and asking to be moved to another parish. Secondly, some priests persisted in giving Holy Communion from the reserved sacrament to parishioners, such as nurses, whose work prevented them attending church on Sunday, which was not envisaged by the 1928 rubrics. Fourteen hundred members of the Federation of Catholic Priests announced that they would ignore the rubrics and Winnington-Ingram lost control of a special diocesan synod in London called to discuss Reservation.[73]

In February 1929, the bishops agreed to establish an episcopal committee to examine the interpretation of the 1928 rubrics 'with special reference to the question of what is or is not a Service in connection with the Reserved Sacrament'.[74] The committee could not agree upon a list of 'special circumstances' for Reservation, and each bishop was left to reach his own decision. There could be no appeal to the archbishops, because the 1928 rubrics were based upon ecclesiastical consent and had no sanctions attached to them. Inevitably, the bishops interpreted the rubrics differently. None interpreted them generously, but some appear to have been more rigorous than others. At least three bishops – Birmingham, Exeter, and St Edmundsbury and Ipswich – refused to institute incumbents to parishes unless they undertook to give up Reservation.[75]

This left Lang in an invidious position. He was obliged to tell complainants that he could not interfere in another diocese, and he reluctantly had to support the right of bishops to refuse institution to clergy who would not abandon Reservation. Lang stamped out related practices, such as Benediction, in his own diocese, but was generous in permitting Reservation for the sick, provided that the 1928 rubrics were fulfilled.[76] Seeing that he could do little to influence things in various diocesan controversies over Reservation in the 1930s, Lang appears to have adopted an attitude of being above the fray. In 1935, Lang declined to receive representatives from the Church Union, the Federation of Catholic Priests and the Confraternity of the Blessed Sacrament, who sought his 'fatherly advice', on the grounds that 'I cannot take any part in the proceedings or policies of party societies.' Curiously, he seems to have been willing to permit religious orders to reserve the sacrament for devotional purposes, on the condition that this practice was restricted to members of the community.[77]

Humphrey Whitby, vicar of the Anglo-Catholic St Mary's Church, Graham Terrace, Chelsea, told Lang in 1936 that one reason why some Anglo-Catholics stressed extra-liturgical adoration of the sacrament and communion outside Mass was as a protest against the disbelief of many evangelicals and some bishops in the objective Real Presence.[78] Lang wrote 'No' in the margin of Whitby's letter, though it is not clear whether he sought to exculpate Anglo-Catholics or evangelicals. What is evident is that many Anglo-Catholics believed themselves to be fighting for their legitimate right to do in England what was done in Scotland and in other Anglican Churches.[79] In November 1934, the Church Union had decided to persuade a diocesan bishop to seek an archiepiscopal 'opinion' about Reservation. 'If it is in favour of Reservation, our battle is won,' they noted, but, 'if it is against us we are no worse off than now, for (as Archbishop [Frederick] Temple pointed out) the "Opinions" have not the force of Law and the hearing is not a Court.' A copy of the correspondence somehow found its way to Lambeth, so Lang knew what they were up to. The bishop of Worcester was asked to raise the matter. Lang sidestepped this initiative by asking Worcester not to press him for a general discussion of Reservation 'because it would be impossible in any discussion . . . to arrive at any formula which would win general consent.'[80]

In June 1936, Lang received a deputation of Anglo-Catholics who came simply to convey their views. Lang questioned them, tried to explain the evangelicals' fears about perpetual Reservation, and reminded them that there were many clergy and laity who did not share their eucharistic doctrine. Lang noted that the Anglo-Catholics were clear that 'unless some greater encouragement was given by the Bishops to the practice of Reservation, there was a real danger of what they called a large landslide to Rome.' Having consulted Temple, Lang asserted at the next bishops' meeting that 'what was needed was a spirit of sympathy and understanding on the part of the Bishops [towards Anglo-Catholics] in interpreting reasonably the regulations which they had laid down in 1929.'[81] There is no evidence that Lang's words made any difference. Much of the responsibility for the muddle over Reservation lies with the ruling that each diocesan bishop should decide about Reservation in his diocese. This resulted in inconsistency across the Church of England, and, where episcopal opposition was determined, Lang's example in Canterbury, and plea for sympathy and understanding, were to no avail.

Preserving Church Unity

'We have to face the fact that a considerable Anglo-Catholic section is contemplating secession as a genuinely practical idea,' Temple wrote to Lang in 1930, continuing: 'I don't know that any of them want it, and most heartily shrink from it, but they are certainly thinking about it.' Both Lang and Temple feared an exodus of disgruntled Anglo-Catholics following the rejection of the 1928 Prayer Book, as had Davidson before them. It is hard to know how real Lang and Temple's fears were, but, in late 1929 or early 1930, Sir William Spens, the Anglo-Catholic master of Corpus Christi College and vice-chancellor of Cambridge University, proposed a round-table conference to discuss the future of Anglo-Catholicism. He was supported by A.K. Ingram, vice-chairman of the National Peace Council, and surprisingly by Joynson Hicks, a leading evangelical opponent of the 1928 Prayer Book.[82] Temple was invited and consulted Lang:

> As you know, the general line to which they incline is the suggestion of the formation of a uniat Anglo-Catholic Church, outside the establishment, Convocation, etc., but regarded as in full communion with Canterbury, and that in this new Church certain actual buildings might be allocated though without any endowments in the form of income.[83]

Lang poured cold water on the idea of an Anglo-Catholic uniat Church and suggested that Joynson Hicks was only involved because he saw this initiative as a way of ridding the Church of England of Anglo-Catholics. He felt that neither archbishop should have anything to do with the proposal, nor should Temple attend the conference, nor offer it the most guarded support, because 'the whole proposal seems to me a definite contemplation of a further sin of schism.'[84] Perhaps Lang thought that Spens' uniat Church proposal was ultimately all about leading a segment of the Church of England, including its buildings, in a Romeward direction. It would be easy to characterise the uniat Church idea as the exaggerated talk of a few Anglo-Catholic 'Young Turks', but the fact that it was advanced by someone as significant as Spens may be an indication that responsible and thoughtful Anglo-Catholics were unsure of themselves and their place in the Church of England of the late 1920s and early 1930s. After Lang's firm line, no more was heard of Spens' projected conference.

What did Lang think about Anglo-Catholics? He was, after all, an Anglo-Catholic himself. He expressed his views in a letter of July 1929, addressed to Arthur Chandler, a retired Anglo-Catholic colonial bishop:

> There is no desire nearer my heart than that the Anglo-Catholic movement should take its proper place in the life of the Church and that that movement and the Liberal Evangelical movement

[sic, Lang probably meant the Liberal and Evangelical movements] should not only carry out their respective principles but make more effort to meet together and understand each other for the good of the whole Church. But I may certainly say that if this aim which we both desire is to have any chance of fulfilment, many of our Anglo-Catholic friends must be prepared to be more considerate than they have sometimes been and not think and talk and pass Resolutions as if they were the Anglican Church and regardless of the effect of what they press upon other members of the Church. I have long felt that if they would only suspend even what they deem to be their lawful rights in certain matters and consolidate their positive and constructive position within the Church their chance of really influencing the whole of that Church and not merely an enthusiastic section of it would be greatly increased. After all very many honoured leaders of the Anglo-Catholics in past days whatever they thought about their full rights were content to be without some of the things which are now ardently claimed, and if there could be a spirit of patience and considerateness I feel sure the whole position would be immensely improved and the influence of the Anglo-Catholic movement made more spiritually real and useful.[85]

The archbishop felt that extremist Anglo-Catholics were tiresome, but he did not wish Anglo-Catholicism to become a self-contained segment within the Church of England, cut off from Anglicans of other churchmanships. Rather, Lang hoped that the influence of Anglo-Catholicism would permeate and enrich the life of the whole Church. Because Lang had solicitude for the entire Church, he was also concerned about liberals and evangelicals and was keen that they and the Anglo-Catholics should talk to each other.

Many Anglo-Catholics shared Lang's hopes about the permeating influence of Anglo-Catholicism, but they did not usually share his solicitude for liberals and evangelicals. In 1933, Professor N.P. Williams, the Anglo-Catholic Lady Margaret Professor of Divinity at Oxford, advocated the purifying of the Church of England 'of all corruptions of foreign protestantism which entered in during the sixteenth century and afterwards', the reabsorption of dissenters and the healing of the breach with Rome, a view which certainly would not have been shared by evangelicals and liberals.[86] Williams probably only represented a minority within Anglo-Catholicism, and certainly a minority within the wider Church of England, but the fact that such views were advocated by the Lady Margaret Professor meant that they could not easily be dismissed as merely the thoughts of insignificant cranks.

How could Lang conciliate disgruntled Anglo-Catholics, whilst also expressing solicitude for the entire Church of England? An important tool available to him was preaching. Mention has been made of his enthronement sermon. Lang repeated his message that there was a proper place for Anglo-Catholics, evangelicals and liberals within the Church of England in another sermon delivered in Canterbury, on 9 November 1930. Interestingly, he said much the same to an evangelical audience in 1936 at the centenary of the death of the evangelical churchman Charles Simeon.[87]

July 1933 saw country-wide Anglo-Catholic celebrations of the centenary of the Oxford Movement. Lang and Temple appointed a 'central committee' ostensibly to organise celebrations, but, according to Dom Anselm Hughes OSB, really to ensure that Anglo-Catholic extremists did not make all the running.[88] Lang preached about the Oxford Movement in Canterbury on 9 July 1933 and was broadcast live by the BBC. His Anglo-Catholic audience would have been pleased by his assertion that 'there is still a need to remember that the Church of England derives its spiritual position and claim not from being "by law established" but from its being the historic Catholic Church of this land.' However, he went on to remind his audience 'that there are other movements and influences which have enriched the English Church', in particular the evangelical and liberal movements. All three movements were continually acting and re-acting upon each other, Lang said, and none of them would be what it was without the others.[89]

With regard to the specific task of keeping Anglo-Catholics in the Church of England, another tool available to Lang was preferment. The view has grown – fostered by Hastings – that Lang was the half-hidden protector of an Anglo-Catholic advance and that he presided over an increase in Anglo-Catholic bishops on the bench.[90] This view must be questioned. Lang took great pains over appointments to high office in the Church and he sought to gather a balanced bench of bishops about him. During Lang's Canterbury archiepiscopate, twenty-two diocesan bishops were appointed or translated in the Province of Canterbury, and he also advised on the appointment of certain suffragan and other bishops.[91] There was a modest increase in the number of bishops who would have called themselves Anglo-Catholics. When Lang became archbishop, only Frere of Truro, Furse of St Albans and possibly Pearce of Derby were Anglo-Catholic. Four further Anglo-Catholics were appointed to diocesan sees: Blunt to Bradford (1931), Rawlinson to Derby (1936), Kirk to Oxford (1937) and Underhill to Bath and Wells (1937), although some Anglo-Catholics thought that Underhill had 'trimmed' in order to secure a mitre and was therefore untrustworthy.[92] Some of the other episcopal appointees were a little high church in the sense that they enjoyed dressing up and ritualistic worship, but they were clearly not Anglo-Catholic in theology, spirituality or outlook.

By the time that Lang came to Canterbury, the vanguard of Anglo-Catholicism was formed by the new and growing phenomenon of Anglican-Papalism, the advocates of which sought to advance reunion with the Holy See by large-scale borrowings from contemporary Roman Catholicism. This was never Lang's version of Anglo-Catholicism, but he always retained the principles that he had absorbed in the late 1880s and 1890s, and, although it is difficult to quantify, the effect of Lang's personal example should not be overlooked. Lang went to Confession, made an annual retreat each Holy Week at Cuddesdon, said Mattins and Evensong every day, and either celebrated or was present at a daily Eucharist in his chapel at Lambeth. He refused to describe himself as a Protestant, and was evidently more Catholic than most of his predecessors. He wore a purple cassock, cape and skullcap, used eucharistic vestments in his chapel and was the first archbishop since the Reformation to wear a mitre. Although some Anglo-Catholics thought Lang liturgically timid, it became known that he personally believed in the objective Real Presence.[93]

According to Hastings, conversions to Roman Catholicism in England during the 1930s were constant at around 12,000 per annum. Many, he says, were the result of mixed marriages, but anecdotal evidence would suggest that some at least were disgruntled Anglo-Catholics.[94] The fact that there was not a large exodus of Anglo-Catholics after 1928 is doubtless due to several reasons, but might indicate a degree of success for Lang's methods.

BISHOP BARNES OF BIRMINGHAM

No account of Lang and inter-war Anglo-Catholicism would be complete without some reference to the Reservation of the Sacrament and Bishop E.W. Barnes of Birmingham. Barnes was a convert to Anglicanism from Nonconformity. A Cambridge don, he had been ordained in 1902 without having attended a theological college and had never worked in an ordinary parish. In 1924, Ramsay Macdonald had appointed him bishop of Birmingham. Bell wrote about Barnes in 1935:

> The Bishop of Birmingham had long been known as a militant liberal Churchman. He was a mathematician and a scientist, and an outspoken champion of the evolutionary view of the origin of man; and he claimed a freedom to remodel Christian theology on that basis. He was also a most decided opponent of distinctively Anglo-Catholic teaching about the Sacraments.[95]

Barnes publicly derided the doctrine of the Real Presence in language that was bound to cause offence, and he crossed croziers with Davidson on the subject in an exchange of correspondence published in *The Times* in 1927. Not surprisingly, there was friction between Barnes and Anglo-Catholic parishes in Birmingham. When the parochial church council of Stirchley complained about their bishop to Lang in 1929, Barnes wrote rather tartly to him, 'I assume that Your Grace will reply that, as Archbishop, you have no general power to review the administrative acts of Bishops of the Province of Canterbury.'[96] For his part, Lang was very worried lest aggrieved parishioners should seek a ruling from the civil courts about Reservation, as he explained to Bishop Frere of Truro:

> It is obvious that the most serious consequences might come. In the first place our whole action is strictly extra-legal and involves

on every part technical breaches of the existing law and I do not
see how the Courts as at present constituted could come to any
other conclusion and if the Law is set in motion and our whole
action were declared illegal it might have the most disastrous
consequences. [97]

Things reached a head in 1930 when the parish of St Aidan, Small
Heath, Birmingham, fell vacant and the Anglo-Catholic trustees, who
were the patrons, nominated the Rev. G.D. Simmonds, curate of St
Mary's, Tyne Dock. Barnes refused to institute Simmonds unless he
first promised to end Reservation at St Aidan's. Barnes' request was
technically improper, and Simmonds consequently refused it. The result
of this impasse was that the Anglo-Catholic trustees announced they
would seek a writ from the High Court obliging Barnes to institute
Simmonds. Barnes refused to attend or to be represented when the case
was heard on 10 February 1930 and a writ was issued directing Lang as
archbishop of the southern province to admit 'a fit and proper person' to
be vicar of St Aidan's. [98]

Lang saw Barnes three days later and quite literally pleaded with him
to institute Simmonds and to come to some friendly understanding
about Reservation. Barnes asked for time to reflect, but Lang was not
sanguine about the chance of success and noted:

> His whole attitude and many of his words confirm my belief that
> he has, with all his abilities, a touch of what can only be described
> as madness. Indeed, when I told him that he had a large element of
> the fanatic in his character he admitted that he had. [99]

Barnes replied four days later that he had decided not to institute
Simmonds 'unless he will give such obedience as I may ask for . . .
[and recognise] in particular, that I have a right to refuse to permit the
practice of Reservation at St Aidan's.' A long legal correspondence then
ensued about what sort of writ could be issued and fittingly received
by Lang, during which Barnes wrote to the trustees demanding that
Reservation should cease and making it crystal clear that no compromise
was possible. [100]

At this point, on 19 April 1930 Lang wrote to the Rev. Dr Charles Harris of the Church Union.[101] The letter is missing from the file at Lambeth, but it is clear that Lang was trying to stop the controversy widening in the Church of England. Following an article by Barnes in the *Modern Churchman*, the notion spread amongst Anglo-Catholics that Barnes' plan 'is to go to prison as a Protestant martyr, with . . . the object of forcing Parliament to intervene on his behalf in an Erastian manner, and in the Protestant interest.' In October 1931, the English Church Union (ECU) paid Barnes' legal costs of £273 6s 10d due by order of the court and sent Barnes a receipted account. Barnes had stated that he was quite prepared to go to prison if the court's order was insisted upon. The ECU thus denied Barnes his last chance of becoming a liberal martyr and of stirring up a parliamentary debate about Reservation.[102]

Lang interviewed Simmonds on 13 May 1931 and found him 'quite sound' and suitable for institution to St Aidan's. On 30 May the archbishop officially informed Barnes that he would institute Simmonds as vicar of St Aidan's in the chapel of Lambeth Palace. He also wrote to Barnes privately, trying to salve the bishop's distress. Barnes responded by publishing a letter to Lang in the national press, in which he condemned Reservation, Simmonds' refusal to give a blanket undertaking never to practise it, and asserted that Lang was over-ruling the Commons' rejection of the 1928 Prayer Book and Reservation. Temple and Henson deemed Barnes' public reply to Lang most improper and urged Lang to make no further reply. Lang instituted Simmonds on 7 July.[103]

The archbishop then sent Barnes another personal letter on 11 July, repeating how distressed he had been at having to institute Simmonds, saying that he had 'pressed upon him the duty of meeting your wishes as far as he conscientiously can', and urging Barnes to 'have a friendly and fatherly talk with him'. The result was a slightly sarcastic reply from Barnes, thanking Lang for the tone of his letter, asserting that educated men did not take seriously the doctrine of the Real Presence, and stating that he might make public reference to Lang's actions. Two days later, he published another letter to Lang in the national press, in which he condemned the 'ecclesiastical procedure adopted by Your Grace which allows a man to make pledges, although there may even be an expectation that he will not keep them', and asserted that '[the idea] that a spiritual presence is to be found in the consecrated elements of Holy Communion is regarded as a superstition, properly rejected at the Reformation.' The Commons, he said, had rejected the 1928 Prayer Book because it feared that continuous Reservation would open the way 'to the erroneous belief in a miraculous change in the consecrated elements'. The Commons had been wiser than a majority of the bishops, and the law should be obeyed.[104] Barnes was here playing a clever game: in his letter to Lang of 13 July he revealed that his motivation was modernism, but he presented himself as a defender of the Reformation and of Erastianism, a position more likely to garner support.

Some evangelicals rallied to Barnes, but others saw through him. For example, Bishop Whittingham of St Edmundsbury and Ipswich, a doughty opponent of Reservation, published a letter in *The Times* on 28 July, explaining that different views of the Eucharist were held in the Church of England and affirming that there was a place for those who believed in the objective Real Presence for purposes of Communion only. Lang sent Barnes a private acknowledgement, observing that it was distasteful to him to have a public correspondence with one of his bishops, 'as I have not your aptitude for letters to the Press'.[105]

Lang could hardly allow such an attack on the doctrine of the Real Presence to pass unanswered, especially if he sought to retain Anglo-Catholics in the Church of England, and he busied himself with various drafts of replies to Barnes.[106] On 21 July, Lang sent a public reply to Barnes, explaining again why he had been compelled to institute Simmonds, and defending the doctrine of the Real Presence:

> I cannot but ask, is it charitable, is it just, to brand as mere superstition a belief, whatever you yourself may think about it, which is held by multitudes of your fellow Churchmen, and which is consistent with the formularies of our Church?'[107]

Barnes replied publicly the next day with a virulent attack upon the Real Presence:

> Your Grace, the assertion that a priest by an act of consecration can cause Christ to come and dwell within the bread and wine

of Holy Communion is the so-called 'miracle of the Mass'. It was a crucial issue at the Reformation and is the source of most of our present irregularities in public worship . . . The belief that a Christian priest can by consecration cause the presence of Christ to dwell within the consecrated elements is exactly analogous to the belief held by the Hindhu that his priest can by consecration cause the god to dwell within its image . . . the belief that a spiritual presence can be made to adhere in a piece of bread by consecration is false. It is a cardinal principle of modern science . . . that assertions must be justified by experience . . . The spiritual presence alleged to exist in the consecrated bread no-one can detect, however delicate his spiritual perception may be; and to say that something exists though no-one can detect its existence receives curt incredulity to-day from thinking men and women.[108]

Barnes' reply produced a flurry of letter-writing to the press. Some letters favoured Barnes, but more appear to have supported Lang and affirmed the Real Presence. Temple was especially incensed by Barnes' assumption 'that "thinking men" is a proper description of those who agree with him', and sent Lang a copy of his father Frederick Temple's 1899 primary charge affirming the doctrine of the Real Presence within the Church of England.[109] Lang privately acknowledged Barnes' letter, but declined to enter into a public discussion with him about the Eucharist, adding:

the whole concept of the relations of spirit and matter which seems always to underlie your reiterated utterances on this deep subject seems to me to belong to a past age both of Science and Philosophy, and in this respect I am bound to say I wish you were a better Modernist.[110]

*

The Prayer Book crisis was really composed of two distinct elements. Firstly, there was the crisis of the Commons' rejections of the Revised Prayer Books of 1927 and 1928 and the immediate shock, emotion and uncertainty these events unleashed. The Commons' rejections were probably a bit more than a hiccup in the working relationship between the Church Assembly and Parliament, but they were far from being a full-blown Church–state clash. Secondly, there were the underlying problems of the Church of England's liturgy which were left unresolved.

Bell's criticism in 1947 of Lang's handling of the Prayer Book crisis of 1928–42 needs to be taken seriously, because Bell was a senior diocesan bishop and had previously been Davidson's chaplain and so had an insider's knowledge. It was certainly not Lang's finest hour; and the impression that lingers, after all the letters, sermons and memoranda have been read and digested, is that Lang lacked what might be described as 'sustained pushfulness'. One never quite gains the impression that Lang was *gripped* by Prayer Book reform. It was just another of that day's problems, and one of many needing archiepiscopal attention. Lang sometimes discussed the assorted symptoms of the crisis with Temple, but he had no cabinet or council to whom he might turn for advice. With hindsight, we can say that Lang might have helped the Church–state commission or the round-table conference more than he did. He pressurised the bishops to be more understanding towards Anglo-Catholics' needs and susceptibilities, and to make adequate liturgical and sacramental provision, but ultimately got nowhere. The problems of the eucharistic canon and of Reservation were still unresolved when he retired in 1942. The whole episode shows the limits of archiepiscopal power and influence. These relied upon the personal interest, effort and gumption of an individual archbishop. They could be frustrated by episcopal intransigence or indifference; and the archbishop had no curia to back him up.

However, Bell's criticisms need to be qualified a little, lest Lang's actual achievements be overlooked. To put it bluntly, Engineer Rear-Admiral Emdin and W. Poynter Adams, to take two examples, had radically different ideas about the identity of the Church of England, and even of what it meant to be a Christian, to those of Sir Will Spens or Professor N.P. Williams. There was no danger that the evangelicals or the modernists would leave the Church of England, however much they might huff and puff, for there was nowhere very obvious for them to go. There was a danger, however, that large numbers of Anglo-Catholics might be drawn to the vibrant contemporary Roman Catholicism of Pius XI. The internal balance and coherence of the Church of England, as well as its work in the parishes, would then have been gravely weakened. Lang's achievement was that he helped to *contain* the Prayer Book crisis and to prevent the Church coming badly unstuck. By the outbreak of war in 1939, the 1928 Prayer Book crisis was a distant memory and the Church of England had found a way – albeit not a very intellectually satisfactory way – of muddling through.

Later historical developments sometimes cast light backwards and aid understanding. The liturgical history of the Church of England in the last quarter of the twentieth century might be described – to adapt a phrase of Ninian Comper – as 'unity by inclusion'. The *Alternative Service Book* (1980) and more noticeably *Common Worship* (1998) got around the problem of diverse and sometimes mutually incompatible Anglican churchmanships by providing a wide range of forms of worship, ranging from lay-led family services to provision for Corpus Christi and the Assumption. All were authorised and therefore all might be counted legitimate expressions of Anglicanism. Amongst Lang's successors, Robert Runcie (1980–91) reserved the sacrament in his chapel at Lambeth for purposes of prayer, and Rowan Williams (2002–12) has officiated at Benediction.[111] The ecclesiological glue holding together Anglo-Catholics, evangelicals and liberals in one worshipping body may thus be said to have become progressively dry and brittle. The question left hanging in the air is: was the attempt at Prayer Book revision, with the goal of one Revised Book of *Common* Prayer which could equally be used by Anglicans of all shades, an impossible dream by 1927 and 1928? Subsequent developments suggest that it *may* have been; and that Lang, in consequence, found himself trying to control an unstoppable evolution or decay, depending upon one's viewpoint.

Let the final image be of the Church of England as a moving and dynamic triangle during the 1920s and 1930s, with all three corners tugging in different directions. Lang found himself in the centre, trying to have solicitude for all. 'Always remember', Lang once told the dean of St Paul's, 'that the archbishop of Canterbury has great responsibility but no power.' In retirement in 1943, Lang reflected upon his handling of the Prayer Book crisis. He recognised that large questions remained to be tackled after the war. 'No doubt it was a somewhat makeshift course,' he mused, 'but it has been at least in practice successful.'[112] It would be very hard to quibble with that assessment.

7

The Second World War

A COMMON VIEW OF THE CHURCH of England in the first half of the twentieth century is that it had a rather bad First World War, but a much better Second World War. The truth, of course, is much more nuanced; but insofar as the Church did in retrospect have a good Second World War, the credit is often laid at the feet of William Temple and George Bell. Lang seldom gets a mention. According to Alan Wilkinson, by September 1939 Lang 'had nothing original left to say'.[1] Edward Carpenter, too, is dismissive of Lang's wartime work:

> Lang saw his archiepiscopal wartime function in more patrician terms. Not for him chairing a committee often dealing with minutiae, routine business and domestic chores. Rather he saw his role, when occasion demanded, as one of calling on, being called upon, the Prime Minister; interviewing the heads of the services and sorting things out with them personally. Nurtured in the school of Randall Davidson, his main preoccupation, except in matters of extreme and self-evident concern for the Church, was never to embarass the Government.[2]

This view of Lang's wartime role is unbalanced and misleading. Lang's ministry between 1939 and 1942 helped the Church of England to cope with the worst years of the Second World War. Much of Lang's wartime work centred on keeping the administrative and pastoral machinery of the Church of England running, resolving problems, and offering advice and pastoral care. Lang used the teaching opportunities available to him to support the nation's cause, whilst urging that the enemy should not be demonised and warning preachers not to preach bloodthirsty sermons. He pointed out to Church and state that even in wartime there were still ethical standards below which it was not safe to fall. He also encouraged Church and state to begin thinking about the post-war world. Most of Lang's wartime work went on unseen, except by a few people at Lambeth. It was sometimes humdrum and it was not glamorous, but that does not mean that it was unappreciated at the time. In the long run, its cumulative effect would prove important for both the Church and the nation.

Support from the Archbishop of Canterbury

Readers will look in vain in the indexes of many recent books about the home front in wartime Britain for a reference to Lang. In fairness, Temple and Bell, and the Church of England generally, seldom fare much better. The wartime files at Lambeth Palace tell a different tale – of individuals and organisations seeking archiepiscopal support or reassurance of various sorts in time of hastening crisis and anxiety.

Before the War

Few people in Britain in 1939 can have doubted that a war with Nazi Germany was a strong possibility. In the late 1930s Lang had been a supporter of Neville Chamberlain's policy of appeasement. On Good Friday 1938, for example, during a broadcast on the BBC, Lang expressed support for the League of Nations and condemned 'what was vindictive and arbitrary in the Treaty of Versailles', before urging his listeners to focus afresh upon the Crucifixion and Resurrection. Lang did not support appeasement because he favoured a rapprochement with Nazi Germany – within six weeks of Hitler's coming to power as chancellor in 1933, he received the first of many disquieting reports about the Nazi regime – nor did he do so because he was he a pacificist.[3] Rather, like millions of Britons who had lived through the 1914–18 conflict, Lang could not bear to think that another generation should have to face the carnage of a further world war.

On 28 September 1938, when Hitler's demand to be allowed to annex the Sudetenland from Czechoslovakia appeared to be leading Europe to the brink of war, Lang appeared in the public gallery of the Commons to hear Chamberlain announce that he had delayed general mobilisation by twenty-four hours and was flying to Munich to meet Hitler, Mussolini and Daladier (the Czechoslovak government was excluded from the conference).[4] Lang was in the public gallery because he was interested in what Chamberlain had to say, but he would also have known that his presence would be seen as lending support to the prime minister, and he may well have been there with Chamberlain's foreknowledge. The following day, Lang broadcast on the BBC, urging his listeners to have faith in God and to pray that war might be averted.[5] When Chamberlain returned from Germany on 30 September proclaiming 'peace in our time', Lang joined in the widespread rejoicing. There was a hint of euphoria as well as relief in his BBC broadcast on 2 October:

> I wonder whether ever in the history of our land there has arisen a greater tide of prayer. It has arisen from the hearts and homes of our people, and from our churches everywhere. We cannot doubt that God has answered. I have already said through the Wireless that when the MPs came trooping out into the Lobby in great emotion last Wednesday, more than one said to me 'Here is the hand of God.' I read yesterday of an old farmer in my own Diocese who pointing upwards to the wide heavens above Romney Marsh said quietly 'There is a God up there.' A solemn responsibility lies upon the men whose eyes have looked into the abyss of war and discerned there its actual impending horror. There must be earnest prayer and deep resolve that God helping us Europe will never have to look into the abyss again.[6]

William Temple also agreed that deliverance at Munich was the work of 'the hand of God'. A relieved Lang gave fulsome and largely uncritical support to the government during the debate about the Munich agreement in the Lords on 3 October 1938, but he was assailed by a niggling doubt: 'Is it ever right, can it be right, to base any peace upon an act of injustice?' He concluded that, faced by a conflict 'which might destroy civilisation itself . . . almost any price was worth paying to avoid that calamity'.[7]

During the autumn and winter of 1938–39, however, Lang gradually revised his views and reluctantly concluded that a war with Germany was inevitable and necessary. He was appalled by the attacks upon German Jews and Jewish property by Nazi thugs on Kristallnacht, 10–11 November 1938, and made his feelings plain in a letter published the following day in *The Times*, in which he condemned the cruelty and vindictiveness of the Nazi 'reprisal', found the compliance of the German police 'sinister', and wished 'that the rulers of the Reich could realise that such excesses of hatred and malice put upon the friendship which we are so ready to offer them an intolerable strain'.[8] He followed this up by participating in a public protest meeting held at the Mansion House, London, at which he shared a platform with Clement Attlee, Lord Rothschild, Cardinal Hinsley, Lord Reading and Neville Laski. Lang condemned the Nazi's 'ingenious and elaborate system of persecution, of mental and moral torture, which would be incredible unless it were known that it was actually happening', and urged support for Stanley Baldwin's appeal in aid of refugees. During the November 1938 session of the Church Assembly, over which Lang presided, it was agreed to raise £5,000 in support of 'non-Aryan' refugees. The following month, Lang made a two-minute Movietone appeal for refugees, which was shown in cinemas around the country.[9] By the time of Hitler's occupation of Prague in March 1939, whilst still believing that Chamberlain had done the right thing in September 1938, Lang had largely abandoned his support for the Munich agreement. He told the Lords, 'I quite admit it [the Munich agreement] was not one which should have been hailed as a triumph. There was too much sacrifice demanded . . . and brute force played too large a part.'[10]

As the prospect of war loomed, many local authorities began planning for an emergency, and some kept Lang informed. In January 1939, Lang had two meetings in three days with Sir John Anderson, the home secretary, to discuss air raids, casualties, evacuation and the use of the clergy in the event of war. The mass bombing of London and southern England was widely feared, and in February 1939 Lang established a committee to coordinate air-raid precautions by churches. In June, the Church Assembly passed the Clergy (National Emergency Precautions) Regulations Measure, which, according to Don, 'gives the Archbishops almost dictatorial powers in the event of war'. The government consulted Lang about a wartime Ministry of Information and Lang convened an interdenominational meeting to discuss the ministry's religious division. It is not hard to detect his legal mind behind the decision to establish an informal advisory committee to assist the religious divison, formed of volunteers on their own responsibility. Thus, if necessary, he could disown them. On 10 August, Samuel Hoare, the home secretary, secretly asked Lang to prepare a speech for George VI to broadcast in the event of war.[11]

As the international situation deteriorated, various people seem to have thought of Lang as someone whose voice might be raised in public for peace. In late April 1939 W.R. Matthews, dean of St Paul's, appealed to Lang and Pius XII to appeal for peace. *The Times* and the *Spectator* supported the idea. Lang discussed visiting the Vatican with several senior bishops, but concluded that it was impracticable.[12] At the end of May, Don noted that 'a mysterious German, Herr X, who is a vehement opponent of the Nazi regime', visited Lang in an attempt to relieve tension and avert war. Lang appears to have informed Chamberlain, and was quickly visited by 'a hush-hush man' called Kenneth Grubb. No more appears to have been heard at Lambeth from Hitler's opponents.[13]

Interestingly, it would seem that three months into the war, the Nazi regime itself tried to approach the British government via Lang in order to discuss a negotiated peace. Their intermediary was Bishop Berggrav of Oslo, who visited Lang ostensibly to discuss a possible interdenominational conference. Berggrav presented Lang with a memorandum from Berlin. Lang suggested to Lord Halifax, the foreign secretary, that it would be worthwhile for him to see Berggrav, but was careful not to express any opinion. Berggrav was eventually told that 'at the present time no talk about peace or negotiations would be permitted.'[14]

The Coming of War

Lang was on holiday in Ballure when the crisis between Germany and Poland arose in August 1939. Parliament was recalled on 24 August. Don had earlier warned Lang, but the archbishop seemed very reluctant to return to London. He replied on 23 August that 'at the present [*indeciph.*] of the situation, I see no reason why I ought to go up for the meeting of Parliament,' adding, 'I could not do anything except listen.' Lang did, however, ask via *The Times* and church newspapers for prayers for peace to be said in parish churches. On 25 August Don again suggested that Lang come to London and he reluctantly returned on 30 August. As Lang entered Lambeth Palace, he said 'What a fuss! I might have stayed where I was – £12 gone all for nothing!'[15]

It is hard to understand Lang's behaviour. One possible explanation is that, alone in the fastness of Ballure, Lang became despondent. Lang was not generally a depressive, but occasionally, when he was ill, he would become temporarily depressed. The archbishop was seventy-five in 1939. He had been ill when he departed for Scotland, and perhaps in isolation in the Highlands he dwelt upon the miseries of the 1914–18 war and worried about his ability to cope in another conflict. Lang broadcast on the BBC at 8 p.m. on 3 September 1939, but, according to Wilkinson, his address was trivial and some people at the BBC feared to use him in the future. Lang's text does not survive and *The Times* and *Church Times* merely reported that he had broadcast, without quoting him.[16] A bad performance from a usually masterly speaker may perhaps be a further indication of depression, and Don felt that the fire had gone out of Lang when he addressed his clergy a few weeks later. In fairness, the next day's entry in Don's diary is a remark about how well Lang preached in Westminster Abbey during a national day of prayer.[17]

There was a flurry of activity at Lambeth Palace in the days immediately after the declaration of war. Thereafter, the work seemed to drop away. Lang even found time to read a novel. This indicates the extent to which much of Lang's pre-war routine work was reactive. Perhaps a lull helped Lang to pull himself together, or the reality of war was more bearable than the fear of it, for there are no further indications of depression. The pressure of work increased over the next few months and in April 1940 Lang collapsed in the chapel. Apart from this incident, Lang seems to have enjoyed reasonable health for the rest of his primacy.[18]

The Early Part of the War

Not everyone supported Britain's war with Nazi Germany. As late as December 1939, Bell was arguing for a negotiated settlement. Several people asked Lang to use his influence to secure an immediate armistice. Lang replied that the Nazi government was untrustworthy and he could not see how peace could be achieved unless they were prepared to make restitution. In November he declined to support a peace conference proposed by the Scandinavian Churches.[19]

Following the evacuation of the British Expeditionary Force from Dunkirk in 1940, Lang was privately approached by Sir James Marchant, an official of the Ministry of Information, who suggested that the archbishop might ask George VI to call 'a council of leading statesman, judges and spiritual leaders' to propound a just settlement and avoid further bloodshed. Lang declined, claiming that Marchant's idea was quite impracticable. Marchant did not mention that he represented anyone else, and the tone of his letter suggests that he was most likely acting alone, but it is impossible to be certain about this. Unusually, Marchant's letter to Lang and the copy of Lang's reply are missing from the files at Lambeth Palace, and the library staff are unable to offer any explanation.[20]

CHRISTIAN TEACHING AND INFLUENCE IN WARTIME

Between 1939 and 1942, Lang supported his country's cause in the conflict, yet he sought to warn about the dangers and excesses surrounding war and to exert a Christian influence at a time when passions were inflamed and oversimplistic judgements all too easy.

The War and the Nazi Regime

Lang never seems to have doubted that Britain's war with Nazi Germany, though tragic, was necessary and just. He made this plain, just nine days after the declaration of war, in a letter to the press, which he signed with leaders of the Church of Scotland and of the English Free Churches. They declared that 'at all costs for the world's peace and order the policy proclaimed by the German Führer must be resisted and overcome.'[21]

It is important to note that Lang did not have a rolling plan of carefully organised, systematic teaching about the war. Most of his teaching was reactive and stemmed from the needs and opportunities of the hour. An important exception was Lang's address to his diocesan conference on 30 October 1939. He repeated many of the themes of this address in subsequent sermons and addresses. Lang did not hide his distress at the outbreak of war, but he unequivocally condemned the Nazi regime and said Christians were justified in supporting Britain's cause:

> As you know, I have not hesitated to describe the issue before us as one that concerns the eternal verities of right and wrong. Can we doubt that the war is now confronted by the menace of a force that is really and truly evil? Consider the persecution and cruelty inflicted upon people whose only crime was their blood or their loyalty to religion and conscience. Consider all the almost incredible miseries suffered in concentration camps, which stain the record of the present rulers of Germany. Consider the principles they have openly professed, often in words, certainly in deeds, of which the names of Austria, Czechoslovakia and Poland are sufficient symbols. Then it is clear that we are using no mere language of exaggeration when we describe this spirit armed with ruthless force as in truth satanic. Certainly it is a negation of all that Christianity has tried to effect in the life of nations. Indeed, it is a manifestation of anti-Christ.[22]

Lang also spoke about attitudes towards the enemy. He was clearly keen to avoid a repetition of some of the bloodthirsty anti-German preaching of the 1914–18 war:[23]

> I have already warned you, my brothers of the Clergy, against the temptation to indulge in what are called patriotic sermons. The real voice of the Church must always be that ultimately evil can only be overcome by good. War may avert the evil. It cannot of itself achieve the good . . . It is for the Church to proclaim that no true victory is possible unless a strong spirit of good – the Christian spirit, the spirit of Christ – enters and prevails. It is for the Church to see that during and beyond the struggle this spirit is kept clean and strong.

The archbishop did express some qualifications in his support of the war. He reminded his audience that there were limits 'below which we shall not fall'. Lang drew a distinction between the German people and the 'present rulers' of Germany who 'misrule' over them. He ended his address with a warning to the Church of England:

> A Church which emerges from the war crippled, inert, dispirited, or a Church which retires into its own cloisters from the turmoil of the world except to go out again with renewed strength, cannot meet the demands of the time that is coming. It must be a Church united, holding the faith committed to it with clearer thought and deeper fervour, eager to launch out into the deep and to win new spheres for the Kingdom of God. It must be a Church which keeps before its eyes, not as a vague hope but as a spur to purposeful ambition, the vision of the time when the kingdoms of the world shall become the kingdoms of Our Lord and of His Christ.[24]

Radio offered Lang a platform for wartime teaching. He broadcast eleven times between 1939 and 1942 and twice after his retirement. He repeated some themes several times. For example, in May 1940 he said 'it is ultimately in the realm of the spirit that the war will be lost or won.' He repeated this again in December, observing: 'The fall of France was mainly due to a failure of spirit. The spirit failed because there was a failure of faith.'[25]

'Spirit' had been a theme of some of Lang's 1914–18 wartime addresses; but whereas during the First World War Lang equated a right spirit with avoiding lust, alcohol and German militarism, by 1939 he had refined his ideas and believed that a right spirit was the fruit of a healthy relationship with God. Lang often spoke about the importance of prayer in wartime, commending short, heartfelt prayers and the placing of men's wills at God's disposal. Unlike Temple, Lang had no qualms about praying directly for a British victory and urged such intercessions.[26]

Lang frequently praised the armed forces and the merchant navy in his broadcasts. He tried to offer help or encouragement during critical moments. During the retreat to Dunkirk, for example, Lang broadcast on the BBC overseas service, seeking to rally the peoples of the British Empire to the mother country. In September 1940, when Churchill was seeking to enlist Roosevelt's aid, Lang broadcast to the USA asking for

American support. During the Battle of Britain, Lang sought to help his listeners with the slogan 'It all depends on me, and I depend on God.' In December 1940, he expressed sympathy with those who had lost their homes during the Blitz and spoke of finding strength in neighbours. His broadcasts could perhaps be summed up by some words he spoke on 7 September 1941: 'For it is nothing less than the worth and dignity of human life, indeed all that makes human life worth living, that is at stake.'[27]

At the start of the war, Lang had cautioned against a spirit of vindictiveness and hatred towards the enemy.[28] His criticism of Hitler and the Nazi regime grew stronger as the war progressed. In September 1940, he called the Nazi system 'a really Evil Thing,' a claim he repeated in December. In March 1941, he said that the Nazis were bent upon enslaving the peoples of Europe. In September 1940, he condemned their wrong principles and cruelty.[29] Lang's attitude towards the Nazi regime hardened as the war progressed. In 1940, he contemplated a just punishment of Germany after the war:

> Mr Chamberlain and Lord Halifax have repeatedly assured us that we seek no vindictive peace. That does not mean an easy peace, any kind of letting off. In the face of wrong doing, justice is stern. The punishments which justice inflicts are stern. But there is all the difference between . . . sternness of justice and vindictiveness of angry passion. Here again, warned by experience, we may expect strong temptation. Self-restraint will be alike necessary and hard.[30]

A just punishment after victory was one thing, but reprisals against Germans during the war were quite another. Before the war, in June 1939, Lang had written to Sir Kingsley Wood, the air minister, and secured an assurance – 'which', he told the bishops, 'was satisfactory in so far as it went' – that RAF pilots and personnel had not received instructions intentionally to bomb enemy civilians in wartime. In autumn 1940, when a call for reprisals against Germany might have been expected after the Blitz, Don spent some time collecting signatures from 'clerical warriors' who had won the Victoria Cross or Distinguished Service

Order in 1914–18, to be appended to a letter from Lambeth to the press condemning reprisals. In the event, it was not judged neccessary to send the letter.[31] In May 1941, during a meeting of Convocation, Lang refused to be swayed by public clamour for indiscriminate bombing of German civilians. His words are little known and worth quoting at length:

> But are there not signs of the danger that just indignation may lose its moral strength by degenerating into mere vindictive passion? One of these signs is the demand in certain quarters provoked by the indiscriminate bombing of our civil population, that we should inflict upon the enemy's country the same ruthless treatment as that which he is inflicting upon ours, a claim for mere retaliation. It is very natural, very human. But it ought not to be allowed to prevail. It is one thing to bomb military objectives, to cripple industries on which the prosecution of the war depends and, alas! on many civilians. It is a very different thing to adopt the infliction of this loss and suffering as a deliberate policy. What advantage would such a policy bring? It would certainly mean a waste of resources which we have every need to husband. It would not shorten the war. It is vain to think that it would rather urge the German people to clamour that the war should cease. Rather, there, as here, it would only embitter passion against their enemy and stiffen the determination to defeat him. It would not lessen, it would only increase, the savagery of the German attacks upon our own people. It would achieve nothing except the satisfaction among a section of our people of feelings which, however natural, do not spring from the better part of human nature.
>
> Again, it may well be asked if we were to adopt a deliberate policy of retaliation, whither would it lead? Where are we to draw the line and say thus far and no further? In any such competition with the enemy we are bound to lose, for there are some limits below which we could not fall without violating the best and oldest instincts of the British character. Even if we were to win, it would be at the cost of bringing lasting shame and dishonour to our cause. I do not believe that the great majority of British folk even in the bombed areas really want such a policy. It is to be hoped that the

Government, some of whose members have been using disquieting language, will resist any pressure and make it clear that they will adhere to what was once declared, as recently by the Secretary of State for Air, to be their own policy. Beyond all questions of advantage, surely from a Christian point of view any contrary policy would be simply wrong. The Christian tradition, even when it has justified war, has always set itself against any deliberate destruction of human life which is not necessary for the conduct of the war. Let me repeat the words which I used at the very beginning of the war, adapting the famous phrase of Edmund Burke – 'Let us strive so to be patriots as not to forget that we are Christians.'[32]

Bell's condemnation of the blanket bombing of German cities later in the Second World War is well known; but it is surely significant that in 1941, which was probably the most difficult year of the war for Great Britain, the archbishop of Canterbury publicly warned members of the government who had been using 'disquieting language' about the dangers of reprisals and of bombing civilians. With the benefit of hindsight, Lang's words were prescient.

Pacifists and Conscientious Objectors

During the First World War there were some 16,500 British conscientious objectors to compulsory military service. Pacifism grew in Britain during the 1930s as the possibility of another war with Germany returned.[33] In November 1936, Lang and Temple received a group of pacifist clergy led by Dick Sheppard of the Peace Pledge Union, and, whilst making it clear that they did not share their pacifist views, said:

> they did not question for a moment the personal sincerity of those whose consciences led them to adopt the full pacifist position, nor did they regard them as disloyal to the Catholic faith or to the Spirit of Jesus Christ.[34]

In fact, Lang and Temple appear to have viewed pacifism slightly differently. Both archbishops disagreed with pacifism, but Temple declared in 1935 that it was 'heretical in tendency'. In 1936, he told Lang that he had 'very publicly committed myself to the view that pacifism is false in principle'. Lang's view was milder. He believed that there were circumstances in which Christians were morally justified in bearing arms, but condemned war as an instrument of national policy, and regretted the harsh treatment meted out to many conscientious objectors between 1916–18.[35]

In April 1939, the government announced a Military Training Bill introducing conscription. Lang was troubled both by 'the thought of the multitude of conscientious objectors who will certainly be revealed', but also anxious about their treatment.[36] The archbishop addressed the subject comprehensively when the Bill came before the Lords on 22 May 1939. He said that he believed that the number of conscientious objectors would be far greater than in the First World War. Moreover, he emphasised that many of them would be well educated and hoped that Parliament and the country would respect their consciences. He hoped that tribunals hearing applications for exemption from conscription would comprised impartial and insightful persons whose 'bias should rather be to respect, not suspect, the genuineness of the convictions of those who come before them'.[37]

On 21 February 1940, the Rev. C.P. Gliddon, secretary of the Anglican Pacifist Fellowship, which was comprised entirely of communicant Anglicans, asked Lang and Temple to receive a delegation of clerical members.[38] Mindful of the failure of Sheppard's pacifist delegation to reach any concrete results in 1936, Lang replied that he and Temple felt that a meeting would serve no really useful purpose, except to provide them with an opportunity to repeat the assurances of appreciation and understanding which they had given three years earlier. Lang was evidently touched by Gliddon's disappointed reply: 'If we cannot turn to our archbishops at a time like this, to whom can we turn?' Don wrote to Temple on 5 April that 'His Grace is on the whole disposed to think that a certain waste of his and your time would be preferable to leaving these good people with a sense of grievance,' and arranged for both archbishops to meet a delegation on 11 June 1940.[39] When the meeting took place, it was as bad as Lang had feared. The delegation of fifteen priests bombarded the archbishops with disconnected statements and questions. Temple replied first, saying that he and Lang had had no time to prepare their answers. His response was inevitably piecemeal, but he made two important points. His real point of disagreement with pacifists, he said, was that whereas he regarded pacifism as a vocation for some, they regarded it as the normal practice in the Christian Church. He further recognised that war occasioned moral problems and drew a distinction between reprisals and the deliberate bombing of open towns, condemning the latter.[40]

Lang answered that he sought bridges across the chasm which separated pacifist from non-pacifist. He had never ceased to recognise their sincerity or their right to hold and propagate their views in the Church of England. He thought the burden borne by the pacifists would increase as the war went on and urged them, in Christian charity, to remember how deep were the feelings of others. He personally had no qualms about praying for victory, but thought clergy ought not to enlist in the Local Defence Volunteers. He urged them not to abandon retreats and quiet days, and thought it would be helpful for pacifist clergy to discuss their views with their fellow priests. He asked them not to abandon high hopes for the post-war world.[41]

The delegation's meeting with Lang and Temple appears to have been quickly forgotten, but the fact that it had taken place at all gave satisfaction to the Anglican Pacifist Fellowship and indicated that their views might not easily be dismissed under the exigencies of war. Lang received reports of ill-treatment of conscientious objectors from time to time during the rest of his primacy. He tried to help individual cases whenever he could, particularly in the Canterbury diocese. Lang's sympathetic words about conscientious objectors and insistence that they be treated humanely, combined with his very evident support of the war effort, may have affected the overall tone with which conscientious objectors were dealt. For the most part, conscientious objectors appear to have been fairly well treated during the Second World War. Some received occasional ill-treatment, as Lang was aware, but this was not on the institutional scale of the First World War.[42]

Peace Aims

There was much discussion during the Second World War about the aims of the conflict and about the world that would emerge from it.[43]

Lang expressed his own hopes during a debate on 'War and Peace Aims' in the House of Lords on 5 December 1939. He began with an assertion that the first task was to win the war and 'cast out' the 'evil things' which compelled Britain to fight.[44] Lang spoke of a sense of shame that the high hopes and sacrifices of the last war had not been fulfilled and claimed that many younger people would not put their whole effort into the present war unless they knew not merely what they were fighting against, but also what they were fighting for. He recognised that 'the language in which any peace aims are described must be of the most general kind,' and consequently, 'we must be content with stating the principles rather than the terms of peace.' Lang said that many would regard the war as having been waged in vain if the common reign of law did not replace the rule of force in international life. Some people contemplated a reconstituted League of Nations, whilst others proposed a federal union of states. This involved nations regarding themselves as fellow members of one community and 'an abatement of the claims of national sovereignty'. He argued that the post-war world would have to be based upon Christian principles because 'only that faith will be strong enough to overcome those ingrained tendencies which lie behind the claims of national sovereignty.'[45] Lang hoped that the popular perception of Christianity would be changed after the war:

> I must at once admit that I hope it will be a Christianity very different from the conventional type to which we have for too long been accustomed. I hope . . . that it will be a Christianity far more sensitive to the social conditions and injustices of our people at home. I hope it will be more sensitive to the duty of regarding other nations as neighbours to whom we owe understanding and good will.[46]

Lang's speech is noteworthy because it shows that, three months into the war, he was giving very careful thought to the future. Many of his points received fuller consideration during the conference organised by Temple at Malvern on 7–10 January 1941, but it should not be overlooked that Lang first enunciated them thirteen months earlier.[47]

In 1940, Lang became involved in the publication of a joint letter to *The Times* about the future peace from the principal English Christian leaders. The instigator was Edith Ellis, a remarkable if slightly formidable Quaker, much given to espousing causes. 'I am so well accustomed in the past to Miss Ellis' well-intentioned but extremely vague talks,' Lang warned the earl of Halifax, 'and to her habit of supposing that the patient sympathy with which one listens can be regarded afterwards as expressing approval.' Ellis latched on to an address given by Pius XII on Christmas Eve 1939 advocating five peace points: (1) the assurance to all nations of their right to life and independence; (2) that nations be delivered from the slavery imposed by the race for armaments; (3) that some juridical institution should guarantee internationally agreed conditions; (4) that the real needs and just demands of nations, populations and racial minorities be adjusted to remove the incentives to violent action; and (5) that peoples and rulers be guided by the laws of God. During the first half of 1940, Ellis urged Lang that the leaders of other Churches should adopt and promote Pius XII's five points. Lang told Ellis that it was impossible in wartime to obtain opinions from the leaders of the other European Churches, but she was not to be deterred and gradually the plan evolved of sending a letter to *The Times* supporting the pope's five points and adding five economic standards derived from the ecumenical Conference on Church, Community and State, which had been held in Oxford in 1937.[48] The five standards were: (1) extreme inequality of wealth and possessions should be abolished; (2) every child should have equal and appropriate opportunities of education; (3) the family as a social unit should be safeguarded; (4) the sense of work as a Divine vocation should be restored; and (5) the resources of the earth should be used considerately as God's gift to the whole human race. After long and careful negotiation, the letter was printed by *The Times* on 21 December 1940 over the signatures of Lang, Cardinal Arthur Hinsley, archbishop of Westminster, Walter Armstrong, moderator of the Free Church Federal Council, and Temple.[49]

Over thirty years later, Cardinal John Heenan, archbishop of Westminster, who had been a Roman Catholic parish priest in 1940, clearly recalled the letter's 'powerful effect on public opinion'. It was the first time that the archbishops of Canterbury and York, a cardinal archbishop of Westminster, and the moderator of the Free Churches had signed such a joint letter about agreed religious matters, and it was hailed by members of all denominations.[50] Probably only the archbishop of Canterbury could have provided the focus for such a letter in 1940. Part of the impact of the letter was due to its timing: Britain stood alone, bombed by the Luftwaffe, the future of the war uncertain. Yet from Lambeth Palace came a letter signed by the leaders of the main English Churches setting out a carefully agreed basis for the future. A deputation of MPs saw Lang on 12 February 1941 to thank him for the letter and urge that it be given widespread publicity. The letter was adopted by Convocation as an 'Act' and Churchill sent Lang a letter of warm interest.[51]

In May 1941, Lang once more urged Convocation that careful thought should be given to the post-war settlement:

> But we dare not wait till this [victory] has been achieved before trying to think out not only the terms of peace, but the kind of policy, national and international, which can justify and reward all the sufferings and sacrifices of the war. The reason why the hopes and dreams which were so freely expressed during the last war faded away so quickly when that was over was that they lacked clear thought and definite purpose. We must not make the same mistake again. Men must even now be setting themselves to think out plans for that better order which we all desire.[52]

These may have been the words uttered by an old man less than a year away from retirement, but they are not the words of an embarrassing relic of a bygone age who had nothing relevant left to say. Rather, they are the words of a clear and experienced thinker who was giving careful thought to the future.

The Sword of the Spirit

In August 1940, Cardinal Hinsley inaugurated a Roman Catholic campaigning movement called the Sword of the Spirit.[53] Hinsley had a number of objectives in mind. The Sword of the Spirit's fundamental aim was 'the restoration in Europe of a Christian basis for both public and private life, by a return to the principles of international order and Christian freedom'. Hinsley sought to achieve this through 'more united and intense prayer and study and work among Catholics in the cause of the Church and our country'.[54] He was also keen to demonstrate the loyalty of British Roman Catholics to Britain's war effort and 'to make clear our desire to be associated with Catholics all over the world in the work of reconstruction after the war'. According to Moloney, Hinsley wished the Sword of the Spirit to constitute a bridge between British Roman Catholics and their fellow, non-Roman Catholic countrymen. The Sword of the Spirit proved controversial with some Roman Catholics, who feared a dilution of their Catholicism, especially in the north of England.[55]

Lang became involved in the Sword of the Spirit in a roundabout way. In February 1941, A.C.F. Beales, a member of the executive committee of the Sword of the Spirit, contacted Bell on his own initiative to solicit an offer of cooperation from Lang. Lang agreed to approach Hinsley, but he told Bell that he was concerned lest the Sword of the Spirit should be used to put 'the Roman Church in this country forward as the one really active agency on the Christian side of patriotism . . . comparing it with the apparent inactivity of the Church of England'. Lang wrote to Hinsley on 11 February 1941, enquiring whether he 'would wish the Sword of the Spirit to co-operate actively in such matters with any similar movements within other Christian Communions'. Hinsley replied that membership of the Sword was restricted to Roman Catholics, though other Christians could become associate members. Reflecting on this response, Lang wrote to Bell on 15 February that the Sword of the Spirit 'is really quite frankly a Roman Catholic organisation . . . I do not think it would be possible to encourage [Anglican] Chuch people in these circumstances to join it.'[56] Lang overcame his scruples sufficiently to deliver a talk entitled 'A Christian Order for Britain', about his vision of post-war Britain, at one of two mass meetings organised by the Sword at the Stoll Theatre, London, on 11 May 1941. This was the worst weekend of the Blitz. Hinsley had spoken on the previous evening, but no Roman Catholic dignitary greeted Lang upon his arrival.[57] Lang spoke about the five standards from the 1937 Oxford conference on Community, Church and State, which had been included in the ecumenical letter to

The Times of 21 December 1940. A recording of Lang's speech reveals that he was greeted warmly and was frequently interrupted by applause.[58]

Lang's address was the high-water mark of Anglican cooperation with the Sword of the Spirit. Although his address received praise, there was also criticism in the evangelical *English Churchman* journal, the Protestant Truth Society led a campaign of opposition, and Archdeacon J.L. Fosbrooke of Blackpool sent Lang five letters in ten weeks complaining about cooperation with Roman Catholics. On the Roman Catholic side, Bell reported to Lang on 24 July 1941, there was a fear that the Sword of the Spirit might be swamped by Anglicans. Archbishop Amigo of Southwark wished to keep the movement as Roman as possible in order to retain control. According to Moloney, there were also serious divisions between members of the committee.[59]

Moloney says of Lang that 'close contact with a movement such as the Sword of the Spirit, which exuded enthusiasm and crusading fervour, seemed to make him fidgety and withdrawn, broadly suspicious of his less inhibited colleagues,' but cites no evidence for this statement.[60] It is possible that Lang concluded that the Sword was unstable and he may have felt that the Church of England would not be well served in wartime by an unneccessary Protestant agitation about cooperation with Roman Catholics. It should be remembered that it is part of the job of an archbishop of Canterbury to be a little cautious – or perhaps discerning – about new religious movements. Lang and Bell agreed in July 1941 that no further action should be taken in connection with the Sword and that it should be made plain that there was no official connection, though individual Anglicans were free to join. According to Moloney, by the time of Hinsley's death in 1943, the Sword of the Spirit had largely failed.[61]

The Soviet Union

The entry of Soviet Russia into the war on the Allies' side in 1941 caused a stir amongst many Christians in the western world. Before the war, Church leaders had repeatedly criticised the Soviet Union because of its atheism and persecution of Christians. Lang had appointed a day of intercession for the suffering Russian Church and had aided exiled Orthodox Christians. In return, the Soviet regime abused Lang and pilloried him in their Museum of the Godless in Leningrad. According to Lawson, many Anglicans regarded the 1939 Molotov–Ribbentrop pact between the USSR and Nazi Germany as a 'diabolical alliance'.[62]

On 22 June 1941, Hitler invaded the USSR, and Great Britain and the Soviet Union found themselves co-belligerents. Many British Christians were uneasy at their country's alliance with a regime they abhorred. Lang sought to address their concerns in his diocesan gazette in August 1941. He acknowledged the widespread misgivings and observed that 'it may seem strange to combine alliance with Bolshevist Russia, with the claim that we are contending for a Christian civilisation.' Lang suggested four reasons why such misgivings were misplaced. Firstly, the aim of the war was 'to overthrow the tyranny of evil embodied in the rulers of Germany', and all who are engaged in that cause 'must needs be our allies'. Secondly, a Nazi victory would destroy any tolerable form of human government. Thirdly, Russia was only the latest country to suffer an unprovoked attack from Nazi Germany and was contending for the same principles of national freedom and independence as the British Empire and USA. Fourthly, Lang hoped that the war might lead the Soviet government to be more tolerant of religion and claimed that it was significant that thousands had flocked to church to pray in Moscow and elsewhere upon the outbreak of war.[63]

Lang's gazette article feels slightly makeshift. By the time he spoke in the Lords debate on aid for Russia on 23 October, he had refined his ideas. Lang began by reminding the Lords that he had protested very strongly in the past against the 'oppressive tyranny, the cruelties and persecution, which marked at least the earlier stages of the Russian revolution'. He said he thought the Soviet government had made 'many modifications and abandoned some of the mistakes of their earlier régime'.[64] Whilst the teaching of religion was forbidden, worship was permitted and the churches had been crowded: 'the truth is that the instinct of religion which is so deeply implanted in the Russian peasantry has proved to be too strong to be suppressed.' He hoped that there might be greater religious freedom after the war. The burden of Lang's speech was to suggest that 'we are not dealing now with the past but with the present.' Whilst there were some features of Communism that were compatible with Christianity, the whole Nazi spirit was incompatible

with Christianity or indeed human civilisation. 'The battle of Russia is
our battle,' Lang claimed, and he added that much depended on whether
Russia stood or fell.[65]

Lawson has suggested that Lang sought to justify Britain's alliance
with the USSR and did so with 'the seamless transformation of Nazism
from an element in a totalitarian alliance into a specific "supreme enemy
of mankind"'.[66] There is no doubt that Lang was obliged to acquiesce
in Britain's co-belligerency with the USSR, but the word 'justify' might
be interpreted to mean 'approve', which is not quite the same. Lang was
probably simply making the best of things. He could hardly have sat in
grumpy silence in the Lords, for his silence would have spoken volumes,
nor could he reasonably disown his country's co-belligerency with the
USSR, for that would not have helped the British – and frequently
Anglican – sailors endangering their lives on the Arctic convoys.

Lang's speech may also have been motivated by two contrasting
currents. Hitler's invasion of Russia was seen by many Roman Catholics
on mainland Europe and in Latin America as a crusade against
Bolshevism, and German propaganda broadcasts claimed that Germany
was protecting Europe from Bolshevism.[67] This was likely to pose more
of a problem for Hinsley than for Lang, but he may have been keen
not to lend credence to such a view of the German invasion of Russia.
Lang's hopes for greater religious freedom in the Soviet Union may have
proved a delusion, but tsarism had crumbled under the pressure of one
world war and perhaps Lang hoped for similar changes in Russia after a
second.

Lang subsequently authorised prayers for Russia. In November 1941,
he appealed for donations for Russia and the following month spoke
warmly of the resistance of the Russian people to 'the common enemy'.
In his speeches after June 1941, Lang spoke about the armies and peoples
of Russia, but carefully distinguished between them and their Soviet
government. He said nothing in support of the latter.[68]

Lang's approach to the USSR was in keeping with his approach to
the rest of the war effort. He fully and repeatedly supported the British
government and roundly denounced the policies and methods of the
Nazis. Yet Lang never offered support at any price. He was careful to
try to avoid compromising Christianity and endangering his Church for

the future. He was quite clear that there was a level of ethical behaviour below which it was not safe to go, and was determined as far as possible, given the exigencies of war, that the nation should emerge with honour intact.

WARTIME PROBLEMS

The Second World War has sometimes been called a 'total war'. It affected almost every aspect of daily life in Britain. Not only was there conscription into the armed forces, but also the direction of labour, including the compulsory employment of women. Aerial bombing meant that civilians were in the front line in a way which they had not been in 1914–18. The government tried to preserve as much of normal life as possible – for example, by reopening theatres and cinemas after the first few weeks of the war – but inevitably there was widespread dislocation of pre-war ways of life and expectations. Problems of various sorts arose, and many people – including sometimes the British government – looked to Lang for a lead, advice or support. Lang also took the initiative from time to time, in order to exert Christian influence, to assist, and to warn of moral and ethical dangers.

Evacuation, Children and Family Life

'The bomber will always get through,' Baldwin had declared in 1932.[69] The British government feared widespread casualties and loss of life from aerial bombing and in September 1939 inaugurated an unprecedented scheme to evacuate children from urban areas, which it was feared would be bombed, to the provinces, which were thought to be less at risk.

On the eve of the war, the government sought Lang's support for this policy and asked him to publish a letter in his diocesan gazette requesting clergy to promote the evacuation scheme from the pulpit. The evacuation proved a mixed success. Some children were well cared for, whilst others were neglected and sometimes abused. Lang quickly became aware of problems caused by the evacuation. Small country parishes, for example, found themselves suddenly swamped overnight with 300–500 children. Clergy and schools struggled to cope and churches were pressed into service as schoolrooms.[70] Some children from good city schools ended up in bad village schools. Lang used a debate in the Lords on 1 November 1939 to express his concern:

> It seems to me certain that family life must be broken up in a two-fold way: evacuated children lose their hold upon their own homes, and the parents of those homes lose largely their sense of responsibility. That is all very well for a short time, but what is to happen if it goes on for a year or two years? Again, in the reception areas the home life of these good people who have been so willing to receive the children from the towns is necessarily interrupted and fundamentally changed by the inclusion of children of a quite different outlook, environment and habits. Here again, is it not possible that we are making needlessly elaborate provision for safety and breaking up the home life of the nation?[71]

Lang used a second debate, on 7 February 1940, to repeat his anxiety about evacuees. He drew attention to those children who had returned home to find their schools closed. It was 'lamentable', Lang said, that between 400,000 and 500,000 children had received no schooling between September 1939 and the beginning of January 1940. He alleged that they were running wild, many had lost free or cheap milk or meals, and they had been deprived of medical services. The archbishop urged the government to reopen schools in evacuated areas immediately.[72]

Lang was updated on the treatment of evacuees by the National Society, the Church of England body which promoted Church schools and religious education. Armed with their information, he endeavoured to assist the evacuees by contacting two of the responsible authorities, the National Council of Social Service and the London County Council, and asking to be kept informed about the ways in which evacuees were being helped. The London County Council thereafter regularly sent him details of the educational work and facilities provided for evacuated London children. By the summer of 1940, Lang had come to doubt the wisdom of sending young children away from their homes and breaking up family life, as he explained in letters declining an offer from the American Protestant Episcopal Church to resettle Anglican evacuees in the United States.[73]

An evacuation of a different sort took place after Dunkirk, when a German invasion was widely feared. On 2 July 1940, Sir John Anderson, the home secretary, informed Lang that preparations were in hand to evacuate up to ninety per cent of the population of south-east Kent if an invasion was imminent. On 5 July, Lang was advised by Malcolm Macdonald, the minister of health, 'to encourage persons who could conveniently leave and who might be in the way in the event of an invasion to leave quietly, but not at present to press other persons to go'. Four days later, Macdonald emphasised the gravity of the situation by sending Lang confidential plans for the evacuation of East Anglian coastal towns as well as those of Kent.[74] Macdonald need not have shared these plans with Lang, and he may have thought that public support by Lang might be useful if an evacuation were attempted. Lang's thoughts turned to the care of those left behind in the invasion zone and he made arrangements for some clergy to remain for essential pastoral work.[75]

Lang became involved in a diocesan problem concerning the evacuation of elderly people in the summer of 1940. A large number of old people from Margate had been persuaded by the local authority to undergo voluntary evacuation and had ended up in Poor Law institutions in Wales, Devon and Cornwall, where husbands and wives were separated, letters were censored and medicines frequently unavailable. News of this situation caused a great stir in the diocese. Lang made detailed enquiries, and, armed with the results, wrote on 2 August to Macdonald asking him to investigate. Macdonald replied a fortnight later that complaints had been few and that everything possible was being done for the comfort of the old people, and repeated this assurance on 3 September.[76] This incident is an example of the careful pastoral care which Lang, who was busy with many other things during wartime, continued to exercise during the war. It also shows that, despite many other demands, government ministers still found time to deal swiftly with enquiries from the archbishop.

Refugees and Nazi Persecution of the Jews

In the months before the outbreak of war, a large number of German and Austrian Jewish refugees sought sanctuary in Great Britain. In November 1939, Sir Robert Waley Cohen, a Jewish former lord mayor of

London, drew Lang's attention to the Kitchener Camp at Richborough, in the diocese of Canterbury, where 160 refugees were being housed.[77] Lang arranged to visit the camp and his words to the refugees made a deep impression on some of them:

> I hope that this country may have the help of the service which you would all be willing to render at this time to the country's need . . . It will be a great thing when we in this country can look upon you not only as refugees but as fellow workers in a common cause in which we can all join. That is my hope.[78]

A number of Jewish refugees in England appealed to Lang to help get their families to safety in England, and in every case he made enquiries or wrote a letter of support to the authorities and tried to cheer the refugees. Perhaps the most poignant request came in March 1940 from 201 men at the Richborough Camp who implored Lang to obtain permits for their families to travel to England. Lang forwarded their letter to Sir John Anderson, with the comment, 'it is, as you will admit, a very natural plea and one which on every ground of human sympathy one would wish to meet.' Anderson replied that there was nothing he could do whilst the men's families were in enemy territory. Lang evidently fully understood the concern of the Jewish refugees, and he probably entertained private apprehensions for the safety of their families. Before the war, he had expressed concern about Nazi ill-treatment of Jews in speeches in the Lords, Canterbury Convocation, the Church Assembly and at a public meeting in 1933. He had also written to *The Times* to condemn anti-Semitism in the Nazi newspaper *Der Stürmer* and had sponsored the collection of a fund for Jewish refugees.[79]

A number of refugees did manage to bring their families to England, but were separated when enemy aliens were interned in 1939. Some two thousand men interned on the Isle of Man sent Lang a telegram in June 1940 urging that they be not evacuated overseas without their children. Lang saw Anderson on 2 July and was told that it would be impossible for families to travel together, should evacuation of internees prove necessary. Lang was reluctant to accept Anderson's assertion as final. On 8 July, he wrote to Anderson to ask him to state that the government 'views their special position with understanding and sympathy'. He also appealed to him to separate interned pro-Nazis and Fascists from opponents of those regimes.[80]

Throughout the summer of 1940, reports reached Lang that the internment programme had been muddled and many refugees badly treated.[81] The archbishop expressed his anxieties to the Home Office, which eventually authorised the release of eighteen categories of the least dangerous 'C' class Austrian and German refugees on 31 July. Lang spent much time during the remainder of the year trying to assist individual refugees with their problems. His concern was appreciated, and at Christmas 1940 many of the former Richborough Camp refugees sent him 'sincere wishes'.[82]

In June 1941, Nazi troops began their invasion of the USSR and by late August the SS Einsatzgruppen were murdering Jews in newly occupied territories. In January 1942, the Wannsee Conference in Berlin determined upon the extermination of Jews in Nazi-occupied Europe. Tom Lawson claims that: 'There is no doubt that the Church was explicitly aware of the annhilation, as its leaders were in receipt of detailed reports *throughout the war* [my italics].'[83] Lawson unfortunately provides no footnotes to verify this assertion. The Wannsee Conference occurred around the time that Lang announced his forthcoming resignation, and he finally left Canterbury at Easter 1942. He was thus in office for the first eight months of the Nazi extermination of the Jews. I have found no trace amongst Lang's papers of any indication that he knew of the systematic murder of the Jews. Lang was in the habit of dictating memoranda of his conversations and meetings, and it is highly likely that he would have left such a record, had he known about the extermination of Jews in central Europe. Nor did Lang mention this matter in the private notebooks which he kept throughout the war.[84] Given his pre-war record, it is possible to speculate that Lang would probably have condemned the Nazi extermination of the Jews, had he known about it.

Wartime Moral Problems

As in the First World War, so again during the Second World War, the dislocation of peacetime patterns of life, compulsory conscription and the movement of troops led to a rise in sexual promiscuity. This expressed itself in the spread of venereal disease, the use of brothels by soldiers, and cohabitation. In each case, Lang was called upon to offer a moral lead to the nation. His approach in each instance was firm but pastoral, sometimes in the face of opposition from pressure groups which wished him to adopt a more condemnatory attitude.

Before war was declared, Lang heard that venereal disease was proving a significant problem in the British army. Lord Gort, commander of the BEF in France, also recognised the problem and on 9 September 1939 sent his aide-de-camp, Lord Munster, to ask Lang if they might consult one another about the moral and spiritual life of the army.[85]

Lang sought guidance about venereal disease from Lord Dawson of Penn, who advised him that it should be dealt with medically. Dawson added that the 'blunt and casual advice' given by Royal Army Medical Corps staff might be improved by allowing 'men of special knowledge and also with some gifts of speech, who would not only deal frankly with the purely medical side but also try to lift the matter up to a higher moral plane to give lectures'.[86]

Lang wrote to Gort on 17 October, advocating Dawson's idea that Royal Army Medical Corps advice to soldiers about venereal disease might be supplemented. Gort replied on 26 October that he had issued an order that troops in France 'must always prove worthy' of the welcome the French had afforded them, explaining, 'I implied all that you had in mind and I feel it would be unwise for me at this moment further to stress the matter.' Gort offered to write to the director-general of medical services if Lang wished to visit him, but suggested that Lang might think this was no longer necessary. Lang replied on 31 October, saying that he regretted that Gort had not been able to speak as directly as Kitchener in 1914, but understood his 'inability' to write further. He would contact the director-general of medical services directly.[87]

Lang continued to gather information about venereal disease throughout the winter of 1939–40. Lord Dawson sent him a detailed memorandum and he was in regular communication with the Rev. Gilbert Russell, who was both a priest and a doctor specialising in venereal disease, and was a member of the Church Moral Welfare Council.[88]

A further controversy which blew up in the first year of the war concerned the issue of prophylactics to troops by the Royal Army

Medical Corps. The use of prophylactics had proved controversial before the war amongst Roman Catholics and some Anglicans. The British Council of Hygiene, which campaigned against venereal disease, favoured their issue, but this was opposed by the National Council of Women Workers and yet more strongly by the Association for Moral and Social Hygiene, which sought to promote Christian morality. Lang was asked by the Association for Moral and Social Hygiene to sign a letter condemning the use of public money to provide prophylactics, 'which may result in a serious loss of moral restraint and chastity of many young men and women'. Lang took the view that the issue at stake was more complex than the association realised and declined to sign their letter.[89] The archbishop saw the director-general of the Royal Army Medical Corps on 16 November 1939 to discuss the problem. As a result of this conversation and subsequent correspondence, Lang was informed that the advertising of prophylactics in barracks would cease, that prophylactics would only be available upon application to a medical officer, who would issue advice and a warning about venereal disease, and that there would be no objection to chaplains being present when medical officers spoke to troops about venereal disease or to their lectures being supplemented by civilian experts. Lang's more nuanced and pastoral approach to combatting venereal disease was not shared by the bishops' war committee, which prepared a draft statement on 14 November 1939 condemning the army's issuing of prophylactics as 'repulsive' and insisting in the name of the Church that it be discontinued. On 5 December 1939, Lang questioned the wisdom of issuing such a statement and in February 1940 the idea was dropped.[90]

The frequent use of *maisons tolérées*, or brothels, by British troops in France proved equally troublesome. Lang was warned of a problem by the chaplain-general on 7 December 1939. On 17 January 1940, he saw Sir Robert Finlayson, the adjutant-general, and told him that he had reason to think the French authorities would be willing to close *maisons tolérées* if approached by the British. Finlayson replied that up to five per cent of soldiers would insist on having some outlet for their sexual passions or would run amok 'like mad dogs'. He informed Lang confidentially that German propagandists were telling French troops that British soldiers were interfering with their women. If *maisons tolérées* were closed, some troops might force their attentions on French civilian women, playing into the hands of the German propagandists, and the prostitutes would set up elsewhere. Finlayson conveyed Lang's concerns to the Army Council, which replied on 9 February 1940 that it was neither desirable nor practical to shut brothels, and said placing them 'out of bounds' might lead to troops forcing their attentions upon respectable women in their billets, which could be used by enemy propaganda.[91]

Lang informed the Association of Moral and Social Hygiene on 14 February that the Army Council had said that the brothels could not be closed. He later received letters from the president of the Catholic Alliance Jeanne d'Arc and from the president of the Fédération Protestante de France, expressing concern about the army's use of *maisons tolérées* and giving details of the degradation of the women involved.[92] 'I have received a great deal of information', Lang told Bishop Batty of Fulham on 22 March, 'which makes it difficult for me to acquiesce in this official view [of brothels] and I must give further consideration to the whole question.' The archbishop spoke on 12 April to Bishop Fisher of London, chairman of the bishops' war committee, who suggested that an ecumenical delegation should confront the prime minister with their objections to brothels, 'and then leave the responsibility of acting or refusing to act upon them to the military authorities'. Lang once more consulted Lord Dawson, who suggested that a small deputation containing no one with extreme views would probably be more effective.[93] Lang confided in Bell that he was irritated by the Association for Moral and Social Hygiene, which was stirring up a public agitation and not helping his efforts behind the scenes. The archbishop was trying to arrange a delegation when the German offensive began in May 1940. After Dunkirk, the problem of *maisons tolérées* ceased.[94]

A problem from 1914–18 which arose again in the Second World War was the position of unmarried women cohabiting with soldiers. On 18 October 1939, Leslie Hore-Belisha, secretary of state for war, told the Commons that an unmarried woman living with a soldier would receive the same allowance as a soldier's wife, 'provided that she was wholly or substantially maintained by him on a permanent domestic basis for a continuous period of not less than six months immediately before the date of his joining the Colours'. Lang saw this as undermining marriage and wrote to Hore-Belisha on 23 October pressing for reconsideration. He reminded Hore-Belisha that in 1915 a distinction had been drawn between wives and unmarried dependants, and that full evidence had been required before an unmarried dependant received an allowance. He asked what evidence of a relationship between a soldier and a woman would be sought, and requested clarification of Hore-Belisha's use of 'substantially'. 'Very probably the matter may arouse further public notice,' wrote Lang, before adding a touch of pressure: 'before I take any action about it I should be grateful if you could tell me on what grounds you think the decision you have announced is sufficient and what you think about the considerations I have urged in this letter.' Hore-Belisha replied on 8 November that no allowance could be made until it was clear that the relationship between a soldier and a woman corresponded to a marital relationship apart from being married, and that the soldier made his partner the same allowance as a married man made to his wife. He was unable to offer a formal definition of 'substantially'.[95]

As Lang reflected upon this issue in the early part of 1940, he became increasingly unhappy about the official use of the term 'unmarried wives'. It occurred to him that if a man died on active service, his pension might go to his mistress and not to his wife. The archbishop saw Oliver Stanley, the new secretary of state for war, on 28 February. They settled on the term 'unmarried dependants living as wives' as an alternative to 'unmarried wives', and this was officially accepted the following month. The government reassured Lang that a legal wife had prior claim to a pension.[96]

It is perhaps not too fanciful to see in the elderly Lang dealing with these problems in 1939–40 an echo of the younger Lang who had been a 'live wire' as vicar of Portsea at the turn of the century. Pastoral work in Portsmouth's largest parish would have exposed Lang to the realities of naval family life and to the moral problems found in ports. In dealing with wartime moral problems, Lang proclaimed high Christian moral standards, but he was realistic in his expectations of men and women under the stresses and strains of war. He never thought that moral problems would be resolved simply by issuing condemnations or by placing brothels out of bounds. Perhaps his attitude to 'unmarried wives' might be seen as symbolic of his whole approach: he sought firmly to uphold marriage and family life, but he did not wish 'unmarried wives' to suffer unneccesary financial hardship, should their 'unmarried husbands' be killed.

The problems surrounding evacuees, refugees and morality reveal the limits of Lang's wartime influence. He had no direct power to help children separated from their families by evacuation and perhaps ill-treated in their new homes, nor could he offer much practical help to refugees. Some men and women tempted to wartime promiscuity might have been swayed by an archiepiscopal warning, but many probably would not. Yet, in wartime, many more people turned to Lang for help and support, and his word obviously counted for something. The files at Lambeth contain copies of Lang's many replies to the sad and often-desperate letters sent to him by refugees and others. He strove to send each a personal letter and to offer them hope, often where there was little reason to be hopeful. Perhaps providing hope may be judged to have been a major part of Lang's wartime ministry.

Keeping the Church of England Going During Wartime

Keeping the machinery of the Church of England going is the bread-and-butter work of any modern archbishop. Lang had to do this during three of the worst years of the Second World War, including the period when a German invasion was widely believed to be imminent. Lang had his own experience from the First World War to guide him, as well as Davidson's example between 1914 and 1918, but although some problems in the Second World War were similar to those of the First World War, others were not.

The Bishops

When war was declared, the bishops found themselves immediately confronted by an array of wartime problems.[97] Lang adopted two measures to help his bishops run their dioceses. As an experienced administrator, Lang fully understood the importance of the bishops adopting consistent policies when dealing with wartime conditions in their dioceses. He also knew that it would be of great practical benefit for the bishops to pool their resources and exchange information. On 25 September 1939, therefore, the archbishop decided to establish a bishops' war committee.[98] He asked Geoffrey Fisher, bishop of London, to act as chairman. Fisher appears to have been responsible for setting the agenda for meetings, but he discussed the committee's work with Lang on a regular basis. The bishops' committee occasionally interviewed various experts, and discussed topics as diverse as petrol, evacuation, use of Roman Catholic property in France, venereal disease, Sunday Schools, church records, altar linen and telephones. The committee had no authority to issue orders, but essentially provided a forum for bishops to exchange or elicit information and to issue advice. Lang attended at least eight meetings of the bishops' committee and may have been present at three more. Temple appears never to have been present.[99] The committee initially met at the start of each month, but meetings became less frequent as the war progressed and travel became more difficult. Nevertheless, the minutes suggest that from an administrative angle, Lang's episcopal war committee was of practical help to over-stretched and sometimes isolated bishops.

Secondly, after the first year of the war, Lang decided to help his bishops by organising a time of shared spiritual renewal and discussion. A committee was established in October 1940 to make the arrangements for an episcopal conference, to be held the following year at St Edmund Hall, Oxford. The English diocesan bishops were joined on 2 July by diocesan bishops from Scotland and Wales. Each day had a set theme: 'The understanding of God's Will at this Time', 'Evangelism', 'The Presentation of the Christian Faith' and 'Worship'. Each subject was introduced by a devotional address in St Peter's Church, followed by a practical address and discussion in the college. Papers were delivered by Temple, Williams (Durham), Barry (Southwell), Woodward (Bristol), David (Liverpool), Kirk (Oxford) and Blunt (Bradford). No minutes were taken of the discussions, but fortunately Bell's private daily notes survive.[100]

In his later recollections, Lang noted, 'the Conferences were well sustained; all the speakers said just what they thought, but there was throughout a delightful atmosphere of harmony and fellowship.'[101] In fact, Bell's notes reveal that episcopal disagreement was rife. Lang had to intervene on the first day when Williams (Durham) and Headlam (Gloucester) introduced irrelevant subjects, ranging from urban squalour to the divine right of kings, during a debate on God's will. Haigh (Coventry) and Bell clashed over concepts of sin, Danson (Edinburgh) used the opportunity to laud the Scottish Episcopal Church, and no one was keen to discuss the suggestion of Underhill (Bath and Wells) that the bishops depressed their clergy. Things got worse the next day when Furse (St Albans) praised sacramental Confession and Havard (St Asaph) said that the Church was too sacerdotal, whilst Warman (Manchester) claimed that the clergy said idiotic prayers. On the third day Lang asked that bishops' contributions should be short and to the point. Hunkin (Truro) and Rawlinson (Derby) argued about the Virgin Birth, the Resurrection, the divinity of Christ and contemporary adoptionism. Bell recorded a good debate about different styles and problems of education. Disagreement returned on the final day during a debate on worship. Hunkin said that he had no desire to go to Communion every week and he objected to a language of eucharistic sacrifice. Blunt answered that Mattins was unpopular and stressed the importance of Holy Communion and of Reservation. Headlam countered that abandoning Mattins for a sung Eucharist had emptied churches. Warman asked Blunt not to speak of 'Mass' and 'biretta'. Temple tried to divert attention to the Scottish liturgy. Hone (Wakefield) remarked that he did not mind the transfer of the 1662 prayer of oblation. Fisher said that Hone could not permit this transfer, and complained about Benediction and the 'fetish' of fasting Communion, the custom of the communicant not eating or drinking after midnight and of making Holy Communion the first thing to be consumed in the day.[102]

People squabble for a variety of reasons, not all of them obvious. The bishops may simply have been letting off steam, in much the same way that a roomful of modern clergy seem always to end up moaning about funerals. Perhaps, although the bishops grumbled about the Church, they were really giving vent to the difficulties of their wartime lives. They certainly appear to have been starved of opportunities for debate, and, from a pastoral point of view, Lang's conference was a good idea. Despite their differences, the archbishop detected a 'spirit of fellowship' amongst the bishops. Garbett, who had opposed the calling of the conference, said that it was much better than he had expected and it had done the bishops good.[103]

Throughout the war, Lang continued his regular correspondence with bishops, tried to answer their questions and offer them advice. He assisted with the selection of new bishops and advised on the translation of others. This was all the routine work of an archbishop, which Lang managed to keep up even after he had been bombed out of Lambeth Palace in 1940. It was not glamorous, but it helped to keep the Church of England functioning.

The Clergy and Combatant Service

There is a long tradition forbidding Christian clergy from shedding blood.[104] The clergy were granted exemption from conscription during the 1914–18 war. As another war plainly drew near, Lang was troubled to learn, on 18 January 1939, that the clergy were not included in the government's category of 'reserved occupations'. On 6 May, he formally asked the government whether the clergy 'would be exempted from compulsory service of a combatant nature'. On 8 June, the Ministry of Labour decided to exempt the clergy from conscription. During the Second World War, however, a small number of clergy felt compelled to undertake combatant service. Lang stated that this participation was incompatible with ordination.[105] In 1940, he approved a recommendation by the episcopal war committee that all clergy embarking upon combatant service would be required to produce testimonials of good conduct throughout their military career. He adopted this practice in his diocese. He was evidently making the best of a difficult situation, and attempting to uphold high standards and expectations of clerical life and behaviour.[106]

Service Chaplains

The Second World War saw an increased demand for priests to become chaplains in the armed services. Before hostilities began, Lang realised that recruitment of service chaplains would need to be carefully managed, for a willy-nilly rush of parish clergy into uniform would disrupt and weaken the Church's parochial ministry. From April 1938, all English dioceses had maintained a system of lists of clergy judged suitable by the bishop to be commissioned as wartime chaplains. Once the war started, this system seems to have proved too cumbersome and fizzled out. Lang quickly became concerned that priests were applying directly to the armed forces for commissions as chaplains, and not applying via their diocesan bishops, who were supposed to be coordinating recruitment and parochial cover. Lang took steps to remind bishops of their responsibilities, and asked the Army Chaplains' Department to make the proper procedure clear to the clergy.[107]

Lang exercised a pastoral oversight towards chaplains of all three services until his retirement in 1942. Not everything went smoothly and Lang had to intervene from time to time with the army's chaplain-general. Haigh, for example, complained that two priests were posted to military units after only two days' preparation. Lang told the chaplain-general that this was quite inadequate and urged him to establish more adequate training facilities in England and France. Learning from private sources that troops preferred older chaplains who had seen a bit more of life, Lang 'strongly pressed' for the recruitment of chaplains aged over forty. The chaplain-general arranged for the recruitment of chaplains aged up to fifty and established training centres for chaplains at Aldershot, Woolwich and Chester. By 10 January 1940, after some further action by Lang, three 'refresher' schools for chaplains were planned in England and France.[108]

On 14 December 1939, Lang sent a letter to every chaplain in the three services:

> I know well the difficulties which you have often to meet. But I also know that you regard it, as indeed you must, as a very high privilege to be fulfilling your ministry among the men who are foremost in serving their country's cause. You hold a key-post . . . For these men form the largest part of the vigorous manhood of their generation. You are among them to help them win some inward security of soul, some sure foundation for all their energies of mind and body. You are there to cheer and sustain their spirit, and to keep them in remembrance of the Eternal Father and of Christ the Divine Comrade who is ever present in their midst.[109]

Lang's letter showed remarkable insight and sensitivity into the lives of chaplains and the men to whom they ministered. He urged the chaplains to 'identify themselves with [the troops], share all their interests, take a leading part in providing them means of recreation and wholesome entertainment'. Lest the attractions of the officers' mess or the military ethos prove too beguiling to the priests, he reminded them of their sacred calling and urged them to take as their daily motto, 'For their sakes I consecrate myself.' He was sympathetic to the chaplains' lack of privacy and their loneliness, and he recognised that few in the armed forces would understand their responsibility as priests. When they were unable to enjoy the worship to which they had been accustomed, Lang urged the priests to remember the unfailing presence of Christ with them, and to keep their hearts as consecrated shrines. Lang was frank about the temptations which beset troops, and urged the chaplains to help them as a brother rather than as a preacher, 'with a full human understanding'. He announced that he hoped to arrange for bishops to visit the forces from time to time to carry out confirmations and give counsel, and to establish 'schools for chaplains'. He assured the chaplains of the prayers of the Church at home, adding 'will you sometimes think of your brethren sticking to their posts on the home front, many of them wishing they could be where you are, and facing difficulties at this time as real as yours, though of a different kind.' Lang was evidently anxious to avoid any cleavage between parochial clergy and service chaplains, for he added, 'at whatever front we may be serving, let us all as one great brotherhood be striving to keep the high standards of the Christian Faith and life in these testing days of war.' Lang's letter showed him to be in touch with the reality of military life, and it is clear that he highly valued the chaplains' work.

One persistent difficulty would appear to have been the army chaplain-general's department. During the First World War, Davidson had managed to remedy deficiencies in the then chaplain-general's administration and pastoral care by getting Bishop Llewellyn Gwynn sent to France as a deputy chaplain-general. When Lang mooted the idea of sending a bishop to the army in France on 28 September 1939, a touchy chaplain-general claimed that this would cause administrative difficulties, and suggested that a panel of bishops might occasionally be made temporarily available. Lang persuaded the chaplain-general to allow Bishop Batty of Fulham to carry out confirmations in France in December 1939. Batty's visit was a great success and many chaplains begged him to return. Lang quickly sought to exploit this enthusiasm and told the chaplain-general that if Batty was not available, he would arrange for other bishops to go. The chaplain-general reluctantly consented, but refused to have Bishops Talbot or Hudson, who had been chaplains in 1914–18. 'If we can put a very large bomb under the Chaplain-General's department at the end of the war,' commented Temple, 'it would be very useful – but you have yourself intimated that such treatment of the entire C. of E. might be salutary!'[110]

Ordinands

During the First World War, the supply of ordinands had dried up, with serious repercussions for the Church's ministry for several years after the Armistice. In 1939, Lang determined to avoid a repetition of this problem by securing exemption from conscription for ordinands. He first raised the position of ordinands with Sir Herbert Creedy of the Army Council on 6 June 1939, but received no satisfactory reply. On 8 June, Don was informed by the Ministry of Labour that ordinands would not be exempted. On 18 July, Don wrote on Lang's behalf to Ernest Brown, minister of labour, claiming that it would be a very serious matter if the supply of ordinands petered out again during a war, and enquiring what action the government might take.[111] It is interesting that Lang fully expected the state to be concerned for the maintenance of the Church of England's parish ministry.

On 31 August 1939, Don was told that some ordinands close to their ordination might be added to the schedule of reserved occupations, as medical students were.[112] On 2 September, Lang pressed Brown by letter for exemption to be granted to all ordinands. Lang met him five days later, but their discussions proved inconclusive. Lang next sent Brown a long letter on 16 September, carefully arguing for exemption for ordinands and claiming that the work of the clergy in wartime was as important as that of doctors. Lang reminded Brown that Cardinal Hinsley had recently secured exemption for his seminarians, and he asked to see him again. A week later, Brown replied that inclusion on the schedule of reserved occupations would be granted to:

a man who was, before September, 1939, established in his course as a student at an institution recognized by any religious denomination as a training institution for Holy Orders or for regular Ministers of that denomination, while he continues as such a student and intends to qualify for Holy Orders or for appointment as a regular Minister.[113]

Superficially, this seemed a satisfactory outcome. However, Lang spotted that there might be difficulties of interpretation: did Brown's definition, for example, cover men reading Theology at university, who had definitely been accepted for ordination? Lang asked Bishop Warman of Manchester, chairman of the Central Advisory Council for Training for the Ministry, to provide a memorandum on such difficult cases, which he submitted to Brown on 2 October. Lang's efforts were rewarded on 11 November when Brown informed him that he had widened the schedule of reserved occupations to include any man who was regarded before September 1939 by any religious denomination as a candidate for ordination.[114]

Lang's campaign to secure exemption for ordinands was not uncontroversial. Bishop Haigh wrote to Lang on 21 July 1939 expressing annoyance at the prospect of ordinands being exempted from conscription, unlike other men of military age.[115] More sustained opposition came from W.R. Matthews, dean of St Paul's, who sent Lang six letters between May and July 1940 claiming that exemption had been interpreted by some as meaning that the bishops disapproved of ordinands fighting in the war. He was supported by Paul de Labilliere, dean of Westminster. Exemption appears to have had an unexpected effect upon some of the ordinands themselves. On 24 May 1940, the principal of King's College, London, reported a 'morbid and unhealthy' atmosphere amongst his ordinands who had been evacuated to Bristol and said he thought that half were pacifists or conscientious objectors. He appealed to Lang for a clear statement that public service was not incompatible with the vocation of an ordinand. Lang and Temple wrote jointly to theological college principals on 12 July 1940, stating that there was no general discouragement of ordinands who consciously wished to serve in the armed forces.[116]

It is clear that Lang believed, firstly, that the heart of the Church of England was located in its parishes, and, secondly, that the Church could best respond to wartime needs at a parochial level. It was therefore imperative for adequate numbers of clergy to be deployed across the parishes. Hence Lang's concern about the supply of ordinands and insistence that some priests should remain in any areas evacuated in anticipation of an invasion. But Lang's support of the war effort had its limits. He held combatant service to be incompatible with ordination and he reminded service chaplains in the clearest terms that they were first and foremost Christian priests.

Wartime Liturgy

Liturgical questions occupied Lang throughout the Second World War until his retirement in 1942. The Church of England had a tradition dating from the sixteenth century of organising days of national prayer at the request of the state, usually in connection with wars, agriculture or epidemics. During the First World War, there had been national days of prayer at the start of each year and on the anniversary of the declaration of war. At the beginning of the Second World War, it was agreed to hold a national day of prayer on Sunday 1 October 1939. Rather than wait for instructions to come from the Privy Council, the traditional manner of authorising a day of prayer, Lang obtained permission to announce that the day of prayer was being held 'with the approval of His Majesty the King'. Lang issued a pastoral letter commending the national day of prayer and composed many of the prayers specially issued for use on the day.[117]

Lang discussed national days of prayer with Neville Chamberlain at 10 Downing Street on 20 February 1940. The archbishop believed that the old method of the Privy Council ordering the Established Church to hold a national day of prayer was cumbersome and offensive to other denominations, and Chamberlain agreed. Lang noted:

> I thought it much more natural and would not give rise to obvious misunderstandings on the part of the Allies or enemies if the anniversary of the war (September 3rd) or a Sunday near it were to be observed, and I suggested that it should not be by Royal

Proclamation or by an Order of the Privy Council but that the King might express his hope that the Day would be generally observed.[118]

Lang's reluctance to arrange too many days of prayer irritated some evangelicals in April 1940.[119] Nerves were evidently frayed and Lang took prompt action when the German offensive in the west began in May. He asked George VI to announce a day of prayer on 26 May as soon as possible. Lang and Temple issued a statement asking 'the whole nation [to join] in acts of united prayer to submit to the protection and blessing of Almighty God the cause to which with its Allies it has pledged all of its strength'. Lang wrote to *The Times* commending the day of prayer and asked the leaders of other Churches to send messages of support to the press. On 26 May, he broadcast on the BBC and preached before the king and queen and the government in Westminster Abbey.[120]

Lang again approached George VI in August 1940, after a conversation with the prime minister, and asked if the king would express the desire for a day of prayer on 8 September, the Sunday nearest the anniversary of the declaration of war. George VI agreed and asked Lang to suggest a form of announcement. Lang issued a press statement and again asked the leaders of other Churches to issue press statements. A pattern had now been established of inaugurating days of prayer by request of the king, in coordination with the leaders of other Churches, and of employing the press and BBC to promote them. Lang followed this pattern when he arranged days of prayer on 23 March 1941, 17 August 1941 and 29 March 1942. In 1941, Churchill suggested reviving the old title of 'prayer and humiliation'. Lang feared 'humiliation' would be misunderstood. Luckily, George VI disliked the word and Lang got round it with a reference to a 'day of humble prayer to Almighty God'.[121]

Another liturgical problem was Armistice Day, 11 November. Armistice Day, and particularly the two minutes' silence at 11 a.m., had evolved into an important communal expression of grief and loss after the First World War. The home secretary, Sir John Anderson, and Lang discussed on 3 October 1939 what to do about Armistice Day in the changed circumstances of another world war. Anderson proposed that there should be no large open-air services on 11 November, lest they be targetted by the Luftwaffe, and Lang agreed that it would be 'proper' for the government to issue such a notice. Lang was, however, anxious that the sacrifices of the previous war should not be overlooked. He proposed that the government's announcement 'should make special mention of the desire that the men who fell or were wounded in the last war should not be forgotten', and should refer to the British Legion's Poppy collection. He further suggested that the following Sunday, 12 November, 'should be observed as a Day of Remembrance and Dedication thus linking together the numbers of men in the last war with the struggle in which the nation is now engaged'. George VI and the War Cabinet approved of Lang's proposal. The archbishop informed the leaders of other Churches and issued a press statement. This pattern was repeated in 1940 and 1941.[122]

Army parade services were a problem from 1914–18 which resurfaced during the Second World War. Soldiers were obliged to go to church, but there had been complaints in the First World War from some Anglo-Catholic soldiers who were obliged to attend parade services, which were an abbreviated form of Morning Prayer, but who were discouraged by the army from additionally attending the Eucharist. Things had improved by 1939, when Lang was informed that troops desiring to attend the Eucharist had only to notify the chaplain and their breakfasts would be kept for them.[123]

In June 1941, Lang was drawn into a controversy surrounding Father Hugh Bishop, a member of the Community of the Resurrection (CR) at Mirfield in Yorkshire, serving as a military chaplain, who had substituted a simplified Eucharist for parade services. Bishop enjoyed some success amongst the troops, but the chaplain-general ordered him to revert to Morning Prayer. Bishop refused and appealed for support to Edward Talbot CR, a former chaplain from 1914–18. Talbot laid Bishop's case before Lang on 4 June 1941 and endorsed his position.[124] Lang consulted the chaplain-general. He then wrote to Talbot on 16 June:

> personally I agree with you that the best way of promoting a sense of worship is the Holy Eucharist rather than Morning Prayer, but you know well it has taken English folk a long time to realise the fact and it is very imperfectly realised now.[125]

However, he added that so long as troops were obliged to attend parade services, some form of service had to be the norm and it was very difficult to expect the chaplain-general to countenance another sort of service than Morning Prayer. He pointed out that Father Bishop's objections to Morning Prayer were not shared by Father Shearburn CR, also serving as an army chaplain.

The Community of the Resurrection considered Lang's reply and on 28 July 1941 submitted a formal memorandum to Lang and Temple asking that 'the possibility of establishing the Holy Eucharist as a Parade Service be not ruled out and that where conditions are favourable a Chaplain may be free to establish it.' Lang consulted Temple, and replied to the Community of the Resurrection on 22 August. He said that the crucial difference was that parade services were compulsory. He felt that, under the mobile conditions of modern warfare, it would be difficult for chaplains to prepare troops for compulsory attendance at the Eucharist and was worried that new men would be drafted to units and expected to attend the Eucharist with no preparation. Lang was unhappy about non-communicating Eucharists and said that he could not 'reconcile myself to the idea of departing in this way from the old principle of excluding catechumens from the Holy Mysteries'. Both these points would have been understood at Mirfield. For these reasons, Lang was unable to press the chaplain-general to authorise the Eucharist for parade services. The Community of the Resurrection accepted Lang's decision and thanked him for considering their memorandum.[126] Although Lang as an Anglo-Catholic and believer in the Real Presence would have had considerable sympathy with Father Bishop's aims, he once again put the well-being of the whole Church of England before advantage to the Anglo-Catholic party.

Lang used liturgy between 1939 and 1942 for a variety of purposes. He saw it as a means of expressing the Church's support for the state and endorsement of the war effort. This policy would have been particularly significant after Dunkirk, when Britain and its empire alone confronted Germany and there was pressure in some quarters to seek a negotiated peace. Lang fully realised the power of worship to unite, and its pastoral significance, hence his concern that Armistice Day should flow into

Remembrance Sunday, when the sacrifice of the past and the struggle of the present might be united.

Lang's use of the heads of other denominations to endorse national days of prayer was a departure from precedent. During the First World War, Davidson merely informed the other denominations about national days of prayer, but did not seek their endorsement or concomitant call to prayer. There are several possible explanations for this change. By 1939, the educational controversies which had previously caused great friction between the Church of England and the Free Churches were well on the way to being resolved. Lang had cultivated cordial relations with the leaders of the Free Churches in the 1930s. His relationship with Cardinal Hinsley was warmer than that with his predecessor, Cardinal Bourne.[127] Most significantly, Lang had a view of himself as something like the chief spokesman for Christianity in England. In the circumstances of the war, he would have felt that a coordinated interdenominational day of prayer was of greater value than a specifically Anglican one.

Sunday

Before the outbreak of war in 1939, Sunday had largely been observed as a day of worship and rest, with shops, cinemas and theatres closed. From summer 1940, Lang began to receive reports that this traditional British Sunday was being disturbed by Home Guard drills, school continuation classes, air-raid wardens' practices and Red Cross examinations during the morning hours of worship. Additionally, at the start of 1941, the government was contemplating permitting cinemas and theatres to open on Sunday afternoons for munitions workers.[128]

Lang sought to resist what he called the 'invasion of Sunday', but it was a difficult fight for him to win. He took the view that Christians were not bound by the prohibitions of the Jewish Sabbath, but believed that the weekly observance of the day of Resurrection helped rest the body and recreate the spirit, and had had a great impact upon the national character. On 6 February 1941, Lang told the Ministry of Labour that whilst he appreciated the grounds upon which the government wished to open cinemas on Sundays, and did not feel able to oppose them under the circumstances, he was concerned that it would be extremely difficult if not impossible to close them after the war. Lang's anxieties were shared by the Commons and a majority of MPs voted against the proposal.[129]

Other encroachments upon Sunday were less easy for Lang to address. The National Society kept Lang informed about educational classes held on Sundays. In February 1941, the archbishop suggested that the Board of Education, the government department responsible for schools in Britain, might forbid classes on Sunday mornings. The board felt that it could not object to Sunday classes organised by local education authorities, but took the line that attendance for pupils and teachers must be voluntary. They would urge education authorities to hold classes on Sunday afternoons. Lang concluded that 'this is as satisfactory as we could expect.'[130]

The bishops' war committee was also concerned about the secularisation of Sunday. In February 1941, Fisher told Lang about a notice issued by the Admiralty emphasising that prayers must be said onboard ships. The committee wondered whether a statement about Sunday observance might be obtained from the prime minister and the heads of the armed services, if not from the king. On 6 March 1941, Lang asked the committee to prepare a letter for the prime minister, which he forwarded with a letter of his own. The prime minister's reply to the committee was disappointing. Churchill promised to draw the Admiralty's instructions to the attention of the army, Royal Air Force, and the civil departments. He said that he was sympathetic to a general appeal to employers to give facilities for Sunday observance, but he indicated that there were difficulties in wartime. In answer to an enquiry from Anthony Bevir, the prime minister's ecclesiastical secretary, Lang said that he had no comment to make about Churchill's reply.[131] Lang did, however, write to *The Times* on 3 April 1941 to assert that:

> each single instance of encroachment on the rest and quiet of Sunday which the Government at such a time has felt compelled to sanction must be capable of justification . . . [because] the national effort will gain, not lose, in strength if we make time to look not only at the things that are seen and temporal but also at the things which are unseen and eternal.[132]

The temptation to regard these 'encroachments' upon the British Sunday as a sudden wartime spurt forward of secularisation should be resisted as over-simplistic. The British sabbatarian tradition appears to have been in very gradual decline since the late nineteenth century.[133] If some pre-war customs, including the observance of Sunday, were challenged by the Second World War, Lang knew from his correspondence that increased numbers of people were being brought into contact with Christianity through the war. Children evacuated to the countryside often found themselves being taken to Sunday School for the first time in their lives. The millions conscripted into the armed forces were obliged to attend church parades and received instruction from chaplains. English and Welsh sabbatarianism revived itself to some degree after the war and lingered on for a further half a century, until the 1994 Sunday Trading Act finally delivered the *coup de grâce*.

LANG'S LIFE IN WARTIME

For the first year of the war, Lang managed to continue his custom of spending weekdays at Lambeth Palace and weekends in the diocese of Canterbury. Parts of Kent were shelled from across the Channel by German artillery in France, and Lang frequently visited the affected towns to offer comfort. On one occasion he had to take shelter when German aircraft flew overhead.[134] Lang also visited hop-pickers from the East End of London, and continued his regular round of preaching, as he noted in 1941:

> I have been going the round of small country parishes – such as Stanford, Servington, Whitfield, Swalecliff, Stourmouth, Sheppey (Minster), etc – with visits to the coast areas, Margate, Ramsgate, Birchington, Sandwich – and several addresses to troops, the best of them the London Scottish at Bridge – it was delightful to hear the old Scottish paraphrases [of the Psalms], and being rather picked men they were so intelligent and attentive that it was an inspiration to speak to them . . . All this is well worth doing, though it is not spectacular and it is not easy to vary one's themes.[135]

In London, Lang opened the crypt of Lambeth Palace as a public air-raid shelter, and frequently over 200 people would spend the night there. On Christmas Day 1940, a party for local children was held, complete with a Christmas tree. Members of the armed forces who found themselves stranded in London were sometimes accommodated overnight in parts of the Palace.[136]

Lang spent most of the Blitz in 1940 in London. Bombs were dropped on or around Lambeth Palace on six occasions. Lang noted:

> The night bombing of London reached its highest intensity on the nights from September 7th–11th [1940]. I was at Lambeth on the nights of the 11th, 12th and 13th. No-one who has not gone through it can realise the almost intolerable strain. All night long, from about 9.30 pm to 5.30 am usually, a continual droning of German aeroplanes and crashing of bombs . . . On the night of the 11th there was a welcome change. Anti-aircraft guns had been brought into play . . . and they kept up a continual barrage . . . [On 12 September] many bombs crashed down. One fell in the garden . . . another, with a ghastly screaming, hit and destroyed part of St Thomas's Hospital over the way . . . the public shelter in the crypt chapel [was] full – 200 people every night . . . I have tried to sleep somehow, though the din is often bad. And this strain, to say nothing of the damaged houses, and homeless families and death and woundings, is going on all over the city. So far the behaviour of the people has been wonderful – but what will be the end, thereof? St Paul's [Cathedral] is isolated, a delayed action bomb quite near: the same at the Abbey.[137]

Lang visited parts of London damaged by the Blitz. On 17 September 1940, he decided to shut up most of Lambeth Palace for the duration of the war and to evacuate most of his staff. For the rest of his time as archbishop, Lang was based at the Old Palace in Canterbury. Life here was not much easier, as Canterbury was a frequent target for German bombers.[138] Garbett recorded one incident in 1941:

> Canon Bradfield sees much of the Archbishop and says he has no fear. Bradfield and the staff were lunching with him after a

meeting in Canterbury when bombs exploded close by without warning: the two archdeacons darted under the table, the chaplain to a recess in the wall, another crouched behind a chair, but the Archbishop sat upright in his place, merely remarking, 'You are all behaving in a very strange way.'[139]

Following Dunkirk, a German invasion was widely feared. The army drew up contingency plans to transport Lang from Canterbury to a house near Farnham, as they did not want him falling into the hands of German invaders. Lang expressed a reluctance to abandon his diocese, and said he would not budge unless he was told that an invasion was imminently expected and was ordered to leave by the army.[140]

Sir Alan Lascelles, assistant private secretary to George VI, told Don that in 1940 the king and Churchill 'seriously considered' awarding the George Medal to 'that brave old man at Lambeth' in recognition of Lang's wartime role, but in the end they did not do so as Lang 'would not have wished for such a mark of Royal favour.'[141]

During the summer of 1941, Lang began to feel that he ought to resign. He discussed resignation privately with Fisher, Garbett and Bishop Herbert of Norwich, and with Churchill, who thought he ought to remain until the victory.[142] Lang was unconvinced:

> [I experienced] the growing conviction that these tremendous times called for qualities of mind and spirit in such leadership as the Archbishopric involves which I could not expect to have in my age – in my 78th year. It had become clear that this awful war would last longer than had once been expected – at least till say 1944. I would then be 80. And indeed before the end of the war, great problems of reconstruction in Church and State would emerge which a man of that age could not be expected to tackle. If so, the man who would be reponsible for meeting those problems *then* ought to be preparing for them *now*. And there was the next Lambeth Conference due to meet as soon as possible after the war ... Two things were plain: one, that *I* would be too old to preside

over such a Conference; the other, that he who would preside ought now to be in a position to prepare.[143]

On 21 January 1942, Lang announced to Convocation his decision to resign. His last official duty was to confirm Princesses Elizabeth and Margaret on 28 March 1942.[144] He was succeeded, as he wished, by Temple.

Temple did not inherit a Church of England on its knees, but rather one which under Lang's guidance had survived and surmounted some of the worst years of the Second World War. Lang had ministered during a period when a German invasion was daily expected. By the time Temple succeeded Lang, Hitler had invaded the USSR and the USA had entered the war. An Allied victory was distant, but inevitable. Between 1939 and 1942, the Church of England under Lang had neither compromised nor discredited itself and its reputation was intact. It is surely significant that neither Temple (archbishop 1942–44) nor later Fisher (1945–61) appear to have greatly departed, during the rest of the war, from the patterns already established by Lang.

Reading Lang's speeches about war aims and the post-war settlement, it is hard to sustain the image of him as an embarrassing relic of a bygone age, with nothing relevant left to say. Nor does Edward Carpenter's claim that Lang avoided 'minutiae, routine business and domestic chores' stand up to closer examination.[145] Carpenter also alleged that Lang's 'main preoccupation, except in matters of extreme and self-evident concern for the Church, was never to embarrass the Government'. It is true that Lang did not deliberately seek to embarrass the government, but in wartime, and particularly when things were not going well for Great Britain, it would not have been wise to antagonise the government. Lang realised that he could best influence ministers quietly, behind the scenes, with a word or a letter. He was prepared when appropriate to challenge the government – for example, over bombing – and he sometimes threatened public comment, but he probably realised that the success of such archiepiscopal confrontations is in inverse proportion to their frequency. He also knew when to abandon an impossible struggle – for example, that with the government over the observance of Sunday.

Hastings has commented that between 1939 and 1945 'organised religion appeared . . . now more spiritually mature than it had in 1914–1918.'[146] This was doubtless due to several factors, but one of them must surely have been the mature and shrewd wartime leadership of Lang. Lang's 1941 quotation from Burke – 'Let us strive so to be patriots as not to forget that we are Christians'[147] – might sum up his whole attitude to the war. He felt that it must be waged and that there could be no surrender. Yet, although he proclaimed the work of the Nazis to be evil, he never demonised the German people. He was clear that his Church, whilst fully supporting the war, should not become so intertwined with the war effort that it stored up trouble for the future. He never remotely implied, for example, that the existence and goodness of God was bound up with an Allied victory. Yet Lang worked and prayed for such a victory. His omission from histories of the home front during the Second World War reflects the priorities of modern authors, but by such omissions they present an incomplete picture of wartime Britain. Far from becoming an irrelevance, pushed to the margins of national life, Lang was afforded, through the war, even greater prominence, and many more people turned to him for advice or succour.

The question is left hanging in the air: was Lang's part in the Second World War his finest hour? In wartime, the Church needs charismatic leaders who will inspire men and women in moments of pain and perplexity; but it has equal, if not greater, need of shrewd, painstaking and experienced leaders, who will remain calm under pressure and prove adaptable in changing and frequently tragic circumstances. Was the most significant achievement of Lang's primacy the way in which he held together the Church of England, and gave Christian witness to the nation, in the darkest days of the Second World War, thereby helping both to begin thinking about post-war reconstruction? The evidence suggests that it may well have been.

8

Lang's Last Days

L ANG SPENT HIS LAST FEW days as archbishop of Canterbury in a whirl of activity. As well as confirming Princesses Elizabeth and Margaret at Windsor Castle, he attended a farewell service in Canterbury Cathedral, and consecrated a bishop in St Paul's. He lunched with Don at the Athenæum on 31 March 1942, his last full day as archbishop of Canterbury. Two days later, newly ennobled as Baron Lang of Lambeth, he assisted at the Royal Maundy service in Westminster Abbey. His old chauffeur, Walter Wells, then drove Lang to spend a few days at Cuddesdon, after which he no longer had an official car. He settled at King's Cottage, Kew, a grace and favour house of some thirty rooms placed at his disposal by George VI.[1]

Lang seems to have been very happy in retirement at Kew. He was looked after by his old butler McDade and his wife, and two maids. Hilda Neal, who had worked for Lang as his secretary when he was archbishop of York, was re-engaged and became very fond of the old man. She left a description of the chapel set up by Lang in King's Cottage, where she recorded that he spent much time in prayer:

> At Kew today. The archbishop showed me his private chapel, just finished. Very much larger than I'd expected, big enough to hold 2–3 dozen people at a squeeze. Quite a large imposing altar, draped in blue damask and gold, with side wings, whitewashed walls, white, the lower part curtained in rose and gold-thread damask. The Sistine Madonna was over the fireplace, and a smaller Madonna in gilt over the left wall. There were some small oak seats and a prie-dieu: big windows, so quite light, but it all looked

rather formal and new. It will be better when it has been more used by household and visitors and the newness has faded a bit.[2]

Hilda Neal noted that Lang found his first few weeks at Kew very difficult, but he quickly settled down.[3] He pressed Churchill to consider Temple as his successor and was most thankful when he was appointed. Lang did not appear to pine for the archbishopric, nor did he interfere with his successor's administration. He visited Ballure, assisted occasionally in Kew parish church, preached at special services, wrote a little biography *Tupper* about his friend Canon A.D. Tupper-Carey, and broadcast twice on the BBC.[4] Lang's close relationship and emotional dependency upon Ann Todd continued after his retirement. He even took Don to see her in a play, and a little over a fortnight before his death wrote to her, '*Do* come . . . I do so much want to see you again.'[5]

Kew Gardens were another source of continual pleasure to Lang. Don recorded:

> To Kew for a walk and tea with C.C. – the gardens are lovely, though the apple-cherry blossom is past its best. C.C. as comic as ever. Addressing a rhododendron named 'Isabella Manglar' which was beginning to fade, he said: 'O my dear Isabella – you are going all to bits. How pitiable – how pitiable. O dear me,' etc. We had some talk at tea about my affairs – my name has evidently been mentioned in connection with the impending vacancy at St George's, Windsor, along with others no doubt – he is a very human, understanding creature. I shall miss him greatly when he is gone – but he shows no sign of going yet! And I may go before him – who knows?[6]

Lang was devastated by Temple's death on 26 October 1944 and told Don it was 'the most severe test of his faith in Providence that he has ever experienced'. On his eightieth birthday, he attended Temple's funeral in Canterbury. According to some sources, Lang believed that Temple had been killed by his job and he was overheard muttering that he would have stayed on as archbishop himself if he had known Temple would die so soon. Churchill sent Anthony Bevir, his appointments secretary, to see Lang to discuss the vacant archbishopric and Lang recommended Fisher.[7]

Lang had long possessed a parsimonious streak. In 1941, Don noted that 'it is with the utmost reluctance that he parts with 2/9 for his lunch and 2/- for a taxi – he thinks he is thereby heading for bankruptcy.' Lang had always been poor at mathematics – he used to joke that the three things he had never mastered were mathematics, cricket and marriage – and as his retirement approached he formed the misapprehension that he would soon be hard up, which he mentioned to a number of people. In truth, Lang was comfortably off, thanks to his pension, an insurance policy and some financial help from his friend J.P. Morgan. However, old habits died hard and in retirement Lang reverted to being what he called a 'bus and bag Bishop', as he had been in his Stepney days, travelling around London by public transport rather than in a hired car. 'My Scottish nature revolts', he once wrote, 'against paying ten pounds for a car when I can go to the House of Lords and back for one and sixpence.'[8]

His parsimony was to prove Lang's final undoing. On 5 December 1945, he was visited by Mrs Lionel Ford, the May Talbot of his far distant days as a curate in Leeds. As she was leaving, she asked Lang if he would say a prayer in his chapel for her son Christopher, who had been killed in Italy in the war. This delayed Lang's departure for Kew Gardens underground station. Unbeknownst to Mrs Ford – and indeed to Lockhart – Lang had arranged to see Ann Todd that afternoon. After Mrs Ford had driven off, Lang began to hurry up the hill to Kew Gardens underground station. The exertion brought on a heart attack and Lang collapsed outside a fishmonger's shop. The customers found him a chair. Lang kept repeating, 'I must get to the station, I must get to the station,' and soon became unconscious. A passing police car was flagged down and took him to Richmond Hospital. A doctor said that Lang was dead, but the hospital refused to accept his corpse, so the police unloaded it at the public mortuary. Lang's old friend Lumley Green-Wilkinson managed to retrieve Lang's body and took it back to King's Cottage. The waiting Ann Todd heard the news from Mrs Opie, Lang's former housekeeper, who must have known of her old employer's attachment to the young actress.[9]

Lang's funeral was held five days later on 10 December 1945 in Westminster Abbey, whilst a Requiem Eucharist was simultaneously celebrated in Canterbury Cathedral. His body was taken to Canterbury for another service in the cathedral, after which it was cremated. Lang's ashes rested overnight in the chapel in the Old Palace. On the morning of 11 December, they were taken to the chapel of Our Lady Undercroft in the cathedral, where another Requiem was celebrated, and then he was finally laid to rest in the St Stephen's Chapel in the north transept.

There is often no clear logic to explain the way in which reputations are formed or coagulate. Much of a man's life passes unseen, save by a very few people. His reputation will be based on a comparatively small part – one might say, a sliver – of his life. He will largely be judged on the basis of a few of his words and deeds, successes and mistakes, and these not always accurately remembered. Additionally, figures from the past are often perceived through an existing film of hopes or prejudices. Historians and writers frequently repeat what other people have written, without checking sources or accuracy, and these views are then accepted as 'fact'. The old English proverb, 'Give a dog a bad name', applies to the reputations of men and women.

By the time that Lockhart's biography, *Cosmo Gordon Lang*, was published in 1949, Lang was becoming a distant and fading memory. Something similar happened in the case of Stanley Baldwin. Few people after 1945 were interested in looking back to the 1930s, the decade of unemployment, the abdication, dictators and appeasement. Lang's reputation has suffered unfairly in the sixty years since his death, in part because of a largely unquestioning tradition of prejudice.

Lang's reputation has also suffered because of the view, held by some writers, of twentieth-century secularisation as an inevitable and unstoppable force.[10] If Christianity was believed to be in terminal decline, the corollary must have been that an archbishop, especially such a complex one as Cosmo Lang, was a largely irrelevant figure to much of the population. This book has provided grounds for challenging that perception of Lang. The picture that has emerged is more complex than a simple narrative of secularisation would allow. Lang's papers at Lambeth

Palace show that the archbishop expected to comment widely on public affairs, and not to be limited to the realm of the purely ecclesiastical. Furthermore, many other people expected the archbishop of Canterbury to behave in this way. Malcolm Macdonald, minister of health, for example, sought a public expression of archiepiscopal support for the government's policy of evacuation at the start of the Second World War, in the expectation that this would somehow encourage families to take in evacuees. Many of the members of the government, royal household, civil service, the professions and senior military figures with whom Lang corresponded shared a common Christian upbringing and language with him, as Hugh Mcleod has observed.[11] It is impossible to quantify their individual degree of commitment to Christianity, but they all treated the archbishop of Canterbury with a great deal of respect and tried to answer his questions, often by return of post. Likewise, there is no way of understanding the religious views of the proverbial man on the Clapham omnibus, unless he wrote them down somewhere, but the files at Lambeth contain many letters from ordinary people to Lang, seeking his help or advice, and they would hardly have written if they felt that the archbishop or Christianity was a complete irrelevance to their lives. Following the declaration of war on 3 September 1939, Lang's post dried up for a few weeks, and then after the initial shock had worn off, the letters started arriving in ever greater numbers: an indication that, amidst the turmoil and disruption of war, the thoughts of many people still turned to the occupant of Lambeth Palace.

Was Great Britain still a consciously Christian society in the inter-war period, as Callum Brown has argued? The answer must surely be a qualified 'Yes'; or at least a recognition that British culture and national identity were still predominantly Christian, and, in England, Anglican. Churchgoing peaked at the start of Lang's archiepiscopate and then began its gradual decline. But some Christian values were widely shared, even amongst those who were usually absent from the pews on Sunday. The most obvious of these was marriage. The majority of Britons between the wars married rather than cohabited. Divorce was a comparative rarity, and, in most cases, marriage was for life. Edward VIII had to abdicate because he ignored this convention. Had he married someone suitable like Lady Rosemary Leveson-Gower,[12] the royal household and government might have concealed his weaknesses. But by choosing to marry a twice-divorced woman with both husbands still living, the king broke with the commonly held view of marriage. Baldwin and Lang saw that, in consequence, Edward VIII had to abdicate, because if he kept his throne and married Mrs Simpson, he would have become a divisive figure in Church and state.

The Church of England remained an important part of English national life and identity throughout Lang's archiepiscopate. The government certainly did not regard the Established Church as one voice clamouring amongst many other, equal, religious voices, but instead afforded the Church of England special consideration. One instance of this was the coronation of George VI in 1937. Lang believed that 'the ceremony is the Consecration of the English King by the English Church in accordance with ancient English rites.' When English Nonconformists and the Church of Scotland asked for a role in the service, Lang took the view that the coronation was set within an Anglican Eucharist, and that conseqently 'it would not be consistent with due ecclesial order that any minister not qualified by his Ordination should take part in it.' The Coronation Executive Committee and prime minister's office accepted the archbisop's contention without demur.[13] Similarly, during the Second World War, Lang expected the government to be concerned for the maintenance of the Church of England's parochial ministry. For its part, the government did everything that the archbishop asked to ensure an adequate supply of ordinands. The government even shared items of confidential wartime information with Lang. The overall picture that emerges from this study of Lang is of a Church of England that was woven into the fabric of English life and identity. Perhaps for many people, the strands were very loose and becoming looser, but nonetheless they still existed.

This book has sought to demonstrate that Cosmo Lang mattered far more than has generally been understood. It is important to note that Lang's handling of the crises surrounding the abdication of Edward VIII, the Revised Prayer Book, and the Second World War bore fruit not just during his archiepiscopate, but also after he had retired. For a start, Lang closely supported Baldwin during the abdication crisis, suggested a course of action to him and tried to help him put it into action. Lang's concept of the ideal expression of monarchy undoubtedly stemmed from his experience of the court of Queen Victoria. His handling of George V's silver jubilee in 1935 and death in 1936, and the coronation of George VI and Queen Elizabeth in 1937 helped to promote a popular view of the British monarchy as something good and benign, the embodiment of Christian duty and service. During the testing years of the Second World War, George VI and Queen Elizabeth fulfilled this image and proved figures around whom the nation could unite.

All Churches are complicated organisations and the twentieth-century Church of England often seemed particularly so. Whilst Roman Catholicism and Eastern Orthodoxy contained divisions and differences, their members for the most part agreed about the basic tenets of their common faith. By Lang's time, the Church of England had come to contain people holding diametrically opposite views, especially where such subjects as the Real Presence and eucharistic sacrifice were concerned. The clash over the 1928 Prayer Book, though it focused on liturgy, was actually a tussle for the identity of the Church of England. Like Tait, Benson, Frederick Temple and Davidson before him, Lang adopted an attitude of being above the fray. He promoted a vision of one Church, containing many mutually enriching strands. Himself an Anglo-Catholic, Lang never used his office to favour Anglo-Catholics over evangelicals or liberals, although he was sensitive to the needs and problems of Anglo-Catholicism. His aim was to hold the Church together and encourage Anglicans of differing hues to talk together and find a way of rubbing along. It might not have been exactly satisfactory from an intellectual point of view, but the twentieth-century Church of England often seemed to cope by simply muddling along. Lang's Church did hang together, and by his retirement the problems of 1928 seemed very outdated.

On the whole, the Church of England emerged from the Second World War with very little for which to reproach itself. It had learnt the lessons of 1914–18 and was more mature Church. One of the undoubted reasons for this was Lang's wartime leadership. To echo a song from the previous war, Lang kept the home fires burning and did so very successfully. His personal pastoral nature and administrative ability came to the fore between 1939 and 1942. He helped the Church to readjust and cope with changed and changing situations, and he dealt sensitively with a variety of thorny pastoral issues. Temple and Fisher may be said to have endorsed Lang's policies by largely continuing them for the remainder of the war. Lang also made good use of the opportunities presented by the war to offer sensible Christian teaching and reflection in sermons and broadcasts. He upheld the nation's war effort, even after 1940 when some voices called for a negotiated settlement, and he believed the conflict must be continued until the twin evils of Nazism and Fascism were overcome. At the same time, Lang taught clearly that there were levels of moral behaviour below which it was not safe to sink, even in the pursuit of victory. He also managed to avoid saying anything that might be seen as endorsing the Soviet regime. Lang was the first to insist that the Church must not wait until the victory to begin preparing for the post-war world, but should begin its planning whilst the conflict was still being waged.

According to Hastings, there was something of a feeling of revival in the Church of England for about twelve years after the end of the Second World War.[14] If some parts of the Church were left feeling run down, other parts experienced numerical growth and a burgeoning sense of confidence. The literary and intellectual life of the Church certainly seemed healthy.[15] This outcome could probably not have happened in the way that it did if the Church of England had had a bad war, and had emerged into the peace more divided than before, unable to cope with post-war realities and saddled with an accumulation of extremist wartime sermons and statements which had seemed acceptable at the time but now appeared inexcusable after the war. Archbishop Lang, quietly getting on with the bread-and-butter work of keeping the machinery going, must take the credit for at least part of what led the Church of England, by contrast, to have a good war.

For all that, a certain sadness attaches itself to the character of Cosmo Lang. When showing some visitors the famous portrait of him by Orpen, he said, 'It is a portrait of a very hardworking, very well-meaning, very lonely and very disappointed man.'[16] One suspects that, to adapt a phrase of Stanley Baldwin about the monarchy, Lang's life as archbishop of Canterbury was really rather a dog's life. He sat at the top of an ecclesiastical pyramid, the focus of all sorts of unrealistic hopes and expectations, trying to hold together and to guide his Church, and coping with an unenviable workload. Lang's workaholism and loneliness would have conspired to make this a circle from which it was difficult to break out. The contrast with the teenage Lang's hopes of a glittering career and full family life, expressed in his spoof *Who's Who* entry, is stark and sad. As archbishop of Canterbury, Lang simply kept going, doing his best for long hours, day by day, filled with an almost Calvinistic sense of duty and obligation.

In the Introduction, it was noted that W.R. Matthews wrote in 1949 that if posterity understood the conditions of the time in which Lang lived, it would certainly say that he had been a great archbishop of Canterbury. Was Lang a great archbishop of Canterbury? Probably not. Great archbishops, like great diocesan bishops, are comparatively rare. If Lang was not a great archbishop, he was undoubtedly a good archbishop, and one might even go so far as to say, a very good archbishop. It was hardly his fault that he was appointed archbishop of York too soon, and translated to Canterbury too late in life. His principal difficulty was that he was both a loner and a workaholic. If devotion to duty is a sign of goodness, then he was undoubtedly a good primate. The machinery of ecclesiastical government which he inherited was ramshackle. Too much fell upon his shoulders, so that his burden was indeed 'incredible, indefensible and inevitable'.

Lang does not deserve the bad reputation which has been unfairly accorded him in the sixty years since his death. The greatest problem, as far as Lang's reputation was concerned, was his complex personality. Yet for all that, he was a very human figure, a caring pastor, sensitive to the needs and pains of others. Let almost the last word go to Alan Don, the man who arguably knew Lang the closest whilst he was at Canterbury. Learning on 15 January 1942 of Lang's decision to resign, he wrote:

> Over to Lambeth at 8pm to see C.C. He looks very well – much better than he did ten years ago and it seems a pity that he should be resigning – but he has made up his mind that in the interests of the Church he ought to make way for a younger, more forward-looking man – and I think he is right, all things considered. But I am wretched at the thought of his going – for Lambeth and The

Old Palace have been real homes to me for the past ten years and it has been a great experience to serve so 'intriguing' a Chief. Those who serve him become increasingly devoted to him, strange as it may seem to those who only know him in his difficult moods. His 'funny' ways (as A.J.C. says: 'He is a funny man'), his 'surface irritation' (to which he frequently refers), his complex character, his mingled childishness and consummate ability, his warm heart concealed beneath an entirely undemonstrative exterior, his elaborateness and simplicity, his not fully regenerate humanity – all combine to make him an intensely interesting and indeed unique being, the like of whom I shall not meet again.

I never regret for one moment that I so strangely joined him in 1931 – and I think that I have been able to help him just a little in ways he appreciates.

It is not everyone who could have lived perfectly happily with him for ten years – but after all we are both Scotsmen![17]

It would be hard to disagree with Lockhart's conclusion that if Lang failed to solve all of the problems that he had inherited, at least he left the Church of England in better shape in 1942 than it had been when he became archbishop in 1928.[18] Many another archbishop might yearn for such an epitaph.

APPENDIX 1

'Cosmo Gordon Lange'

Spoof *Who's Who* entry written by Cosmo Lang when a teenager, printed in J.G. Lockhart, *Cosmo Gordon Lang*, London, 1949, 460–61 (It has not been possible to trace Lang's original manuscript).

William Cosmo Gordon Lange was born on the 31st of October 1864. His parents were the well-known Dr. Marshall Lang, of the Barony Church, Glasgow, and Hannah Agnes, daughter of the Rev. Dr. Keith, Minister of Hamilton. His birthplace was Fyvie, Aberdeenshire, where his father was clergyman, and where his godfather, Col. Gordon of Fyvie Castle, resided. His father then became Minister of Anderston Church, Glasgow, to w. city the family removed. Morningside Church, Edinburgh, was his father's next appointment, where the family resided for four years. Dr. Marshall Lang was then appointed successor to Dr. Norman McLeod in the Barony Church of Glasgow. Cosmo in Glasgow attended the school of the historian Dr. W.F. Collier, for whom he always had a great regard. Thence, at the somewhat early age of 14, he went to Glasgow University. There, after a successful career of four years, he graduated as Master of Arts. He then went up to Cambridge, graduated there, and entered the Law Classes of Glasgow University for three years. Taking the degree of LL.D., he was called to the Scotch Bar in 1888, aged 23 years. His business at the Bar being not at first remunerative, he turned to literature, where he achieved a marvellous success as novelist, poet, historian. A few leading cases fell to his care, and this, with the fortune he had made in literature, settled him comfortably at the age of 28. Then in the year 1894 he married the younger daughter of the Earl of Kintore. Aged 30, he stepped forward into politics as candidate for North Ayrshire against the Liberal candidate. It was a Liberal seat, and he lost the contest. Fortune was kinder in a little, and in the General Election of 1897 he gained the seat for the Conservatives. At once he was a marked man. He moved the Address of 1897, and in a few months was Lord Beaconsfield's secretary. In the year 1900 he became Under-Secretary of State for Ireland. In 1902 he became Under-Secy. for Foreign Affairs. During the severe illness of Lord Salisbury in 1903–04 he acted temp. Secretary, was appointed Secy. of State for War in 1907, Lord Claverton in the same year, Secy. for Foreign Affairs in 1908, Earl of Norham and Prime Minister in 1912. His career has been one long success. In literature, in oratory, in statesmanship, he has been equally successful, and equally admired.

The Rt. Hon. William Cosmo Gordon, Earl of Norham, K.T., D.C.L., LL.D.
Emily, sister to the Rt. Hon. The Earl of Kintore, Countess of Norham.

1. Lady Emily Gordon Lange, now Her Grace the Duchess of Richmond and Gordon, b. 1895. M.1916. has issue – Alexander Douglas Gordon, Marquis of Gordon.
2. Hon. William Cosmo Gordon Lange, Viscount Claverton, b. 1897.
3. Hon. Douglas Kintore Marshall Gordon Lange, b. 1899.
4. Lady Anne Mary Keith Gordon Lange, b. 1900.
5. Hon. Keith Gordon Lange, R.N., b. 1901.
6. Hon. Norman Hamilton Gordon Lange, b. 1902.
7. Lady Hannah Buchanan Gordon Lange, b. 1903, d. 1910.
8. Hon. George Victor Albert Gordon Lange, b. 1905.

Seats: Norham Hall, nr. Norham, Norfolkshire.
Claverton Park, nr. Calne, Wiltshire.
Glendonald Castle, by Oban, Argyllshire.

Town Address: 10 Downing Street. Carlton Club, Conservative Club, Beaconsfield Club, Literary Club, London.

APPENDIX 2

'Past and Present'

The text of Archbishop Lang's broadcast on Edward VIII's abdication, 10 December 1936, Lang Papers, volume 271, folios 209–16.

During the last ten days we have seen strange things. Very rarely in the long course of its history has this Nation passed through a week of such bewilderment, suspense, anxiety. Within twenty-four hours one King went and another King came. Yet there has been no confusion, no strife, no clash of parties. Truly it has been a wonderful proof of the strength and stability of the Throne. It has been an even more striking proof of the steadiness of the people of this country and throughout the Empire. It seems as if some strong tide of instinct rather than of reasoned thought, flowing deep beneath the surface eddies of excitement, has borne them through the rapids of the crisis. It is right to be proud of the way in which the Nation has stood the test. Yet let there be no boasting in our pride. Rather let it pass into humble and reverent thankfulness for this renewed token of the guidance of the Nation's life by the over-ruling Providence of our God.

What pathos, nay, what tragedy, surrounds the central figure of these swiftly moving scenes! On the eleventh day of December 248 years ago King James II fled from Whitehall. By a strange coincidence on the eleventh day of December last week King Edward VIII, after speaking his last words to his people, left Windsor Castle, the centre of all the splendid traditions of his ancestors and his Throne, and went out into exile. In the darkness he left these shores.

Seldom if ever has any British Sovereign come to the Throne with greater natural gifts for his Kingship. Seldom if ever has any Sovereign been welcomed by a more enthusiastic loyalty. From God he received a high and sacred trust. Yet by his own will he has abdicated – he has surrendered the trust. With characteristic frankness he has told us his motive. It was a craving for private happiness. Strange and sad it must be that for such a motive, however strongly it pressed upon his heart, he should have disappointed hopes so high, and abandoned a trust so great. Even more strange and sad it is that he should have sought his happiness in a manner inconsistent with the Christian principles of marriage, and within a social circle whose standards and ways of life are alien to all the best instincts and traditions of his people. Let those who belong to this circle know that today they stand rebuked by the judgement of the Nation which had loved King Edward. I have shrunk from saying these words, but I have felt compelled for the sake of sincerity and truth to say them.

Yet for one who has known him from childhood, who has felt his charm and admired his gifts, these words cannot be the last. How can we forget the high hopes and promise of his youth, his *most* genuine care for the poor, the suffering, the unemployed, his years of eager service both at home and across the seas? It is the remembrance of those things that wrings from our hearts the cry – "The pity of it. O the pity of it!" To the infinite mercy and protecting care of God we commit him, wherever he may be.

There are two other figures who will always stand out among the memories of those fateful days. One is our ever honoured and beloved Queen Mary. She knows, for in her moving message she has told us so, that the respectful sympathy of the whole Nation and Empire surrounds her. During all the strain of tense anxiety, deep as her distress has been, her wonderful calmness, self-control, steadiness of judgement have never failed. The thought of her Reign by the side of her beloved husband for twenty-five years, of the sorrow which came to her when he passed from her sight, and of the fresh sorrow which within less than a year she has had to bear is a threefold cord which binds her fast to the hearts of her People.

The other person who has earned our gratitude and admiration is the Prime Minister. With great courage he took the whole burden on himself. As one to whom throughout all these anxieties he has given his confidence I can personally testify that he has combined, as perhaps only he could, the Constitutional responsibility of a Minister, the human understanding of a man, and the faithfulness of a friend. History will record he was the pilot who by God's help steered the Ship of State through difficult currents, through dangerous rocks and shoals into the harbour where it now safely rests.

So much for the past, and now the future. The darkness of an anxious time is over. A new morning has dawned. A new Reign has begun. George VI is King. You can readily imagine what it means to him to be summoned so suddenly, so unexpectedly, in circumstances so painful to himself – for he was bound to his brother by ties of closest affection – to face the immense responsibilities of Kingship. Sympathy with him there must be, deep and real and personal. But it passes into loyalty, a loyalty all the more eager, strong and resolute because it rises from this heart of sympathy. It is this wholehearted loyalty which with one mind and voice the peoples of this Realm and Empire offer him today. He will prove worthy of it.

What I shall venture to say of him will be no mere conventional eulogy. It will be said from the personal knowledge – I am sure he would allow me to say – of many years of friendship.

In manner of speech he is more quiet and reserved than his brother (And may I here add a parenthesis which may not be unhelpful. When his people listen to him they will note an occasional momentary hesitation in his speech. But he has brought it into full control, and to those who hear, it need cause no sort of embarrassment for it causes none to him who speaks). He is frank, straightforward, unaffected. The six thousand boys from our Public schools and from the homes of working folk whom for the last fifteen years he has gathered in the comradeship of a Summer Camp know that he has been himself a boy among them. In the varied fields of service – in the Navy, in the Air Force, in association with all manner of public and charitable causes – he has gained a wide experience. He has made the welfare of industrial workers his special care and study. There is no branch of industry where he is not at home. In his visits with the Queen to Central Africa, to Australia and New Zealand he has studied the peoples and problems of the great Empire over which he is now called to rule. He has high ideals of life and duty, and he will pursue them with a quiet steadfastness of will. He inherits the name, he will follow the example, of King George V to whose memory let us offer now the homage of our undying affection and respect.

No passage in the last message of the Duke of Windsor, as we must now learn to call our late King, was more touching than that in which he spoke of his brother's "matchless blessing – a happy home with wife and children." King George will have at his side the gentle strength and quiet wisdom of a wife who has already endeared herself to all by her grace, her charm, her bright eager kindliness of heart. As for her dear children, I will only say that they are as delightful and fascinating as she was in her own childhood as I remember it over thirty years ago. Truly it is good to think that among all the homes of the Empire – the homes from which all that is best within it springs – none can be more happy and united than the home of our King and Queen.

A King has gone. God be with him. A King has come. God bless him, keep him, guide him now and ever.

Only a few moments are left in which to say what I had most chiefly wished to say. I must now reserve it for the message which I hope to broadcast a fortnight hence on the last Sunday of the year. My desire is then, if God will help me, to make to the Nation a somewhat solemn Recall to Religion. Who can doubt that in all the events of these memorable days God has been speaking. It has been a time of shaking – a shaking, in possibility, thank God not in fact, of the very Throne itself; a shaking of confidence, of seemingly assured hopes. Is there not a call to us to see that "those things which cannot be shaken may remain" – Faith in God, in His Will, in His Kingdom? We are all rallying to our new King. Will there not also be a rally to the King of Kings? There is I am pursuaded a real deep instinct of religion in the heart of the people. But instinct if it is to hold in times of stress such as these in which we are now living must be made strong by conviction and kindled by conscious faith. We still call ourselves a Christian Nation. But if the title is to be a reality and not a mere phrase, there must be a renewal in our midst of definite and deliberate allegiance to Christ – to His standards of life, to the principles of His Kingdom. We are now able to look forward with hope and joy to the Coronation of our King. He himself and his

Kingship will then be most solemnly consecrated to the service of the Most High God. But the august ceremony will be bereft of a great part of its true meaning unless it is accompanied by a new consecration of his people to the same high service. So may King and people alike acknowledge their allegiance to God and dedicate themselves to seek first His Kingdom and His Righteousness. "Wherefore we receiving a kingdom which cannot be moved, let us have grace whereby we may serve God acceptably with reverence and godly fear."

Glossary

Anglo-Catholic Someone who believes the Church of England to be the historic Catholic Church of the land (*Anglo*-Catholic instead of *Roman* Catholic), and stresses the Church of England's essential continuity with the pre-Reformation English Church. Anglo-Catholics emphasise the doctrinal, ecclesiological, sacramental and liturgical aspects of Christianity, and have generally sought agreement and ultimately unity with Roman Catholicism and Eastern Orthodoxy.

Benediction A eucharistic devotion in which a consecrated wafer is displayed in a special container called a monstrance. The Blessed Sacrament is honoured with incense, portions of hymns are sung, scripture read and prayer offered. The people are blessed as the sign of the Cross is made over them by the priest with the monstrance.

Charge An address delivered by a bishop, archdeacon, or other senior cleric to those under his authority.

Churchmanship The different strands of theology and spirituality to be found within the Church of England. Broadly speaking, these are Anglo-Catholicism, evangelicalism, and liberalism, sometimes known as modernism.

Kensitite A follower of John Kensit (1853–1902), a Protestant propagandist and agitator, who in the late 1890s orchestrated an increasingly violent campaign of prosecution and intimidation of Anglo-Catholic priests and parishes. He died in Liverpool after being injured in a fracas.

Nonconformist A member of the Protestant churches and chapels that have separated from the Church of England; for example, Baptists, Congregationalists, Methodists, Presbyterians (in England), Quakers, etc.

Suffragan bishop A bishop who assists a diocesan bishop in a diocese.

Thirty-Nine Articles The set of formulae dealing with issues of dogma passed by Convocation in 1563 as the Elizabethan Church of England grappled with its own identity vis-à-vis Roman Catholicism and continental Protestantism.

Tractarian An Anglican inspired by the *Tracts for the Times*, published between 1833 and 1845 by J.H. Newman, E.B. Pusey, John Keble and others, to propagate the Oxford Movement (also known as the Catholic Revival), an intellectual movement which opposed theological liberalism within the Church of England and stressed its Catholic inheritance and identity. Later followers became known as Anglo-Catholics.

Uniat Eastern Churches which are in full communion with the pope, whilst retaining their own liturgical traditions, language, canon law, married clergy, etc.

Short Biographies

These outline biographies are intended to give some background information on people who were important in Lang's life, but are perhaps less familiar to readers.

Edward White Benson (1829–96), archbishop of Canterbury 1883–96. While bishop of Truro (1877–82), he devised the Christmas festival of Nine Lessons and Carols. As archbishop, Benson was forced to revive the 'Court of the Archbishop of Canterbury' in 1889 to try Edward King, bishop of Lincoln, for alleged ritual offences. In the subsequent 'Lincoln Judgement' (1890), he largely upheld Bishop King and ruled that many traditional Catholic liturgical practices were compatible with the Book of Common Prayer, ignoring previous decisions by secular courts and the Judicial Committee of the Privy Council.

Randall Thomas Davidson (1848–1930), archbishop of Canterbury 1903–28. The son of Scottish Presbyterian parents, he converted to Anglicanism whilst a schoolboy at Harrow. He became a chaplain to A.C. Tait (archbishop of Canterbury 1868–82, a fellow Scot and convert to Anglicanism). Queen Victoria appointed Davidson dean of Windsor in 1881. In 1891 he became bishop of Rochester, before being translated to Winchester in 1895, and Canterbury in 1903. Cosmo Lang got on very well with Davidson during his time as archbishop of York (1908–28), and, succeeding Davidson at Canterbury, ministered to him on his deathbed in 1930.

Alan Campbell Don (1885–1966), priest and diarist. Originally from Dundee, Don studied at Cuddesdon and was ordained in the Church of England. He returned to Scotland to be provost of the Episcopal cathedral in Dundee. Between 1931–41 he was chaplain and private secretary to Cosmo Lang at Lambeth Palace. Don became a chaplain to the king, and also chaplain to the speaker. In 1941 he was made a canon of Westminster and rector of St Margaret's Church, Westminster. Between 1946 and 1959 Don was dean of Westminster. His marriage to his wife Muriel was rather unhappy: she stayed away when he suffered a heart attack at Lambeth Palace, and Don was cared for by Cosmo Lang and Martha Saville, Lang's indefatigable Cockney housemaid.

Geoffrey Francis Fisher (1887–1972), archbishop of Canterbury 1945–61. Fisher was the son of an Anglican priest. He was ordained in 1913 and became headmaster of Repton School the following year. Fisher was never a parish priest. He became bishop of Chester in 1932, and was translated to London in 1939, to succeed Winnington-Ingram, who had been the bishop since 1900 and left behind rather a muddle. Fisher became archbishop of Canterbury in 1945 following the unexpected death of William Temple. Always a somewhat headmasterly figure, Fisher was first and foremost an administrator and began the revision of Canon Law.

Cyril Foster Garbett (1875–1955), archbishop of York 1942–55. Garbett was the son of an Anglican priest. He was ordained in 1899 and went as curate to St Mary's Church, Portsea, where he stayed for twenty years, becoming the vicar in 1909. In 1919 he was appointed bishop of Southwark, and in 1932 was translated to Winchester. He succeeded William Temple as archbishop of York in 1942.

Alexander (Alec) Henry Louis Hardinge (1894–1960). After serving in the Grenadier Guards in the First World War, where he won the Military Cross, Hardinge was appointed assistant private secretary to George V in 1920, working with Sir Clive Wigram, the king's private secretary. In 1936 Hardinge was appointed private secretary to Edward VIII, but became disillusioned with the king. He was retained as private secretary by George VI upon his accession in 1936, but the two did not always see eye to eye and Hardinge retired in 1943, aged 49.

Herbert Hensley Henson (1863–1947), Fellow of All Souls College, Oxford, clergyman, diarist and controversialist. Henson was the son of English Nonconformist parents. He was ordained in the Church of England in 1887. After dallying briefly with Anglo-Catholicism, Henson became a theological modernist of a highly individualist kind. He was a gifted writer and preacher, and commented publicly on affairs of Church, state and society. Politically, Henson was a Conservative. Personally, he was a kind and witty man, but could also be very caustic: his diaries had to be carefully expurgated before they were published as *Retrospect of an Unimportant Life*. Henson became bishop of Hereford in 1917 and was translated to Durham in 1920.

William Temple (1881–1944), the only son of an archbishop of Canterbury (Frederick Temple, archbishop 1897–1902) also to have become archbishop. Temple combined great intelligence with an avuncular, down-to-earth charm. He established his reputation with a series of books on philosophy, theology and the New Testament. He became bishop of Manchester in 1921 and was translated to York in 1928, following Lang's appointment to Canterbury. The two men quickly established a close working relationship (something that not all archbishops of Canterbury and York have managed): Lang habitually addressed Temple as 'My dear William', and Temple affectionately pulled Lang's leg from time to time. In 1942 Temple published his most famous work, *Christianity and the Social Order*, setting out his vision for post-war society. Lang sought to ensure that he was succeeded at Canterbury by Temple, and he was devastated when Temple died after only eighteen months in office. At Temple's funeral, Lang was overheard saying sadly that he would willingly have soldiered on himself as archbishop of Canterbury if that might have preserved the younger man's life.

Clive Wigram (1873–1960). Wigram served as assistant private secretary to George V between 1910 and 1931, when he succeeded Lord Stamfordham as private secretary to the king. He was ennobled as Baron Wigram of Clewer in 1935. Following the death of George V and accession of Edward VIII in 1936, Wigram, like other members of the royal household, remained in office for the first six months of the new king's reign. He retired in June 1936 and was succeeded by Alec Hardinge. Wigram returned to act as temporary private secretary to George VI for the first three months of 1937 whilst Hardinge recovered his health after the strain of the abdication crisis.

Notes

1 INTRODUCTION

1 Dr G. Hughes to the Rev. A.C. Don, 11 Nov. 1949: LPL, MS 1469, f. 173. W.R. Matthews, press cutting of a review of *Cosmo Gordon Lang*, 1949: LPL, MS 1469, f. 199, pasted into book. Newspaper unknown.
2 Diary of the Rev. A.C. Don, 29 Dec. 1942. Sir E. Ford, interview, 19 Oct. 2001.
3 A. Hastings, *A History of English Christianity, 1920–2000* (London, 2001), 251–2, 255.
4 A. Wilkinson, *Dissent or Conform* (London, 1986), 261.
5 Hastings, *English Christianity*, 49. Lang to Sir L. Dibdin, Dean of Arches, 28 Feb. 1929: LP, vol. 96, f. 7.

2 FROM FYVIE TO LAMBETH: THE MAKING OF AN ARCHBISHOP

1 J.G. Lockhart, *Cosmo Gordon Lang* (London, 1949), 6.
2 Lockhart, *Lang*, 7.
3 C. Herbert, *Twenty Years as Archbishop of York* (London, 1929), 5. W. David H. Sellar, Lord Lyon King of Arms, to the author, 14 Jul. 2008.
4 Herbert, *Twenty Years*, 5. Lockhart, *Lang*, 4.
5 Lockhart, *Lang*, 14. Herbert, *Twenty Years*, 6.
6 Herbert, *Twenty Years*, 23.
7 Herbert, *Twenty Years*, 24, 37. Sir E. Ford, interview 19 Oct. 2001.
8 Lockhart, *Lang*, 42–6.
9 Herbert, *Twenty Years*, 17. LP, vol. 192, f. 171. LP, vol. 222 *passim*.
10 Lockhart, *Lang*, 75, 80.
11 See P. Dearmer, *The Parson's Handbook* (London, 1899), and some of the publications of the Alcuin Club and Henry Bradshaw Society.
12 A. Hughes, *The Rivers of the Flood: A Personal Account of the Catholic Movement in the 20th Century* (London, 1961), 46–56.
13 Lockhart, *Lang*, 67.
14 The Rev. W.A. Simons to the author, 25 Sep. 2003.

15 Lang to Anson, 28 May 1890: All Souls College, Oxford, Codrington Library, Papers of Sir William Anson, 'Lang' envelope, f. 81. Herbert, *Twenty Years*, 26.

16 Diaries of Mary (May) Catharine Ford, *née* Talbot (1887–1932), 23, 29, 30 Sep. 1891, 1 Nov. 1891, 20, 25, 26, 30 Dec. 1891, 2, 21 Jan. 1892, 7, 10 Jun. 1892. Family papers of Sir E. Ford. E. Ford, interview 16 Nov. 2001. Herbert, *Twenty Years*, 27. Lockhart, *Lang*, 100.

17 All Souls College, Oxford, Codrington Library, Papers of Sir William Anson, 'Lang' envelope, f. 196, 227. Lockhart, *Lang*, 101–2. Herbert, *Twenty Years*, 30. All Souls College, Oxford, Codrington Library, Papers of Sir William Anson, 'Lang' envelope, f. 301, 15.

18 LP, vol. 222, f. 118.

19 Herbert, *Twenty Years*, 33–40.

20 Bell to Don, 17 Oct. 1950: LPL, Bell Papers, vol. 202, f. 297. C.G. Lang, *The Opportunity of the Church of England: Lectures Delivered in the Divinity School of the University of Cambridge in 1904* (London, 1905), 45. Lockhart, *Lang*, 156. Herbert, *Twenty Years*, 44–8. Lockhart, *Lang*, 149–50, 156, 162. Lang, *Opportunity*, 33–7, 45–7, 50–1, 70–5, 127.

21 H.H. Asquith to Lang, 10 Nov. 1908: LP, vol. 189, f. 133.

22 Lang to Asquith, 11 Nov. 1908: Bod., Asquith Papers, vol. 22, f. 1. Lang to Asquith, 12 Nov. 1908: LP, vol. 22, f. 2.

23 Lockhart, *Lang*, 179–80, 193–5. LPL, Bell Papers, vol. 210, f. 199–200, 297–8.

24 LPL, Bell Papers, vol. 210, f. 297. *Vanity Fair*, 19 Apr. 1906.

25 Lockhart, *Lang*, 193–5. Herbert, *Twenty Years*, 65. Lockhart, *Lang*, 195, 214–15.

26 Borthwick Institute, York: Bp.C.&P., vol. XII, *passim*.

27 Lockhart, *Lang*, 212. Herbert, *Twenty Years*, 54, 56–66, 68, 74, 112.

28 Herbert, *Twenty Years*, 62, 85.

29 LPL, Bell Papers, vol. 210, f. 200. Lockhart, *Lang*, 229.

30 Lockhart, *Lang*, 203–4.

31 Lockhart, *Lang*, 262.

32 Herbert, *Twenty Years*, 89. Lockhart, *Lang*, 257. LPL, Bell Papers, vol. 210, f. 92, 93, 203–4.

33 Don, 10 Feb. 1932.

34 LPL, Bell Papers, vol. 210, f. 101. Lockhart, *Lang*, 268–72. LPL, Bell Papers, vol. 202, f. 297. Diary of May Ford, 31 Dec. 1927.

35 Lockhart, *Lang*, 286.

36 G.K.A. Bell, *Randall Davidson, Archbishop of Canterbury* (Oxford, 1935), 1361–4, 1366.

37 Baldwin to Lord Irwin, 15 Sep. 1927: P. Williamson and E. Baldwin (eds), *Baldwin Papers: A Conservative Statesman, 1908–1947* (Cambridge, 2004), 202. The bishop of Oxford was Thomas Strong. Arthur Cook was general-secretary of the Miners' Federation and seen by some as an extremist.

38 Lockhart, *Lang*, 310.

39 R. Ellis Roberts, *H.R.L. Sheppard: Life and Letters* (London, 1942), 186.

40 Lockhart, *Lang*, 311, 316.

41 Lockhart, *Lang*, 458.

42 Don, 28 Oct. 1938. Talbot, 7–10 Jun. 1892.

43 Talbot, 29 Nov. 1891. Don, 28 Mar. 1932, 21 Jan. 1942. Don, 28 Sep. 1938, 30 Sep. 1939, 24 Jul. 1941. Lockhart, *Lang*, 197.

44 Lockhart, *Lang*, 119, 127. There is only evidence of Lang writing a single spoof archiepiscopal signature, and not practising one frequently 'for years', as Hastings asserts in *English Christianity*, 250.

45 Don, 20 May 1931, 2 May 1932, 23 Oct. 1932, 12 Jan. 1933, 20 Apr. 1934, 30 Dec. 1940.

46 I. White-Thomson, 'Chaplain to Three Archbishops: A Study in Personalities' (unpublished text in the possession of Mrs W. White-Thomson), 3. LP, vol. 192, f. 128. H.M. Queen Elizabeth The Queen Mother, audience, 4 Dec. 2001. Don, 24, 25 Dec. 1932. White-Thompson, 'Chaplain', 3. E. Ford, interview 19 Oct. 2001; H.M. Queen Elizabeth The Queen Mother, 4 Dec. 2001; Canon D. Ingram Hill, 8 and 9 May 2002; Mr I. Watson, 10 Jul. 2002; Sir J.R. Maxwell Macdonald, 20 Aug. 2003; Lady A. Eliot, 3 Oct. 2003; Mr J. Green-Wilkinson, 11 Feb. 2004. D. Ingram Hill, interview 9 May 2002. Bishop J. Cavell to the author, 11 Sep. 2002. Lockhart, *Lang*, 215.

47 White-Thomson, 'Chaplain', 3. Don, 22, 27 May 1931, 22 Mar. 1932, 23, 31 Oct. 1932, 9 Nov. 1934, 12 Jan. 1935, 28 Oct. 1935, 14 Dec. 1935. Don, 27 May 1931, 29 Jul. 1934. Lockhart, *Lang*, 172. Don, 15 Jan. 1935, 31 May 1939.

48 Don, 9 Jan. 1938.

49 Lockhart, *Lang*, 120.

50 Lang to Crawley, 24 Mar. 1900: LPL, MS 3355, f. 46.

51 Don, 22 Nov. 1935.

52 Lockhart, *Lang*, 145–6.

53 Don, 1 Aug. 1938. Lockhart, *Lang*, 31.

54 Lang, *Opportunity*, chapter IV. *Parliamentary Debates, Lords*, 1909, vol. 4, 1234. LPL, MS 2881, f. 114. White-Thompson, 'Chaplain', 2. Don, 1 Mar. 1933, 29 Mar. 1939. E. Ford, interview 19 Oct. 2001.

55 *The Miracles of Jesus as Marks of the Way of Life* (London, 1904), *The Opportunity of the Church of England* (London, 1905), *Thoughts on Some of the Parables of Jesus* (London, 1906).

56 Lockhart, *Lang*, 383. Don, 2 Aug. 1934. White-Thompson, 'Chaplain', 3.

57 Don, 20 Jun. 1934, 15 May 1935, 30 Jun. 1935, 16 Oct. 1935, 2 Jul. 1939, 10 Oct. 1939. White-Thomson, 'Chaplain', 2.

58 LP, vols 206, 207, 210, 213, 217. Lockhart, *Lang*, 444. LP, vol. 272, f. 102, 142, 147, 213, 282.

59 J.R. Maxwell Macdonald, interview, 20 Aug. 2003.

60 LP, vol. 147, f. 366. LP, vol. 272, f. 101. LP, vol. 272, f. 181, 212.

61 J. Cavell to the author, 11 Sep. 2002.

62 LP, vol. 288, f. 29.

63 C.G. Lang, *Tupper: A Memoir of the Life and Work of a Very Human Parish Priest* (London, 1945), 9, 14, 15, 17, 19, 26, 28.

64 Lang, *Tupper*, 48–9.

65 Lang, *Tupper*, 45.

66 Lang, *Tupper*, 32, 34, 41, 46–7.

67 Lang, *Tupper*, 43–4.

68 Lang, *Tupper*, 50.

69 D.A. Bellenger and S. Fletcher, *The Mitre and the Crown: A History of the Archbishops of Canterbury* (Stroud, 2005), 158.

70 D. Starkey, *Reinventing the Royals*, Granada Bristol for Channel 4, 17 Dec. 2002. Lord Esher was a courtier of Edward VII and George V and was a secret homosexual.

71 Don, 25 Jul. 1933

72 Lockhart, *Lang*, 14. Norman Lang to Don, 29 Mar. 1946: LP, vol. 192, f. 206. LP, vol. 192, f. 120.

73 Lang to Stafford Crawley, 24 Mar, 1900: LPL, MS 3355.

74 Lockhart, *Lang*, 166; LP, vol. 192, f. 169.

75 Lockhart, *Lang*, 168. Don, 23 Jan. 1934.

76 Lang to N. Crawley, undated: LPL, MS 3207, f. 107; Lang to S. Gordon, 26 Jan. 1942: National Library of Scotland, Seton Gordon Papers, Accession 7451, box 6. O. Chadwick, *Hensley Henson: A Study in Friction Between Church and State* (Norwich, 1994), 326.

77 Ellis Roberts, *Sheppard*, 35.

78 Ellis Roberts, *Sheppard*, 37–9.

79 Ellis Roberts, *Sheppard*, 39.

80 Lockhart, *Lang*, 180.

81 Don, 31 Oct. 1937. Ellis Roberts, *Sheppard*, 47–9.

82 LP, vol. 2881, f. 7, 10, 12, 49, 55. Lang to Parker, 29 Jul. 1910: LP, vol. 2881, f. 49. Lang to Parker, 23 Jan. 1912: LP, vol. 2881, f. 91.

83 Lang to Parker, 17 Sep. 1912: LP, vol. 2881, f. 71–81.

84 Lang to Mrs Parker, 27 Dec. 1911: LP, vol. 2884, f. 255.

85 Lang to Parker, 29 Jul. 1910: LP, vol. 2881, f. 49. Don to George Bell, 4 Oct. 1934: LPL, Bell Papers, vol. 102, f. 132.

86 Gibbs to Lang, 15 Aug. 1917: LP, vol. 190, f. 13.

87 Lang to N. Crawley, 7 May 1918: LP, vol. 190, f. 26.

88 C. Mackenzie, *The Windsor Tapestry, Being a Study of the Life, Heritage and Abdication of HRH The Duke of Windsor, KG* (London, 1939), 394. E. Ford, interview 19 Oct. 2001.

89 Ingram Hill, interview 9 May 2002.

90 'Cosmo Gordon Lange', Appendix 1 below.

91 Don, 24 Jan. 1932, 13 May 1933, 5 Jun. 1934.

92 Bell's secretary to Lockhart, 11 Aug. 1947: LPL, Bell Papers, vol. 210, f. 198–210. Lockhart to Bell, 16 Sep. 1947: LPL, Bell Papers, vol. 210, f. 209. Lockhart, *Lang*, 166.

93 Don, 6 Dec. 1933.

94 Lang to Ann Todd, 9 Oct. 1937: family papers of Mr David Malcolm. Lang to Todd, 27 Oct. 1939: family papers of Mr David Malcolm.

95 Lang to Todd, 9 Oct. 1937, 13 Feb. 1938, 28 Aug. 1938, undated 1939 from Uppark, 27 Oct. 1939, 25 Dec. 1939, 27 Dec. 1940, 17 Nov. 1945: family papers of Mr David Malcolm. Lang to Todd, 17 Oct. 1938: family papers of Mr David Malcolm. Lang to Todd, 15 Apr.1938: family papers of Mr David Malcolm. Lang to Todd, 13 Feb. 1938, Lang to Todd, 27 Oct. 1939: family papers of Mr David Malcolm. Don, 30 Oct. 1937. A. Todd, *The Eighth Veil* (London, 1980), 43–4. Lang to Todd, undated, from Uppark, 1939: family papers of Mr David Malcolm. Todd, *Eighth Veil*, 44.

96 Lang to Todd, 29 Dec. 1941: family papers of Mr David Malcolm.

97 Lang to Todd, 25 Dec. 1939: family papers of Mr David Malcolm.

98 Todd, *Eighth Veil*, 44.

99 Lockhart, *Lang*, 52.

100 Lockhart, *Lang*, 318.

101 F. Watson, *Dawson of Penn* (London, 1950), 233–40.

102 Don, 17 Jan. 1932. Lockhart, *Lang*, 328. Don, 8 Oct. 1931. E. Ford, interview 19 Oct. 2001. Don, 26 Aug. 1932. Fibromyalgia or Fibrositis is 'an ill-defined chronic, achy, stiff, tired and depressing condition and is much commoner in well-educated people – much the same group of people who typically suffer from "M.E.".' Dr L. Spooner to the author, 22 Nov. 2001. Don, 23 Oct. 1934, 12 May 1935, 17 Jan. 1937, 6 Feb. 1937, 2 Aug. 1937. Lockhart, *Lang*, 328.

103 Sir J.R. Maxwell Macdonald to the author, 14 Jan. 2002. According to Gaelic usage, it should be spelt 'Balure' as it is a Gaelic name and there are never two consonants together in Gaelic, but in Lang's time Ballure was always spelt with double 'l'. J.R. Maxwell Macdonald to the author, 16 Dec. 2001.

3 The Archbishopric of Canterbury Between the Wars

1 D.G. Squibb, *Order of Precedence in England and Wales* (Oxford, 1981). The archbishop of Canterbury's place was established by the 1539 Precedence Act.

2 D. MacCulloch, 'The Myth of the English Reformation', *Journal of British Studies*, 30 (1991), 1–19.

3 Hughes, *Rivers*, 15–16, 23–6, 113, 121, 128.

4 M. Grimley, *Citizenship, Community, and the Church of England: Liberal Anglican Theories of the Church and State Between the Wars* (Oxford, 2004), 10, 15, 161–2. Don, 21 Oct. 1932, 2 Feb. 1934, 14 May 1934, 11 Oct. 1935, 19 Mar. 1936, 21 Oct. 1938. Don, 6 Feb. 1934.

5 Don, 11 Mar. 1932, 30 May 1933, 14 Oct. 1933. Don, 9 Jul. 1934.

6 *Church Times*, 13 Jul. 1935. *Church Times*, 13 Jul. 1935. *Baptist Times*, 19 Jul. 1935. *Christian World*, 19 Jul. 1935.

7 Lockhart, *Lang*, 265.

8 Lockhart, *Lang*, 80.

9 Bell, *Davidson*, 430–4, 1374–5. Lockhart, *Lang*, 357. *Church Times*, 3 Jun. 1932. Lockhart, *Lang*, 370. Don, 29 May 1933.

10 Don, 29 Feb. 1934. Don, 29 Oct. 1934. Don, 28 Nov. 1932. Don, 14 Dec. 1935.

11 *Evening Express*, 30 May 1935.

12 Don, 20 Jan. 1932. Don, 24 Jun. 1932. Protocol signed by Henricus Theodosus Johannes, Bisshop van Haarlem, pasted into diary.

13 Don, 24 Nov. 1933.

14 Don, 14–30 Oct. 1931, 5 May 1932. Βέβαιος translates as well-founded, reliable, effective; κατ' οἰκονομίαν as according to economy.

15 Hastings, *English Christianity*, 33. Don, 4 May 1940. LP, vol. 270, f. 284. Don, 27 Jan. 1937. Don, 24 Nov. 1938, 30 Mar. 1939, 17 Jun. 1939, 28 Jul. 1939, 26 Mar. 1940. Don, 10 Feb. 1939, 18 May 1940.

16 Hastings, *English Christianity*, 218–19.

17 Don, 17 Aug. 1931.

18 Don, 5 Oct. 1931, 6 Nov. 1931.

19 'Charge delivered by the Archbishop of Canterbury at his Visitation of the Clergy of the Diocese, October 14th, 15th, 16th and 18th, 1934'. LPL MS H5133.118.

20 Grimley, *Citizenship*, 10.

21 O. Chadwick, *The Victorian Church, Part Two, 1860–1901* (London, 1987), 187. See J. Coombs, *Judgement on Hatcham: The History of a Religious Struggle, 1877–1886* (London, 1969), *passim*. LP, vol. 104, f. 325. LPL, Davidson Papers, vol. 12, 327–40. *Proceedings of the Church Assembly*, vol. XVII, 5 Feb. 1936, 111.

22 D. MacCulloch, *Thomas Cranmer, A Life* (Newhaven, CT, and London, 1996), 129. A.G. Dickens, *The English Reformation* (Glasgow, 1981), 165–72. LP, vol. 96, f. 7.

23 Bell, *Davidson*, 454–61. I am indebted for this observation to the Rev. Dr Jeremy Sheehy, a priest and lawyer, who once underook a private study of Bishop Barnes. Letter, 14 Sep. 2004. Memorandum 30 Apr. 1930: LP, vol. 104, f. 192.

24 Lockhart, *Lang*, 372.

25 K.N. Medhurst and G.H. Moyser, *Church and Politics in a Secular Age* (Oxford, 1988), 78.

26 Medhurst and Moyser, *Church*, 79, 82–98, 95. LP, vol. 104, f. 284.

27 Bell, *Davidson*, 851–82 *passim*. LP, vol. 98, f. 227–8.

28 Chadwick, *Victorian Church*, 331–2. Chadwick, *Henson*, 156. M. Ramsey, *Canterbury Pilgrim* (London, 1974), 176. Bishops in Canterbury Province: LP vol. 118, f. 313–54; vol. 123, f. 239–41; vol. 137, f. 169–87; vol. 148, f. 236–81; vol. 164, f. 314–20; vol. 169, f. 262–4; vol. 181, f. 136–9; vol. 182, f. 238–302. Bishops in York Province: LP vol. 117, f. 18–22, 69–101; vol. 118, f. 312–61; vol. 149, f. 228–70; vol. 154, f. 350–7; vol. 160, f. 77–122; vol. 182, f. 237–302; vol. 191, f. 280–3. This was the reflection of Canon Howard Root, formerly

director of the Anglican Centre in Rome, who worked with three archbishops. Interview with the author, 10 Feb. 2004.

29 Bishop John Cavell, letter to the author, 11 Sep. 2002. LP, vol. 108, f. 98–103. LP, vol. 137, f. 85. LP, vol. 97, f. 128.

30 Bell, *Davidson*, 319. P.A. Bromhead, *The House of Lords and Contemporary Politics, 1911–1957* (London, 1958), 63. Grimley, *Citizenship*, 10, 15, 161–2.

31 Bromhead, *Lords*, 60. Lockhart, *Lang*, 381–2. Don, 8 Mar. 1944.

32 *Proceedings of the Church Assembly*, vols XXI–XXII, 1940–42, 22.

33 Don, 25 May 1936. *Proceedings of the Church Assembly*, vol. XIV, 1933, 98–9, vol. XIX, 1938, 370–88. *Chronicle of Convocation*, July Session 1929, 103.

34 *Proceedings of the Church Assembly*, vol. XIII, 1932, 393. *Chronicle of Convocation*, June Session 1934, 292. *Proceedings of the Church Assembly*, vol. XVI, 1935, 466–7.

35 LP, vols 270–3, *passim*. LP, vol. 271, f. 84. LP, vols 285–92, *passim*.

36 Bell, *Davidson*, 1210–11.

37 LP, vol. 271, f. 339.

38 R.T. Davidson and W. Benham, *Life of Archbishop Tait* (London, 1891), 237.

39 Don, 12 Jun. 1931, 19 Jul. 1931, 28 Apr. 1932, 2 May 1934, 15 Jun. 1934, 5 Jun. 1935, 3 Jun. 1938. Don, 28 Apr. 1935, 20 Jun. 1935, 30 Jun.–2 Jul. 1937, 2 July 1938. H.M. Queen Elizabeth The Queen Mother, audience 4 Dec. 2001. F.R. Barry, *Mervyn Haigh* (London, 1964), 103.

40 Don, 27 May 1938.

41 Don, 21 Mar. 1934.

42 LP, vol. 139, f. 272. LP, vol. 88, f. 185. Don, 9 Jul. 1934.

43 Don, 27 Feb. 1935.

44 LP, vol. 85, f. 94–130. LP, vol. 88, f. 110, 113, 114, 116, 119, 122.

45 Don, 16 May 1934.

46 Bell, *Davidson*, 1179–80.

47 LP, vols 18, 123, 148, 177, 181, 153, 95. LP, vols 7, 18, 86, 99, 110, 123, 154, 168.

48 Bishop Palmer to Lang, 2 Dec. 1937: LP, vol. 148, f. 189.

49 Lang to Palmer, 12 Nov. 1937: LP, vol. 148, f. 184–5. Don to Palmer, 10 Jan. 1938: LP, vol. 157, f. 144–5. Don to Palmer, 20 Jan. 1938: LP, vol. 157, f. 151. Don to Palmer, 6 Mar. 1939: LP, vol. 167, f. 81. Memorandum, 15 May 1938: LP, vol. 167, f. 95. Don to Palmer, 17 Jun. 1939: LP, vol. 167, f. 97. Don to Palmer, 18 Dec. 1939: LP, vol. 167, f. 102.

50 LPL, Davidson Papers, vol. 12, f. 304–16, 327–40. *Croydon Times*, 16 Mar. 1935: LP, vol. 288, f. 116–17.

51 *Croydon Times*, 16 Mar. 1935.

52 *Croydon Times*, 16 Mar. 1935.

53 Lockhart, *Lang*, 388. LP, vol. 271, f. 217.

54 Don, 17 May 1932. LPL, Davidson Papers, vol. 12, f. 327–40. Don, 22 Sep. 1933.

55 BBC Sound Archives, CPRD 1214, 13 Dec. 1936. LP, vol. 271, f. 43, 115, 217, 312, 339.

56 Lockhart, *Lang*, 381–2. *Proceedings of the Church Assembly*, vol. XIII, 1932, 538. Bell, *Davidson*, 1307–12.
57 LP, vol. 270, f. 284. LBL, Bell Papers, vol. 202, f. 297.
58 Don, 25 Jul. 14–18 Oct. 1931, 20 Jan., 11 Mar. 1932.

4 LANG AND THE MONARCHY

1   E. Ford, interview 19 Oct. 2001.
2   V. Mallet (ed.), *Life with Queen Victoria: Marie Mallet's Letters from Court 1887–1901* (London, 1968), 76–7. LP, vol. 223, f. 42. Transcribed and bound together in LP vol. 223. Lockhart used both sets of notes in his biography of Lang. On p. 136 he mixed them together so that they appeared to be a single piece of writing. On pp. 131, 135 and 140 he changed words. On p. 137 he has a paragraph about Queen Victoria's views of President Kruger which I have been unable to trace. It does not feature in either set of Lang's notes about Kruger on pp. 65 or 311–12, or in his letters to his mother in LP vols 187 and 188.
3   LP, vol. 223, f. 42–4.
4   Queen Victoria's Journal, 30 Jan. 1898: Royal Archives, Windsor Castle, VIC/QVJ.
5   Victoria, 7 Aug. 1898. Victoria, 8 Jan. 1899.
6   LP, vol. 223, f. 46.
7   Victoria, 4 Feb. 1900.
8   Victoria, 8 Jan. 1899. LP, box 193, f. 14.
9   LP, vol. 223, f. 312–15.
10 Lang to Mrs H. Lang, 6 Oct. 1902: LP, vol. 188, f. 52.
11 P. Clark, Royal Archives Registrar, letter to the author, 3 Jan. 2002.
12 LP, vol. 223, f. 47–8. Lockhart, *Lang*, 144. LP, vol. 223, f. 70. Duke of York to Lang, 25 Mar. 1900: LP, vol. 188, f. 78.
13 Duke of York to Lang, 7 Apr. 1900: LP, vol. 188, f. 82.
14 LP, vol. 318, *passim*.
15 Bigge to Lang, 16 Nov. 1908: LP, vol. 189, f. 138. Lang to Mrs H. Lang, 27 Nov. 1910: LP, vol. 188, f. 82.
16 Lang to Mrs H. Lang, 11 Dec. 1910: LP, vol. 188, f. 84. LP, vol. 318, f. 13, 15, 21, 45. George V to Lang, 17 Sep. 1931: LP, vol. 318, f. 15. Duke of Windsor, *A King's Story: The Memoirs of HRH the Duke of Windsor, KG* (London, 1951), 273. K. Rose, *King George V* (London, 1983), 362–5.
17 Princess of Wales to Augusta, Grand Duchess of Mecklenburg-Strelitz, 22 Nov. 1908: Royal Archives, Windsor Castle, GV/CC25/13. J. Pope-Hennessy, *Queen Mary, 1867–1953* (London, 1959), 386, 536–7.
18 Pope-Hennessy, *Queen Mary*, 368, 442, 435. Lang to Mrs H. Lang, 12 May 1918: LP, vol. 188, f. 124.
19 Lang to Mrs H. Lang, 15 July 1912: LP, vol. 188, f. 99–102.
20 Lockhart, *Lang*, 216. Lang to Mrs H. Lang, 15 April 1917: LP, vol. 188, f. 119.

21 H. Nicolson, *King George V: His Life and Reign* (London, 1952), 430. LP, vol. 222, f. 253. Stamfordham to Lang, 23 and 29 Dec. 1928: LP, vol. 318, f. 5, 7. Wigram to Lang, 27 Aug. 1931: LP, vol. 318, f. 11. LP, vol. 318, f. 17; vol. 223, f. 233.
22 Don, 19 Jul. 1931.
23 Prince of Wales to Lang, 12 Oct. 1912: LP, vol. 189, f. 305. F. Donaldson, *Edward VIII* (London, 1974), 35, 40.
24 Donaldson, *Edward VIII*, 43.
25 S. Bradford, *George VI* (London, 2002), 69. Prince Albert to Lang, 1 Feb. 1923: LP, vol. 318, f. 142. Prince Albert to Lang, 13 Feb. 1923: LP, vol. 318, f. 143.
26 Queen Elizabeth The Queen Mother, audience 4 Dec. 2001.
27 The Queen Mother, audience 4 Dec. 2001.
28 A. Morrow, *Without Equal* (Thirsk, 2000), 87, 271. The Queen Mother, audience 4 Dec. 2001.
29 The Queen Mother, audience, 4 Dec. 2001.
30 Duchess of York to Lang, 1 Jan. 1933: LP, vol. 318, f. 172; 16 Jul. 1933: LP, vol. 318, f. 173; 12 Jan. 1934: LP, vol. 318, f. 175; 5 Jul. 1935: LP, vol. 318, f. 176.
31 Princess Mary to Lang, 29 Jun. 1937: LP, vol. 318, f. 228; 23 Dec. 1937: LP, vol. 318, f. 230; 17 Oct. 1940: LP, vol. 318, f. 232; Dec. (undated) 1941: LP, vol. 318, f. 235; 19 Dec. 1943: LP, vol. 318, f. 237.
32 LP, vol. 223, f. 305–14.
33 LP, vol. 223, f. 47.
34 LP, vol. 223, f. 62. Lang to Mrs H. Lang, 7 February 1898: LP, vol. 188, f. 7. LP, vol. 223, f. 44–5.
35 LP, vol. 223, f. 44, 46, 60; vol. 188, f. 7. LP, vol. 223, f. 46. 49, 64–5.
36 Hughes, *Rivers*, 47.
37 LP, vol. 223, f. 307. LP, vol. 271, f. 210.
38 Nicolson, *King George V*, 62, 122, 391, 510, 515–17. Bigge to Lang, 8 Dec. 1910: LP, vol. 189, f. 259–60.
39 LP, vol. 288, f. 138.
40 Coronation Programme, 1936: LP, vol. 22, f. 213.
41 LP, vol. 271, f. 77–8.
42 LP, vol. 271, f. 68–9.
43 D. Starkey, *Monarchy: England and her rulers from the Tudors to the Windsors* (London, 2007), 320. LP, vol, 271, f. 1, 43, 316–17; vol. 272, f. 96.
44 LP, vol. 223, f. 248. Diary of H. Hensley Henson, 22 Oct. 1936: Durham Cathedral Library.
45 LP, vol. 271, f. 217.
46 LP, vol. 271, f. 217.
47 P. Ziegler, *King Edward VIII, The Official Biography* (London, 1990), 29. Donaldson, *Edward VIII*, 302. Ziegler, *King Edward VIII*, 556–7.
48 Don, 15 Nov. 1934.
49 K. Middlemas and J. Barnes, *Baldwin: A Biography* (London, 1969), 984.

Middlemas and Barnes, *Baldwin*, 308. Ziegler, *King Edward VIII*, 94–105, 222, 227–9.

50 C. Higham, *Mrs Simpson: Secret Lives of the Duchess of Windsor* (London, 2004), 1–5, 22–30, 54, 57, 63–4.

51 Ziegler, *King Edward VIII*, 227–34.

52 Rose, *George V*, 391–2. Lang to Don, 20 Sep. 1935: letter pasted into Don's 1935 diary, f. 72a.

53 LP, vol. 318, f. 118. Ziegler, *King Edward VIII*, 199. Ziegler, *King Edward VIII*, 233.

54 Lord Cromer, Lord Chamberlain, to Lang, 6 May 1935: LP, vol. 318, f. 37. Pope-Hennessy, *Queen Mary*, 556–7. LP, vol. 223, f. 216.

55 Rose, *George V*, 400. LP, vol. 223, f. 216. LP, vol. 223, f. 217.

56 Don, 19 Jan. 1936.

57 LP, vol. 223, f. 217–18.

58 LP, vol. 223, f. 220.

59 LP, vol. 223, f. 220. Bradford, *George VI*, 200. Windsor, *King's Story*, 264. Princess Royal to Lang, 27 Mar. 1936: LP, vol. 318, f. 220. LP, vol. 223, f. 220.

60 LP, vol. 223, f. 221.

61 Ziegler, *King Edward VIII*, 241. LP, vol. 223, f. 221. H. Hardinge, *Loyal to Three Kings* (London, 1967), 61. LP, vol. 223, f. 222. Higham, *Mrs Simpson*, 136.

62 LP, vol. 223, f. 222.

63 LP, vol. 223, f. 225.

64 Donaldson, *Edward VIII*, 181.

65 LP, vol. 223, f. 227.

66 Don, 21 Jan. 1936. Don, 23 Jan. 1936. Don, 26 Jan. 1936.

67 LP, vol. 223, f. 228.

68 LP, vol. 271, f. 138.

69 LP, vol. 223, f. 231–2.

70 United States War Department, *Instructions for American Servicemen in Britain* (Washington, 1942), 12.

5 LANG AND THE ABDICATION CRISIS

1 Don, 26 Jan. 1937.

2 Lockhart, *Lang*, 403–4.

3 Donaldson, *Edward VIII*, 223. Hastings, *English Christianity*, 221, 223, 247–8. Ziegler, *King Edward VIII*, 241, 250, 265. Ziegler, *King Edward VIII*, 243, 250, 253, 263, 265, 293, 302, 318, 329, 332, 338.

4 H. Montgomery Hyde, *Baldwin, the Unexpected Prime Minister* (London, 1973), 473. Bradford, *George VI*, 299. A. Wilkinson, 'Lang (William) Cosmo Gordon, Baron Lang of Lambeth (1864–1945)', *ODNB*, 313.

5 Windsor, *King's Story*, 331.

6 Hardinge, *Loyal*, 72. Ziegler, *King Edward VIII*, 242.

7 T. Jones, *A Diary with Letters* (Oxford, 1954), 163–4.

8 Middlemas and Barnes, *Baldwin*, 978.
9 Higham, *Mrs Simpson*, 436. Donaldson, *Edward VIII*, 187, 399. Windsor, *King's Story*, 272–4, 384. Lockhart, *Lang*, 395. LP, vol. 223, f. 231–2.
10 Windsor, *King's Story*, 272. Lockhart, *Lang*, 395.
11 Windsor, *King's Story*, 272–3.
12 LP, vol. 223, f. 231–232.
13 Windsor, *King's Story*, 273.
14 LP, vol. 223, f. 232.
15 Windsor, *King's Story*, 273–4.
16 LP, vol. 223, f. 232. Lockhart, *Lang*, 395.
17 Don, 29 Jan. 1936.
18 Donaldson, *Edward VIII*, 185. Hardinge, *Loyal*, 83–4, 89, 103.
19 Donaldson, *Edward VIII*, 186–8, 192.
20 Ziegler, *King Edward VIII*, 122–5, 164, 168. Middlemas and Barnes, *Baldwin*, 1015.
21 Diary of Monica Baldwin, 7 Oct. 1937, quoted in Williamson and Baldwin, *Baldwin Papers*, 418–19.
22 Ziegler, *King Edward VIII*, 163, 194.
23 Pope-Hennessy, *Queen Mary*, 38, 188–95, 318–21, 338. Hardinge, *Loyal*, 86, 90. Donaldson, *Edward VIII*, 188.
24 Ziegler, *King Edward VIII*, 234–9.
25 Donaldson, *Edward VIII*, 184.
26 Halsey to Lang, 13 Dec. 1936: LP, vol. 192, f. 371. Ziegler, *King Edward VIII*, 255. Ziegler, *King Edward VIII*, 255–6. Halsey talked to Lang in February 1936 and mentioned their conversation in a letter to him after the abdication, 13 Dec. 1936: LP, vol. 192, f. 371. Bod., Monckton Papers, vol. 22, f. 11. Don, 16 Dec. 1936. 2nd Lord Linlithgow to G. Dawson, 17 Nov. 1936: Bod., Geoffrey Dawson Papers, vol. 79, f. 14.
27 Lockhart, *Lang*, 233–4.
28 Lang to A. Todd, undated 1939: family papers of Mr David Malcolm.
29 Don, 2 Mar. 1936. Don, 4 Mar. 1936. Don, 5 Apr. 1936. Rev. G.D. Watkins, Priest-in-Ordinary, interview, 6 Jan. 1990. Don, 9 Apr. 1936.
30 Don 1 Nov. 1936, 17 Dec. 1936.
31 Don, 1 Nov. 1936.
32 LP, vol. 318, f. 118.
33 Don, 28 Oct. 1936. Ziegler, *King Edward VIII*, 294. Mrs M. Cook to Lang, 27 Oct. 1936: LP, vol. 22, f. 401. Don to the Very Rev. J. MacRae, 17 Nov. 1936: LP, vol. 22, f. 405. Mrs M. McCartney to Lang, 3 Dec. 1936: LP, vol. 22, f. 406.
34 LP, vol. 318, f. 119.
35 Don, 28 Jan. 1936, 23 Nov. 1936.
36 LP, vol. 318, f. 100. Lockhart, *Lang*, 404–7. Ziegler, *King Edward VIII*, 291. LP, vol. 223, f. 235.
37 Edward VIII to Lang, 20 Jul. 1936: LP, vol. 318, f.8. LP, vol. 223, f. 235. LP,

vol. 223, f. 233–5. Edward VIII to Lang, 23 Jul. 1936: LP, vol. 318, f. 9. Jones, *Diary*, 189. Donaldson, *Edward VIII*, 223 and footnote *10. Windsor, *King's Story*, 331.

38 Don, 9 Dec. 1936. Sargent's notes, King Edward's Abdication, 13 Dec. 1936: LP, vol. 318, f. 122.

39 LP, vol. 223, f. 235.

40 LP, vol. 318, f. 120.

41 LP, vol. 223, f. 235–6. Ziegler, *King Edward VIII*, 283–7. Donaldson, *Edward VIII*, 214. Don, 1 Oct. 1936. Donaldson, *Edward VIII*, 215.

42 LP, vol. 213, f. 110–11.

43 LP, vol. 213, f. 111. Margaret Elphinstone was a cousin to the princesses.

44 Don, 1 Oct. 1936. Montgomery Hyde, *Baldwin*, 447–8. Ziegler, *King Edward VIII*, 292.

45 Middlemas and Barnes, *Baldwin*, 983.

46 Pope-Hennessy, *Queen Mary*, 574.

47 Ziegler, *King Edward VIII*, 293. Donaldson, *Edward VIII*, 227.

48 LP, vol. 318, f. 82.

49 LP, vol. 318, note on verso of f. 89.

50 Hardinge, *Loyal*, 78–9. F. Ponsonby, *Recollections of Three Reigns* (London, 1951), 287–9.

51 Donaldson, *Edward VIII*, 227–8.

52 Henson, 22 Oct. 1936: Durham Cathedral Library.

53 LP, vol. 318, f. 80–1.

54 LP, vol. 318, f. 83. Don, 19, 26 Nov. 1936. LP, vol. 318, f. 80, 85, 86, 90, 94. LP, vol. 318, f. 123.

55 Donaldson, *Edward VIII*, 231. LP, vol. 318, f. 83. Don, 1, 4, 6, 15 Nov. 1936.

56 Unpublished passage from T. Jones' diary, 5 Nov. 1936, quoted by Williamson and Baldwin, *Baldwin Papers*, 388.

57 Report from Superintendant A. Canning to Sir P. Game, 3 Jul. 1935: TNA, PRO MEPO 10/35.

58 Don, 7 Nov. 1936. LP, vol. 192, f. 358. Bod., Dawson Papers, vol. 55, f. 11. Middlemas and Barnes, *Baldwin*, 989.

59 Lang to G. Dawson, 12 Nov. 1936: LP, vol. 192, f. 359.

60 Montgomery Hyde, *Baldwin*, 463.

61 Williamson and Baldwin, *Baldwin Papers*, 390.

62 Williamson and Baldwin, *Baldwin Papers*, 391. Pope-Hennessy, *Queen Mary*, 574–5. The late Earl of Harewood, in a letter to the author of 27 Aug. 2002, recalled receiving a letter at Eton from the Princess Royal on 1 Dec. 1936 announcing the king's decision, which he had to show to his house master. He added, 'you can imagine the frustration of a 13 year-old being asked by his schoolmates about the abdication and not being able to say anything, and being taunted because he didn't know!' Montgomery Hyde, *Baldwin*, 469.

63 Henson, 17 Nov. 1936: Durham Cathedral Library.

64 LP, vol. 318, f. 83.

65 Don, 19 Nov. 1936.

66 Middlemas and Barnes, *Baldwin*, 997.

67 LP, vol. 318, f. 84.

68 Donaldson, *Edward VIII*, 257–8. Middlemas and Barnes, *Baldwin*, 997–8. Montgomery Hyde, *Baldwin*, 470–1.

69 Middlemas and Barnes, *Baldwin*, 999.

70 CUL, Baldwin Papers, vol. 176, f. 36.

71 Lang to Baldwin, 25 Nov. 1936: CUL, Baldwin Papers, vol. 176, f. 76.

72 Montgomery Hyde, *Baldwin*, 473. Lang's writing is notoriously difficult, but Montgomery Hyde has apparently misread 'would' as 'could'.

73 Don, 24 Nov. 1936.

74 TNA, PREM 1/448. S. Williams, *The People's King: The True Story of the Abdication* (London, 2003), 146.

75 CUL, Baldwin Papers, vol. 176, f. 36. Montgomery Hyde, *Baldwin*, 465.

76 Don, 26 Nov. 1936.

77 Middlemas and Barnes, *Baldwin*, 1000–1.

78 LP, vol. 318, f. 121. Bod., Dawson Papers, vol. 55, f. 180. Don, 30 Nov. 1936.

79 Don, 28 Nov. 1936. LP, vol. 318, f. 120.

80 LP, vol. 318, f. 84–5.

81 LP, vol. 318, f. 85.

82 Don, 3 Nov. 1936. Henson, 7 Nov. 1936: Durham Cathedral Library. J.S. Peart-Binns, *Blunt* (Queensbury, 1969), 152.

83 Peart-Binns, *Blunt*, 277.

84 Peart-Binns, *Blunt*, 154–5. Windsor, *King's Story*, 350–3. Ziegler, *King Edward VIII*, 309–10.

85 LP, vol. 318, f. 121.

86 G. Mayfield to Don, 2 Dec. 1936, and indeciph. Winckworth to Don, 2 Dec. 1936: LP, vol. 318, f. 361–2. Don, 4 Dec. 1936. Peart-Binns, *Blunt*, 154.

87 Lang to Bishop Blunt of Bradford, 7 Dec. 1936: LP, vol. 192, f. 366.

88 Donaldson, *Edward VIII*, 266, footnote. Peart-Binns, *Blunt*, 153. Peart-Binns, *Blunt*, 154. LP, vol. 318, f. 121. Peart-Binns, *Blunt*, 119–20. Mackenzie, *Windsor Tapestry*, 209.

89 CUL, Baldwin Papers, vol. 176, f. 36.

90 LP, vol. 318, f. 86–7, Lang's underlining.

91 Montgomery Hyde, *Baldwin*, 489.

92 Bod., Monckton Papers, vol. 14, f. 52–4. CUL, Baldwin Papers, vol. 176, f. 38–9.

93 Canon A. Deane to G. Dawson, 6 Dec. 1936: Bod., Dawson Papers, vol. 79, f. 34; see also below, the end of the next section, for a comment on the authorship of this letter.

94 Montgomery Hyde, *Baldwin*, 489.

95 Donaldson, *Edward VIII*, 276–7.

96 LP, vol. 318, f. 122.

97 Donaldson, *Edward VIII*, 269.

98 Lang to G. Dawson, 3 Dec. 1936: Bod., Dawson Papers, vol. 79, f. 25.

99 The Rev. D. Rea to Lang, 3 Dec. 1936: LP, vol. 318, f. 128. LP, vol. 318, f. 128–31. Lang to Brown, 9 Dec. 1936: LP, vol. 318, f. 132. Brown to Lang, 10 Dec. 1936: LP, vol. 318, f. 133.

100 Donaldson, *Edward VIII*, 117. Ziegler, *King Edward VIII*, 167. Mrs Patricia Gray to the author, 17 May 2012. Proud was relieved to spot Walmsley (who was an old comrade from the Horse Guards) walking along the pavement as he wondered how to cope with the drunk prince of Wales. R. Wollheim, *Germs: A Memoir of Childhood* (London, 2005), 252–3.

101 Lang to Lord Dawson, 12 Dec. 1936: LP, vol. 318, f. 135.

102 Dr B. Armitage to Baldwin, 6 Dec. 1936: CUL, Baldwin Papers, vol. 176, f. 95–6.

103 Dr B. Armitage to Baldwin, 6 Dec. 1936: CUL, Baldwin Papers, vol. 176, f. 95–6.

104 Lang to Dawson, 12 Dec. 1936: LP, vol. 318, f. 135. Armitage to Baldwin, 6 Dec. 1936: CUL, Baldwin Papers, vol. 176, f. 96.

105 *Edward VIII: The Plot to Topple a King,* (Blakeway) Channel 4, 10 May 2012.

106 Canon Anthony C. Deane to Geoffrey Dawson, 6 Dec. 1936: Bod., Dawson Papers, vol. 79, f. 34.

107 LP, vol. 318, f. 88–9.

108 LP, vol. 21, f. 114.

109 LP, vol. 318, f. 88.

110 Henson, 6 Dec. 1936: Durham Cathedral Library.

111 Montgomery Hyde, *Baldwin*, 490. LP, vol. 318, f. 123.

112 LP, vol. 318, f. 93.

113 Williamson and Baldwin, *Baldwin Papers*, 405. Middlemas and Barnes, *Baldwin*, 1011.

114 LP, vol. 318, f. 123.

115 Montgomery Hyde, *Baldwin*, 498–501.

116 Don, 17 Dec. 1936. Percival says this was at Marlborough House, Lang at Royal Lodge. LP, vol. 318, f. 124. LP, vol. 318, f. 94.

117 *Parliamentary Debates, Lords, 1936–37*, vol. 103, 731.

118 *Parliamentary Debates, Lords, 1936–37*, vol. 103, 731–4.

119 LP, vol. 318, f. 96.

120 LP, vol. 318, f 101.

121 Bouquet to Don, 11 Dec. 1936: LP, vol. 22, f. 415.

122 Haigh to Don, 12 Dec. 1936: LP, vol. 192, f. 368.

123 Don to Bouquet, 14 Dec. 1936: LP, vol. 22, f. 419.

124 British Library, London, Sound Archives, T8077/0404.

125 Williams, *People's King*, 238–52. LP, vol. 318, f. 89.

126 Don, 19 Jul. 1931.

127 Don, 11 Dec. 1936.

128 Don, 15 Dec. 1936. LP, vol. 318, f. 126. Don, 15 Dec. 1936. LP, vol. 318, f. 125.

129 *Parliamentary Debates, Lords, 1936–37*, vol. 103, 734. Don, 19 Dec. 1936.

130 Baldwin to Lang, 14 Dec. 1936: LP, vol. 92, f. 79.

131 Don, 22 Dec. 1936. Princess Royal to Lang, 24 Dec. 1936: LP, vol. 318, f. 226. LP, vol. 192, f. 370–427. Don, 24 Dec. 1936. Montgomery Hyde, *Baldwin*, 512. Don, 15 Dec. 1936.

132 Don, 31 Dec. 1936.

133 Don, 4 Jan. 1937.

134 LP, vol. 318, f. 99–100.

135 LP, vol. 318, f. 102. Lang to N. Crawley, 27 Dec. 1936: LP, MS 3207, f. 129.

136 Ziegler, *King Edward VIII*, 337, 362.

137 LP, vol. 156, f. 218–21.

138 LP, vol. 156, f. 221. Berriedale Keith acknowledged it in his letter to Lang of 23 Mar. 1937: LP, vol. 156, f. 223. Berriedale Keith acknowledged it in his letter to Lang of 25 Mar. 1937: LP, vol. 156, f. 227. LP, vol. 156, f. 223–5. Lang to Berridale Keith, 27 Mar. 1937: LP, vol. 156, f. 226.

139 S. Batty to Lang, 2 Jan. 1937: LP, vol. 156, f. 210. Memorandum: LP, vol. 156, f. 212–13. Ziegler, *King Edward VIII*, 353.

140 Don to Lang, 6 Apr. 1937: LP, vol. 318, f. 138.

141 Wigram to Lang, 5 Apr. 1937: LP, vol. 318, f. 136.

142 Lang to Wigram, 6 Apr. 1937: LP, vol. 318, f. 138–40.

143 Wigram to Lang, 10 Apr. 1937: LP, vol. 318, f. 141.

144 Chadwick, *Henson*, 232. Mrs I. Madden to the author, 18 Sep. 2002. Bod., Monckton Papers, vol. 22, f. 71.

145 Don, 2 Jun. 1937.

146 Don, 2 Jun. 1937.

147 Don, 3 Jun. 1937.

148 Don, 14 Jun. 1937. Don, 20 Jul. 1937. Don, 20 Jul. 1937, 4 Aug. 1937.

149 W.B. Wells, *Why Edward Went: Crown, Clique and Church* (New York, 1937), 21, 131–69, 212, 214, 218. Wells, *Why*, 3, 167–8, 218, 171–5.

150 Wells, *Why*, 167, 185, 186, 219. Don, 28 Jan. 1938.

151 Bradford, *George VI*, 261.

152 Queen Elizabeth to Lang, 12 Dec. 1936: LP, vol. 318, f. 177.

153 LP, vol. 318, f. 102.

154 Don, 22 Dec. 1936. Henson, 25 Dec. 1936: Durham Cathedral Library. Henson, 25 Dec. 1936: Durham Cathedral Library.

155 George VI to Lang, 29 Dec. 1936: LP, vol. 318, f. 145.

156 LP, vol. 318, f. 102.

157 Bradford, *George VI*, 329. Donaldson, *Edward VIII*, 328–30. Bradford, *George VI*, 336.

158 Lang to N. Crawley, 11 Sep. 1937: LPL, MS 3207, f. 129.

159 Ziegler, *Edward VIII*, 389–96.

160 J.H. Jenson to Lang, 8 May 1936: LP, vol. 21, f. 1. LP, vol. 21, f. 240. LP, vol. 226, f. 240. Privy Council Order, 11 Feb. 1937: TNA, HO144/21056/2. LP, vol. 21, f. 34–5, 86, 325. Undated memorandum: LP, vol. 21, f. 180.

'Coronation Service Music' memorandum, 16 Oct. 1936: LP, vol. 21, f. 92–4. LP, vol. 21, f. 209–12.

161 LP, vol. 152, f. 1–3.
162 LP, vol. 271, f. 217.
163 *Chelmsford Diocesan Chronicle*, Dec. 1936, Jan. 1937, Feb. 1937, Mar. 1937, May 1937. LP, vol. 223, f. 243–4.
164 LP, vol. 223, f. 246. LP, vol. 22, f. 79.
165 *The Times*, 10 May 1937.
166 J.W. Wheeler-Bennett, *King George VI: His Life and Reign* (London, 1958), 312–13.
167 Don, 12 May 1937.
168 George VI to Lang, 13 May 1937: LP, vol. 318, f. 148.
169 Queen Elizabeth The Queen Mother, audience 4 Dec. 2001.
170 Countess of Strathmore and Kinghorne to Lang, 1 Jun. 1937: LP, vol. 22, f. 125. Marchioness of Reading to Lang, 15 May 1937: LP, vol. 22, f. 103. LP, vol. 223, f. 254. Temple to Lang, 22 May 1937: LP, vol. 22, f. 119. Bradford, *George VI*, 285.
171 Lockhart, *Lang*, 403–4.
172 Lang to Baldwin, 25 Nov. 1936: CUL, Baldwin Papers, vol. 176, f. 76. Lang to Dawson, 12 Nov. 1936: LP, vol. 192, f. 359. Lang to Dawson, 3 Dec. 1936: Bod., Dawson Papers, vol. 79, f. 25.
173 Don 7 Dec. 1936. LP, vol. 318, f. 122. Don, 19 Nov. 1936. LP, vol. 318, f. 123–4. LP, vol. 318, f. 122.
174 Don, 15, 17, 20, 22, 24 Dec. 1936, 4 Jan. 1937.
175 Lockhart, *Lang*, 399–406 *passim*.
176 LP, vol. 318, f. 80–102.
177 Lockhart, *Lang*, 404.
178 LP, vol. 318, verso f. 89.
179 M. Barber, 'Randall Davidson: A Partial Retrospective', in S. Taylor (ed.), *From Cranmer to Davidson* (Woodbridge, 2002), 420.
180 LP, vol. 318, f. 81.
181 Lang to Blunt, 7 Dec. 1936: LP, vol. 192, f. 367.
182 Middlemas and Barnes, *Baldwin*, 449.
183 Montgomery Hyde, *Baldwin*, 447. Bradford, *George VI*, 238. P. Williamson, *Stanley Baldwin: Conservative Leadership and National Values* (Cambridge, 1999), 328. Hastings, *English Christianity*, 247.
184 Lockhart, *Lang*, 290. Middlemas and Barnes, *Baldwin*, 1017. Bod., Dawson Papers, vol. 55, f. 24. Windsor, *King's Story*, 402. Lang to Baldwin, 25 Nov. 1936: CUL, Baldwin Papers, vol. 176, f. 76. Lang to Dawson, 12 Nov. 1936: LP, vol. 192, f. 359. Lang to Dawson, 3 Dec. 1936: Bod., Dawson Papers, vol. 79, f. 25.
185 Jones, *Diary*, 288. LP, vol. 318, f. 80. Montgomery Hyde, *Baldwin*, 487–8.
186 LP, vol. 318, f. 93. Middlemas and Barnes, *Baldwin*, 1005.
187 Ziegler, *King Edward VIII*, 168. Don, 20 Jan. 1936. LP, vol. 318, f. 84, 121.

Montgomery Hyde, *Baldwin*, 448. Donaldson, *Edward VIII*, 251. Lang to Baldwin, 25 Nov. 1936: CUL, Baldwin Papers, vol. 176, f. 76.

6 LANG AND THE REVISED PRAYER BOOK, 1928–1942

1 H.H. Henson, *Retrospect of an Unimportant Life* (London, 1943), vol. 2, 28 Jul. 1928.
2 'Archbishop Lang and Archbishop Davidson, Some Reflections': LPL, Bell Papers, vol. 210, f. 205.
3 Lockhart, *Lang*, 377. Hastings, *English Christianity*, 207–8.
4 Lockhart, *Lang*, 327–8.
5 J.R.H. Moorman, *The Anglican Spiritual Tradition* (London, 1983), 60–4, 94, 103, 131. P.B. Nockles, *The Oxford Movement in Context* (Cambridge, 1994), 209–27.
6 Nockles, *Oxford Movement*, 236–7. Nockles, *Oxford Movement*, 236–7.
7 J. Pinnington, *Anglicans and Orthodox, Unity and Subversion, 1559–1725* (Leominster, 2003), 22, 27, 29.
8 See, for example, *The Restoration of Churches the Restoration of Popery* (1844), *'The Catholic Revival', or Ritualism and Romanism in the Church of England* (1866) and also parts of *The Roman Antichrist a 'Lying Spirit'* (1846) and *Semper Idem; or Popery Everywhere and Always the Same* (1851) by the Very Rev. Francis Close.
9 E. Daniel, *The Prayer-Book: Its History, Language and Contents* (London, 1894), v. D. Gray, *The 1927–28 Prayer Book Crisis*, vol. 1 (Norwich, 2006), 11–12. *Church and State, the Report of the Archbishops' Commission on the Relations between the Church and the State*, vol. 1 (London, 1936), 28–9. L. Pullman, 'Prayer Book Revision', *All Saints' Margaret Street Church and Parish Paper*, London, Mar. 1911.
10 Gray, *Prayer Book Crisis*, vol. 1, 30. Bell, *Davidson*, 1326. Bell, *Davidson*, 1357.
11 Chadwick, *Henson*, 185–6.
12 Chadwick, *Henson*, 190. Chadwick, *Henson*, 190.
13 Bell, *Davidson*, 1329–30.
14 Hastings, *English Christianity*, 195–9.
15 B. and M. Pawley, *Rome and Canterbury through Four Centuries* (London, 1981), 261–77. Bell, *Davidson*, 1284.
16 Bell, *Davidson*, 1331. Hughes, *Rivers*, 75.
17 Church of England Liturgical Commission, *Prayer Book Revision in the Church of England: A Memorandum of the Church of England Liturgical Commission* (1957), 10–11.
18 Bell, *Davidson*, 1334–6. J. Maiden, *National Religion and the Prayer Book Controversy, 1927–1928* (Woodbridge, 2009), 106–32. Gray, *Prayer Book Crisis*, vol. 2, 20, 28, 31.
19 Gray, *Prayer Book Crisis*, vol. 2, 32.
20 Gray, *Prayer Book Crisis*, vol. 2, 32–3. Bell, *Davidson*, 1349. Hughes, *Rivers*,

83. Gray, *Prayer Book Crisis*, vol. 2, 39. LPL, Davidson Papers, vol. 16, f. 12. Bell, *Davidson*, 1363.

21 Hughes, *Rivers*, 80–1. Gray, *Prayer Book Crisis*, vol. 2, 32. Chadwick, *Henson*, 206. O. Chadwick, *Michael Ramsey: A Life* (Oxford, 1990), 35. LP, vol. 58, f. 177–301. Bell, *Davidson*, 1355.

22 Gray, *Prayer Book Crisis,* vol. 2, 39–40.

23 Bell, *Davidson*, 1330.

24 See R.W.F. Beaken, 'Wartime Religion in a Garrison Town: The Parish Churches of Colchester During the Great War, 1914–1918,' Lambeth M.A. thesis, 2000. St Peter's (evangelical), Holy Trinity (mildly low church), St Mary-at-the-Walls (choral worship for carriage folk), St Botolph (plain C of E), and St Stephen (Anglo-Catholic), Colchester. St Mary-at-the-Walls magazine, Sep. 1927, Feb. 1928, Aug. 1928. St Botolph's parish magazine, Aug. 1931 and Aug. 1932.

25 Interview with the author, 17 Jul. 2003.

26 LP, vol. 321, f. 33–46. LP, vol. 222, f. 250.

27 LP, vol. 321, f. 39–40, 42.

28 LP, vol. 18, f. 19.

29 *Church Times*, 6 Jul. 1928.

30 LP, vol. 18, f. 19.

31 Harris to Lang, 19 Jul. 1929: LP, vol. 18, f. 21.

32 The Rev. E.D. Merritt to Lang, 8 Nov. 1934: LP, vol. 137, f. 79. Lang to Bishop Bardsley of Leicester, 14 Dec. 1929: LP, vol. 97, f. 128.

33 Bell, *Davidson*, 1345, 1348, 1353–8. Chadwick, *Henson*, 199–200. Gray, *Prayer Book Crisis*, vol. 2, 42–3. Hastings, *English Christianity*, 205–7. Bell, *Davidson*, 1346. Gray, *Prayer Book Crisis*, vol. 2, 30.

34 Bell, *Davidson*, 1332.

35 F.A. Iremonger, *William Temple, Archbishop of Canterbury* (Oxford, 1949), 354. Iremonger, *Temple*, 206.

36 CUL, Baldwin Papers, vol. 53, f. 161–235, *passim.* CUL, Baldwin Papers, vol. 53, f. 168.

37 Emdim to Baldwin, 21 Nov. 1928: CUL, Baldwin Papers, vol. 53, f. 161–3. W. Poynter Adams to A.M. Williams, 1 Mar. 1929: CUL, Baldwin Papers, vol. 53, f. 199.

38 CUL, Baldwin Papers, vol. 53, f. 168. CUL, Baldwin Papers, vol. 53, f. 188.

39 Bishops' Meeting VIII, 29 Jun. 1928, f. 177–8. *Church Assembly Proceedings*, 5 Feb. 1936, 206.

40 Chelwood to Lang, 29 May 1930: LP, vol. 7, f. 31. Lang to the Rev. E. Hellins, 18 Oct. 1930: LP, vol. 7, f. 67. Lang to E. Bennett, 9 Oct. 1930: LP, vol. 7, f. 48. Lang to Temple, 17 Sep. 1930: LP, vol. 7, f. 36. Lang to Temple, 17 Sep. 1930: LP, vol. 7, f. 36. Notice of Preliminary Meeting, 4 Nov. 1930: LP, vol. 7, f. 58. H.B. Vaisey to Lang, 16 Oct. 1930: LP, vol. 7, f. 59. E. Hellins to Lang, 21 Oct. 1930: LP, vol. 7, f. 69.

41 *Church and State*, vol. 2 (evidence).

42 Lang to Baldwin, 3 Aug. 1935: LP, vol. 7, f. 136. Chelwood to Lang, 9 Sep. 1932: LP, vol. 126, f. 22–4.

43 Lang to Chelwood, 14 Sep. 1932: LP, vol. 126, f. 25. Present author's italics.

44 *Church and State*, vol. 1 (recommendations), 49–50.

45 *Church and State*, vol. 1, 58, 87–8.

46 *Church and State*, vol. 1, 62–3.

47 *Church Assembly Proceedings*, 5 Feb. 1936, 65–115, 361; 18 Jun. 1936, 312–63.

48 Lang to Garbett, 1 Nov. 1936: LP, vol. 7, f. 263. Lang to Temple, 1 Nov. 1936: LP, vol. 7, f. 264. Memorandum, 17 Jan. 1937: LP, vol. 7, f. 283. Lang to Temple, 28 Jan. 1938: LP, vol. 7, f. 291. LP, vol. 7, f. 296. Bell to Lang, 17 Aug. 1937: LP, vol. 7, f. 184–219. 27 Aug. 1937: LP, vol. 7, f. 223–8. 20 Sep. 1937: LP, vol. 7, f. 229–35. 30 Sep. 1937: LP, vol. 7, f. 236–44. Memorandum, Oct. 1937: LP, vol. 7, f. 256–9. 3 Jan. 1938: LP, vol. 7, f. 275–9. 14 Jan. 1938: LP, vol. 7, f. 282. Undated 1938: LP, vol. 7, f. 309–12. 3 Jun. 1938: LP, vol. 7, f. 375–7.

49 LP, vol. 7, f. 295.

50 Temple to Lang, 26 Mar. 1938: LP, vol. 7, f. 341–2.

51 Lang to Temple, 29 Mar. 1936: LP, vol. 7, f. 343.

52 Memorandum: LP, vol. 7, f. 387–8. LP, vol. 7. 380, 387.

53 Temple to Lang, 5 Jun. 1939: LP, vol. 7, f. 418. LP, vol. 222, f. 267.

54 LP, vol. 7, f. 420.

55 G. Dix, *The Shape of the Liturgy* (London, 1982), 716. Dix, *Shape*, 725. Bell, *Davidson*, 1331. Dix, *Shape*, 715.

56 Bishops' Meeting, 19 Jan. 1932, BM10 minutes, 20. LP, vol. 149, f. 309–22. Bishops' Meeting, 22 Jan. 1934, BM10, 100.

57 N.P. Williams, *For the Present Distress: A Suggestion for an Interim Rite* (London, 1932); LP, vol. 39, f. 224.

58 Dix, *Shape*, 730.

59 Viscount Halifax to Lang, undated, 1930: LP, vol. 100, f. 374. Lang to Halifax, 17 Jul. 1930: LP, vol. 100, f. 380.

60 Bishops' Meeting, 29 Jun. 1932, BM10, 32.

61 Don to Whitby, 5 Jun. 1934: LP, vol. 39, f. 97.

62 Memorandum, 18 Oct. 1934: LP, vol. 39, f. 100.

63 LP, vol. 39, f. 224. Bishops' Meeting, 21 Jan. 1935, BM10, 160. Blunt to M. Child, 24 Oct. 1934: LP, vol. 39, f. 123. Bell to Bishop Sheddon, 31 Oct. 1934: LP, vol. 39, f. 131. Cecil to Lang, undated: LP, vol. 39, f. 244. Perowne to Lang, 1 Feb. 1935: LP, vol. 39, f. 248. Whittingham to Lang, 2 Feb. 1935: LP, vol. 39, f. 251. Memorandum, 14 Jan. 1935: LP, vol. 39, f. 218. Memorandum, 2 Feb. 1935: LP, vol. 39, f. 250.

64 Bishops' Meeting, 21 Jan. 1935, BM10, 159–60. Bishops' Meeting, 4 Feb. 1935, BM10, 189–90. Bishops' Meeting, 23 Oct. 1935, BM10, 220. Bishops' Meeting, 20 Jan. 1936, BM10, 221.

65 Bishops' Meeting, 21 Oct. 1936, BM10, 246–7. Voting figures not recorded.

66 Lang to Bell, 2 Jan. 1937: LP, vol. 149, f. 314.

67 Bishops' Meeting, 19 Jan. 1937, BM10, 256. Bishops' Meeting, 19 Jan. 1942, BM11, 171.

68 Hughes, *Rivers*, 91. Stamfordham to Lang, 22 Jan. 1928: LP, vol. 58, f. 32.

69 H. Maynard Smith, *Frank, Bishop of Zanzibar* (London, 1926), 35, 284, 302, 304–5.

70 C. Smyth, *Cyril Foster Garbett, Archbishop of York* (London, 1959), 195.

71 Garbett to Lang, 28 Jan. 1928: LP, vol. 58, f. 52.

72 Warman to Lang, 28 Jan. 1928: LP, vol. 58, f. 60.

73 A. Parr-Mayhew to Winnington-Ingram, 14 Dec. 1928: LP, vol. 58, f. 221. LP, vol. 114, f. 57–70. Hughes, *Rivers*, 93–4.

74 Bishops' Meeting, 12 Feb. 1929, BM8, 202.

75 Lang to Perowne, 11 Dec. 1934: LP, vol. 137, f. 85. Perowne to Lang, 9 May 1935: LP, vol. 137, f. 269. E.D. Merritt to the Clerical Secretary of the Church Union, 8 Nov. 1934: LP, vol. 137, f. 79.

76 White-Thompson to N.E. Marshall, 12 Sep. 1939: LP, vol. 172, f. 125. Lang to Bishop Whittingham, 9 Jun. 1933: LP, vol. 117, f. 61. LP, vol. 317, part 1, *passim*; part 2, f. 391.

77 Lang to Merritt, 23 Feb. 1935: LP, vol. 137, f. 93. Lang to Parsons, 26 Nov. 1932: LP, vol. 114, f. 68.

78 Whitby to Lang, 27 Jul. 1936: LP, vol. 146, f. 197–204.

79 A.E. Cornibeer to Don, 23 Jun. 1936: LP, vol. 139, f. 195. C. Harris, 'The Communion of the Sick, Viaticum, and Reservation', in W.K. Lowther Clarke and C. Harris, *Liturgy and Worship: A Companion to the Prayer Book of the Anglican Communion* (London, 1933), 541–615. D.H.S. Cranage, *Loyalty and Order: Being Three Sermons Preached Before the University of Oxford 1932–33, to which are Added Two Sermons Preached in the Cathedral Church of Norwich, July, 1933* (London, 1934), 32–3. D. Stone, *The Faith of the English Catholic* (London, 1926).

80 E.D. Merrit to the Clerical Secretary of the Church Union, 8 Nov. 1934: LP, vol. 137, f. 79. LP, vol. 137, f. 79. Perowne to Don, 12 Dec. 1934: LP, vol. 137, f. 86. Lang to Perowne, 11 Dec. 1934: LP, vol. 137, f. 85.

81 Memorandum by Lang, 12 Jun. 1936: LP, vol. 146, f. 186. LP, vol. 146, f. 186, 197. LP, vol. 146, f. 186. Memorandum, 15 Jun. 1936: LP, vol. 146, f. 190. Bishops' Meeting, 1 Jul. 1936, BM10, f. 240.

82 Temple to Lang, 22 Feb. 1930: LP, vol. 7, f. 20. LP, vol. 7, f. 18–20. Bell, *Davidson*, 1355–6. Temple to Lang, 19 Feb. 1930: LP, vol. 7, f. 18.

83 LP, vol. 7, f. 18.

84 Lang to Temple, 20 Febrary 1930: LP, vol. 7, f. 19.

85 Lang to A. Chandler, 10 Jul. 1929: LP, vol. 95, f. 251.

86 Hughes, *Rivers*, 63–4. Hughes, *Rivers*, 38 and footnote 2. W.R. Inge, 'The Future of Protestantism', *Modern Churchman*, XXII (1932), 230–8.

87 LP, vol. 321, f. 33–46. LP, vol. 270, f. 272–85. LP, vol. 321, f. 256–64.

88 Hughes, *Rivers*, 97–8.

89 LP, vol. 321, f. 101–14.

90 Hastings, *English Christianity*, 197.
91 1929 Bell (Chichester), Wilson (Chelmsford)
    1930 Smith (Rochester)
    1931 Haigh (Coventry), Perowne (Worcester)
    1932 Garbett (Winchester), Parsons (Southwark)
    1933 Heywood (Ely), Macmillan (Guildford), Woodward (Bristol)
    1935 Hunkin (Truro)
    1936 Curzon (Exeter), Lovett (Salisbury), Partridge (Portsmouth), Rawlinson (Derby)
    1937 Kirk (Oxford), Underhill (Bath and Wells)
    1939 Fisher (London)
    1940 Brook (St Edmundsbury and Ipswich), Chavasse (Rochester)
    1941 Cash (Truro), Wynn (Ely)
92 Peart-Binns, *Blunt*, 81. Peart-Binns, *Blunt*, 92. E.W. Kemp, *Kenneth Escott Kirk* (London, 1959), 74. Hughes, *Rivers*, 42, 71–2.
93 Lockhart, *Lang*, 444. Don, 13 Oct. 1932, 25 Oct. 1935, 3 Feb. 1939. Don to C. Weston, 2 Nov. 1934: LP, vol. 130, f. 304.
94 Hastings, *English Christianity*, 277. Hughes, *Rivers*, 88.
95 Bell, *Davidson*, 1319.
96 Bell, *Davidson*, 1320–4. Hastings, *English Christianity*, 202–3. Barnes to Lang, 30 Jul. 1929: LP, vol. 98, f. 228.
97 Lang to Frere, 23 Nov. 1929: LP, vol. 98, f. 237.
98 Dibdin to Barnes, 23 Dec. 1929: LP, vol. 104, f. 126. *The Times*, 11 Feb. 1930.
99 Undated memorandum: LP, vol. 104, f. 146.
100 Barnes to Lang, 17 Feb. 1930: LP, vol. 104, f. 149. LP, vol. 104, f. 156–225. Barnes to S. Royle Shore, 8 Apr. 1930: LP, vol. 104, f. 171.
101 Harris to Lang, 23 Apr. 1930: LP, vol. 104, f. 189.
102 Harris to Lang, 23 Apr. 1930: LP, vol. 104, f. 189. *Church Times*, 30 Oct. 1931.
103 Memorandum, 13 May 1931: LP, vol. 104, f. 231. Lang to Barnes, 30 May 1931: LP, vol. 104, f. 246. Lang to Barnes, 30 May 1931: LP, vol. 104, f. 242. Barnes to Lang, 1 Jun. 1931: LP, vol. 104, f. 253. Temple to Lang, 5 Jun. 1931: LP, vol. 104, f. 264. Lang to Simmonds, 2 Jun. 1931: LP, vol. 104, f. 260.
104 Lang to Barnes, 11 Jul. 1931: LP, vol. 104, f. 283. Barnes to Lang, 13 Jul. 1931: LP, vol. 104, f. 284. Barnes to Lang, 15 Jul. 1931: LP, vol. 104, f. 286.
105 Leader, *The English Churchman and St James's Chronicle*, 16 Jul. 1931: LP, vol. 104, f. 292. *The Times*, 28 Jul. 1931. Lang to Barnes, 18 Jul. 1931: LP, vol. 104, f. 295.
106 LP, vol. 104, f. 297–306.
107 Lang to Barnes, 21 Jul. 1931: LP, vol. 104, f. 312.
108 Barnes to Lang, 22 Jul. 1931: LP, vol. 104, f. 315.
109 LP, vol. 104, f. 327, 328, 335, 336, 339, 341, 342, 344–6, 348. Temple to Lang, 23 Jul. 1931: LP, vol. 104, f. 324–5.
110 Lang to Barnes, 23 Jul. 1931: LP, vol. 104, f. 323.
111 Bishop Christopher Hill to the author, 17 Mar. 2008. Walsingham, 31 May

2004, St Alban's Church, Holborn, 10 Sep. 2006, Lourdes, 25 Sep. 2008, witnessed by author.
112 W.R. Matthews, book review of *Cosmo Gordon Lang*, 1949: LPL, MS 1469, f. 199. LP, vol. 222, f. 267, 275.

7 THE SECOND WORLD WAR

1 Wilkinson, *Dissent*, 261.
2 E. Carpenter, *Archbishop Fisher: His Life and Times* (Norwich, 1991), 85.
3 LP, vol. 271, f. 312. Don to the Rev. G.B. Bentley, 31 May 1939; LP, vol. 80, f. 14.
4 Don, 28 Sep. 1938.
5 LP, vol. 271, f. 369.
6 'The Deliverance and After', 2 Oct. 1938: LP, vol. 271, f. 376.
7 LP, vol. 55, f. 142. *Parliamentary Debates, Lords*, 1936–38, vol. 110, 1321.
8 A. Chandler, 'The Church of England and Nazi Germany, 1933–1945', University of Cambridge Ph.D. thesis, 162–76. *The Times*, 12 Nov. 1938.
9 Chandler, 'The Church of England and Nazi Germany, 1933–1945', 19. Don, 8 Dec. 1938. Don, 14–18 Nov. 1938. Don, 14 Dec. 1938.
10 *Parliamentary Debates, Lords*, 1936–38, vol. 110, 319.
11 Lang to J. Anderson, 12 Nov. 1938: LP, vol. 77, f. 29. LP, vol. 77, f. 48. LP, vol. 78, f. 48. Don to Bishop Parsons of Southwark, 20 Feb. 1939: LP, vol. 77, f. 78. Don, 20 Jun. 1939. Hoare to Lang, 12 Jul. 1939: LP, vol. 87, f. 335. LP, vol. 87, f. 350. LP, vol. 87, f. 350. Hoare to Lang, 10 Aug. 1939: LP, vol. 318, f. 151.
12 *The Times*, 27, 29 Apr. 1939. Don, 5 May, 11 May 1939.
13 Don, 29–31 May 1939.
14 Undated memorandum by Lang, 'Christian Churches and Peace': LP, vol. 84, f. 137. Lang to Halifax, 9 Dec. 1939: LP, vol. 84, f. 142. Memorandum, 'Germany in Time of War', 29 Jan. 1940: LP, vol. 84, f. 152.
15 Don, 23 Aug. 1939. Don, 23 Aug. 1939. Lang to Don, 23 Aug. 1939: letter pasted into Don's diary on 24 Aug. 1939. Don, 24–6 Aug. 1939, 30 Aug. 1939.
16 Don, 8 Oct. 1931, 4 Aug. 1939. Wilkinson, *Dissent*, 261. *The Times*, 4 Sep. 1939, *Church Times*, 8 Sep. 1939.
17 Don, 30 Sep. 1939, 1 Oct. 1939.
18 Don, 12 Sep. 1939, 19 Oct. 1939, 17 Apr. 1940, 23 Apr. 1940. LP, vol. 223, f. 286.
19 Hastings, *English Christianity*, 373. Bilton to Lang, 16 Oct. 1939: LP, vol. 84, f. 118. Byard to Lang, 22 Nov. 1939: LP, vol. 84, f. 120. Printed appeal signed by twenty MPs, 10 Nov. 1939: LP, vol. 84, f. 136. Don to Bilton, 20 Oct. 1939: LP, vol. 84, f. 119. Don to Byard, 24 Nov. 1939: LP, vol. 84, f. 123. Don to Paton, 21 Nov. 1939: LP, vol. 84, f. 127.
20 Lang to Marchant, 10 Jun. 1941: Bod., Marchant MSS, f. 87.
21 'Christian Citizenship in Time of War': LP, vol. 322, f. 126–30.
22 *Canterbury Diocesan Gazette*, Dec. 1939, 3.

23 A. Marrin, *The Last Crusade: The Church of England and the First World War* (Durham, NC, 1974), 189.

24 *Diocesan Gazette*, Dec. 1939, 4. *Diocesan Gazette*, Dec. 1939, 4. *Diocesan Gazette*, Dec. 1939, 6.

25 LP, vol. 272, 31 Dec. 1939, f. 86; Easter Day 1940, f. 96; 26 May 1940, f. 111; 1 Sep. 1940, f. 131; 8 Sep. 1940, f. 140; 29 Dec. 1940, f. 177; 23 Mar. 1941, f. 208; 7 Sep. 1941, f. 231; 28 Dec. 1941, f. 280; 1 Nov. 1942, f. 409; 22 Nov. 1942, f. 418. LP, vol. 322, undated transcript, f. 154. LP, vol. 272, f. 111. LP, vol. 272, f. 179.

26 *Yorkshire Herald*, 19 Oct. 1914. *Scotsman*, 10 Dec. 1914. *Parliamentary Debates, Lords*, 1941–42, vol. 221, 182–5. LP, vol. 272, f. 115, 142, 183, 211, 212–13, 231, 233. Iremonger, *Temple*, 555–6. LP, vol. 272, f. 145.

27 LP, vol. 272, f. 111, 134, 137, 140, 178, 209, 232, 280, 236, 283–4.

28 LP, vol. 272, f. 91–2, 131, 177, 208, 231, 240

29 LP, vol. 272, f. 91–2, 131, 177, 208, 231, 240.

30 LP, vol. 272, f. 92.

31 Bishops Meetings Minutes, BM11, f. 35–6. LP, vol. 80, f. 355–86.

32 *Chronicle of Convocation*, 27 May 1941, 2–3.

33 Wilkinson, *Dissent*, 120, 291.

34 LP, vol. 45, f. 278.

35 Wilkinson, *Dissent*, 264. Temple to Lang, 5 May 1936: LP, vol. 145, f. 273. Don to A.A. Hamilton, 13 May 1939: LP, vol. 80, f. 9. *Parliamentary Debates, Lords, 1938–39*, vol. 113, 32.

36 Lang to Bishop Rawlinson of Derby, 28 Apr. 1939: LP, vol. 80, f. 5.

37 *Parliamentary Debates, Lords, 1938–39*, vol. 113, 32.

38 Gliddon to Lang, 21 Feb. 1940: LP, vol. 80, f. 64.

39 Lang to Gliddon, 28 Feb. 1940: LP, vol. 80, f. 69. Gliddon to Lang, 19 Mar. 1940: LP, vol. 80, f. 70. Don to Temple, 5 Apr. 1940: LP, vol. 80, f. 80.

40 'Report on the Deputation of Pacifist Clergy to the Archbishop of Canterbury and the Archbishop of York': LP, vol. 80. f. 114–21.

41 'Deputation': LP, vol. 80, f. 123–5.

42 LP, vol. 80, f. 148–58, 178, 186–264. Wilkinson, *Dissent*, 248, 290. LP, vol. 80, f. 232, 238.

43 J.C. Heenan, *Not the Whole Truth* (London, 1971), 275.

44 *Parliamentary Debates, Lords, 1939–40*, vol. 115, 95.

45 *Parliamentary Debates, Lords, 1939–40*, vol. 115, 97.

46 *Parliamentary Debates, Lords, 1939–40*, vol. 115, 98.

47 Iremonger, *William Temple*, 428–34.

48 Ellis to Lang, 24 Sep. 1939: LP, vol. 84, f. 111. Don to Ellis, 8 Dec. 1939: LP, vol. 84, f. 135. Lang to Halifax, 25 Sep. 1939: LP, vol. 84, f. 114. *Address (In Questo Giorno) of Pope Pius XII to the Sacred College of Cardinals on Christmas Eve 1939* (London, 1940). Lang to Ellis, 17 Aug. 1940: LP, vol. 84, f. 168.

49 LP, vol. 84, f. 177–93.

50 J.C. Heenan, *Crown of Thorns* (London, 1974), 311. LP, vol. 84, f. 195–209.

51 LP, vol. 84, f, 195–209. Dashwood to Lang, 20 Jun. 1941: LP, vol. 84, f. 256. Churchill to Lang, 2 Jul. 1941: LP, vol. 84, f. 258.

52 *Chronicle of Convocation*, 27 May 1941, 3.

53 T. Moloney, *Westminster, Whitehall and the Vatican: The Role of Cardinal Hinsley, 1935–1943* (London, 1985), 186.

54 Heenan, *Thorns*, 312. Hinsley to the English Catholic hierarchy, 7 Aug. 1940: quoted by Moloney, *Westminster*, 186.

55 Moloney, *Westminster*, 187. Heenan, *Thorns*, 311.

56 Moloney, *Westminster*, 189. Bell to Lang, 5 Feb. 1941: LP, vol. 84, f. 284. Lang to Bell, 11 Feb. 1941: LP, vol. 84, f. 285. Lang to Hinsley, 11 Feb. 1941: LP, vol. 84, f. 286. Hinsley to Lang, 13 Feb. 1941: LP, vol. 84, f. 287. Lang to Bell, 15 Feb. 1942: LP, vol. 84, f. 295.

57 Moloney, *Westminster*, 192.

58 LP, vol. 84, f. 295–304. British Library Sound Archives, 29E BBC Archive 1422/3/04S3–4BBC.

59 J.W. Welch to Lang, 14 May 1941: LP, vol. 84, f. 303. *English Churchman*, 5 Jun. 1941. Moloney, *Westminster*, 198. J.L. Fosbrooke to Lang, 30 Jun. 1941: LP, vol. 84, f. 316. 9 Jul. 1941: LP, vol. 84, f. 318. 31 Jul. 1941: LP, vol. 84, f. 326. 7 Aug. 1941: LP, vol. 84, f. 328. 2 Sep. 1941: LP, vol. 84, f. 335. LP, vol. 84, f. 324. Moloney, *Westminster*, 197–200.

60 Moloney, *Westminster*, 193.

61 LP, vol. 84, f. 324. Moloney, *Westminster*, 204.

62 Lockhart, *Lang*, 381. T. Lawson, *The Church of England and the Holocaust: Christianity, Memory and Nazism* (Woodbridge, 2006), 74–5.

63 *Canterbury Diocesan Gazette*, Aug. 1941.

64 *Parliamentary Debates, Lords, 1940–41*, vol. 120, 389–92.

65 *Parliamentary Debates, Lords, 1940–41*, vol. 120, 389–92.

66 Lawson, *Holocaust*, 76.

67 Moloney, *Westminster*, 224, 227.

68 Broadcast, 7 Sep. 1941: LP, vol. 272, f. 233. *Diocesan Gazette*, Nov. 1941. Broadcast, 28 Dec. 1941: LP, vol. 272, f. 281.

69 Middlemas and Barnes, *Baldwin*, 735.

70 W. Elliott, Minister of Health, to Lang, 31 Aug. 1939: LP, vol. 88, f. 35. Experiences related to the author by former evacuees in a pastoral context. LP, vol. 88, f. 69.

71 *Parliamentary Debates, Lords, 1938–39*, vol. 114, 1622.

72 *Parliamentary Debates, Lords, 1939–40*, vol. 115, 469–70.

73 *Parliamentary Debates, Lords, 1939–40*, vol. 115, 469–70. LP, vol. 88, f. 73. E. Rich, London County Council education officer, to Lang, 10 Apr. 1940: LP, vol. 88, f. 94–7. Lang to Perry, 16 Jul. 1940: LP, vol. 88, f. 39. 18 Jul. 1940: LP, vol. 88, f. 32.

74 Lang to Perry, 18 Jul. 1940: LP, vol. 88, f. 32. Lang to Bishop Rose of Dover, 2 Jul. 1940: LP, vol. 88, f. 99. LP, vol. 88, f. 101. Macdonald to Lang, 9 Jul. 1940: LP, vol. 88, f. 102–3.

75 V. Bovenizer, secretary to A. Eden, to Don, 15 Jul. 1940: LP, vol. 88, f. 107.
76 D. Beckingham to Lang, 28 Jul. 1940: LP, vol. 88, f. 110. Beckingham to White-Thompson, 1 Aug. 1940: LP, vol. 88, f. 114. White-Thompson to Beckingham, 31 Jul. 1940: LP, vol. 88, f. 113. Lang to Macdonald, 2 Aug. 1940: LP, vol. 88, f. 116. Macdonald to Lang, 16 Aug. 1940: LP, vol. 88, f. 119. Macdonald to Lang, 3 Sep. 1940: LP, vol. 88, f. 122.
77 Waley Cohen to Lang, 16 Nov. 1939: LP, vol. 85, f. 13.
78 H. Gutwurzel to Lang, 31 May 1940: LP, vol. 85, f. 98.
79 LP, vol. 85, f. 2–5, 26–8, 44. E. Appelbaum, W. Cohn and C. Seckelson to Lang, 4 Mar. 1940: LP, vol. 85, f. 27–8. Lang to Anderson, 6 Mar. 1940: LP, vol. 85, f. 30. Anderson to Lang, 9 Mar. 1940: LP, vol. 85, f. 34. *Parliamentary Debates, Lords*, 1932–33, vol. 87, 225, 30 Mar. 1933. *Chronicle of Convocation*, 31 May 1933, 22–3. *Proceedings of the Church Assembly*, 20 Nov. 1935, 466. *The Times*, 28 Jun. 1933. *The Times*, 17 Nov. 1933, 16 May 1934.
80 LP, vol. 85, f. 119, 131. Lang to Anderson, 8 Jul. 1940: LP, vol. 85, f. 138.
81 L. Masterman to Lang, 18 Jul. 1940: LP, vol. 85, f. 184. Bell to Don, 23 Jul. 1940: LP, vol. 85, f. 167. O. Quick to Don, 31 Jul. 1940: LP, vol. 85, f. 184.
82 LP, vol. 85, f. 206, 212–71. H. Friess to Lang, 15 Dec. 1940: LP, vol. 85, f. 261.
83 Lawson, *Holocaust*, 81. Lawson, *Holocaust*, 82. My italics.
84 LPL, MS 220 ('Notebook A'), MS 221 ('Notebook C').
85 Bishop Herbert of Blackburn to Temple, 1 Aug. 1939: LP, vol. 82, f. 1. LP, vol. 82, f. 36.
86 LP, vol. 82, f. 58.
87 Lang to Gort, 17 Oct. 1939: LP, vol. 82, f. 60. Gort to Lang, 26 Oct. 1939: LP, vol. 82, f. 85. Lang to Gort, 31 Oct. 1939: LP, vol. 82, f. 92.
88 LP, vol. 82, f. 59, 65, 69.
89 LP, vol. 82, f. 69. A. Neilans to Lang, 20 Oct. 1939: LP, vol. 82, f. 73. Lang to Temple, 10 Nov. 1939: LP, vol. 82, f. 110. Don to Neilans, 23 Oct. 1939: LP, vol. 82, f. 79.
90 LP, vol. 82, f. 122, 144. LPL, MS 2448, f. 12–15.
91 LP, vol. 82, f. 152, 177, 206.
92 Lang to Neilans, 14 Feb. 1940: LP, vol. 82, f. 222. P. Depret to Lang, 26 Feb. 1940: LP, vol. 82, f. 248. M. Boegner to Lang, 16 Apr. 1940: LP, vol. 82, f. 301.
93 Lang to Batty, 22 Mar. 1940: LP, vol. 82, f. 281. LP, vol. 82, f. 295, 311.
94 Lang to Bell, 18 May 1940: LP, vol. 82, f. 352. Lang to Temple, 16 May 1940: LP, vol. 82, f. 348.
95 LP, vol. 82, f. 68. Lang to Hore-Belisha, 23 Oct. 1939: LP, vol. 82, f. 76. Hore-Belisha to Lang, 8 Nov. 1939: LP, vol. 82, f. 107.
96 Lang to Astor, 13 Feb. 1940: LP, vol. 82, f. 219. LP, vol. 82, f. 249. Stanley to Lang, 13 Mar. 1940: LP, vol. 82, f. 263. W. Womersley, Minister of Pensions, to Lang, 7 Mar. 1940: LP, vol. 82, f. 257.
97 Don, 25 Sep. 1939.
98 Minutes of the Bishops' War Committee, 1939–1944, MS 2448.

99 Bishops' War Committee, MS 2448. Lang was present on 12 Oct. 1939, 14 Nov. 1939, 5 Dec. 1939, 10 Jan. 1940, 14 Feb. 1940, 10 Jul. 1940, 27 Nov. 1940, 26 Feb. 1940. It is unclear from the minutes whether he was also present on 15 May 1940, 4 Jun. 1940, 25 Mar. 1941.

100 LPL, Bell Papers, vol. 301, f. 35. LP, vol. 223, f. 6–7. BP, vol. 271, f. 43–56.

101 LP, vol. 223, f. 7.

102 LPL, Bell Papers, vol. 271, f. 43–54.

103 LP, vol. 223, f. 7. Smyth, *Garbett*, 268, 271.

104 St Thomas Aquinas, *Summa Theologica*, II-II, question 40, article 2.

105 Don to E. Brown, Minister of Labour, 6 May 1939: LP, vol. 33, f. 203. J. Anderson, Home Secretary, to Lang, 18 Jan. 1939: LP, vol. 77, f. 53. Don to Brown, 6 May 1939: LP, vol. 77, f. 203. LP, vol. 77, f. 289. Lang to J.F. Martin, 11 Feb. 1941: LP, vol. 78, f. 331.

106 Don to J. McLeod Campbell, secretary of the Bishops' War Committee, 29 Aug. 1940: LP, vol. 87, f. 305. Lang to Martin, 11 Feb. 1941: LP, vol. 78, f. 303.

107 LP, vol. 79, f. 5, 63. Temple to Lang, 10 Sep. 1939: LP, vol. 79, f. 72. C.D. Symons to Lang, 7 Sep. 1939: LP, vol. 79, f. 66. J. Walkey to Lang, 7 Sep. 1939: LP, vol. 79, f. 67.

108 Haigh to Don, 17 Oct. 1939: LP, vol. 79, f. 88. C.D. Symons to Lang, 30 Oct. 1939: LP, vol. 79, f. 98. Lang to F.R. Barry, 7 Dec. 1939: LP, vol. 79, f. 117. LP, vol. 79, f. 90, 112, 146.

109 LP, vol. 79, f. 131.

110 S. Batty to Lang, 24 Dec. 1939: LP, vol. 79, f. 143. LP, vol. 79, f. 81, 118, 146, 189. Temple to Lang, 30 Sep. 1941: LP, vol. 79, f. 302.

111 Don to E. Brown, 18 Jul. 1939: LP, vol. 78, f. 18. LP, vol. 77, f. 287, 289. Don to Brown, 18 Jul. 1939: LP, vol. 78, f. 18.

112 LP, vol. 78, f. 79.

113 Lang to Brown, 2 Sep. 1939: LP, vol. 78, f. 84. Lang to Brown, 16 Sep. 1939: LP, vol. 78, f. 150–2. Brown to Lang, 23 Sep. 1939: LP, vol. 78, f. 187.

114 Don to Brown, 28 Sep. 1939: LP, vol. 78, f. 189. Don to Warman, 28 Sep. 1939: LP, vol. 78, f. 193. Don to Warman, 2 Oct. 1939: LP, vol. 78, f. 203. Brown to Lang, 11 Nov. 1939: LP, vol. 78, f. 236.

115 Haigh to Don, 21 Jul. 1939: LP, vol. 78, f. 35.

116 W.R. Matthews to Lang, 16 May 1940: LP, vol. 78, f. 263. 30 May 1940: LP, vol. 78, f. 284. 24 Jun. 1940: LP, vol. 78, f. 305. 27 Jun. 1940: LP, vol. 78, f. 312. 15 Jul. 1940: LP, vol. 78, f. 321. 18 Jul. 1940: LP, vol. 78, f. 324. P. de Labilliere to Lang, 20 May 1940: LP, vol. 78, f. 268. R. Hanson to Lang, 24 May 1940: LP, vol. 78, f. 269. LP, vol. 78, f. 320.

117 LP, vol. 83, f. 121–44, 159, 177. Don, 12 Sep. 1939.

118 LP, vol. 83, f. 199, 419.

119 *Church of England Newspaper*, 5, 12 Apr. 1940.

120 LP, vol. 83, f. 241, 253. Lang to G. Dawson, 23 May 1940: LP, vol. 83, f. 270. Lang to Archbishops of Wales, Armagh, the Primus of the Scottish Episcopal

Church, R. Bond, A. Main and Cardinal Hinsley, undated: LP, vol. 83, f. 242, 244. LP, vol. 83, f. 280. Don, 26 May 1940.

121 Lang to Hardinge, 3 Aug. 1940: LP, vol. 83, f. 359. Hardinge to Lang, 6 Aug. 1940: LP, vol. 83, f. 361. LP, vol. 83, f. 367. Lang to the Archbishops of Wales and Armagh, the Primus of the Scottish Episcopal Church, the Moderator of the General Assembly of the Church of Scotland, the Rev. Dr R. Bond, 7 Aug. 1940: LP, vol. 83, f. 362. Lang to Hinsley, 7 Aug. 1940: LP, vol. 83, f. 365. LP, vol. 83, f. 422–33; LP, vol. 84, f. 10–12, 40–56, 86–7, 90–9, 102–3. Don, 8 Mar. 1941. Lang to A. Bevir, 13 Mar. 1942: LP, vol. 84, f. 93. Hardinge to Lang, 22 Feb. 1941: LP, vol. 83, f. 422. LP, vol. 84, f. 103.

122 Don, 3 Oct. 1939. Anderson to Lang, 5 Oct. 1939: LP, vol. 83, f. 25. Lang to the Rev. Dr Robert Bond, Hinsley, and the Moderator of the General Assembly of the Church of Scotland, 5 Oct. 1939: LP, vol. 83, f. 17, 19, 21. LP, vol. 83, f. 14, 35–6, 54–109.

123 English Church Union, *Religious Ministrations in the Army* (1916). LP, vol. 79, f. 54.

124 Talbot to Lang, 4 Jun. 1941: LP, vol. 88, f. 365. Lang to chaplain-general, 9 Jun. 1941: LP, vol. 88, f. 369.

125 Lang to Talbot, 16 Jun. 1941: LP, vol. 88, f. 371.

126 Temple to Lang, 12 Aug. 1941: LP, vol. 88, f. 383. Lang to B. Horner, CR, 22 Aug. 1941: LP, vol. 88, f. 385. Horner to Lang, 25 Aug. 1941: LP, vol. 88, f. 387.

127 Lockhart, *Lang*, 368. Moloney, *Westminster*, 30–1, 121.

128 Temple to Don, 23 Oct. 1940: LP, vol. 88, f. 329. Fisher to Lang, 27 Feb. 1941: LP, vol. 88, f. 347. R. Assheton, Minister of Labour and National Service, to Don, 30 Jan. 1941: LP, vol. 88, f. 331.

129 LP, vol. 88, f. 354. Don to Assheton, 6 Feb. 1941: LP, vol. 88, f. 337. Lang to *The Times*, 3 Apr. 1941: LP, vol. 88, f. 361.

130 R. Parsons, Director of Religious Education, the National Society, to Lang, 17 Feb. 1941: LP, vol. 88, f. 340. Lang to H. Ramsbottom, President of the Board of Education, 24 Feb. 1941: LP, vol. 88, f. 345. Ramsbottom to Lang, 3 Mar. 1941: LP, vol. 88, f. 349. Lang to Parsons, 5 Mar. 1941: LP, vol. 88, f. 351.

131 Fisher to Lang, 27 Feb. 1941: LP, vol. 88, f. 347. Memorandum, 6 Mar. 1941: LP, vol. 88, f. 354. Lang to Churchill, 17 Mar. 1941: LP, vol. 88, f. 355. Churchill to Fisher, 22 Mar. 1941: LP, vol. 88, f. 358. I. White-Thompson to A. Bevir, 25 Mar. 1941: LP, vol. 88, f. 360.

132 LP, vol. 88, f. 361–62.

133 A. Gilbert, *The Making of Post-Christian Britain: A History of the Secularisation of Modern Britain* (London, 1980), 95.

134 LP, vol. 223, f. 13; Don, 6 Sep. 1940.

135 LP, vol. 223, f. 17.

136 Don, 20 Sep. 1940, 25 Dec. 1940; LP, vol. 223, f. 10.

137 LP, vol. 223, f. 9–11.

138 Don, 15 Jan. 1941; LP, vol. 223, f. 11, 16.

139 Smythe, *Garbett*, 269.

140 Don, 27 Mar. 1941.

141 Annotation by Alan Don on page 434 of his copy of Lockhart's biography of Lang: Family Papers of Mr Robin Don.

142 LP, vol. 223, f. 13, 286.

143 LP, vol. 223, f. 12–13.

144 Don, 21 Jan. 1942. Lockhart, *Lang*, 442.

145 Carpenter, *Fisher*, 85.

146 Hastings, *English Christianity*, 383.

147 *Chronicle of Convocation*, 27 May 1941, 2–3.

8 LANG'S LAST DAYS

1 Don, 31 Mar. 1942, 2 Apr. 1942. George VI to Lang, 21 Dec. 1941: LP, vol. 318, f. 160.

2 Diary of Hilda Neal, 14 Oct. 1942: IWM, Private Papers, 11987.

3 Diary of Hilda Neal, 23 Apr. 1942: IWM, Private Papers, 11987.

4 Don, 11 Dec. 1941, 20 Mar. 1942. LP, vol. 272, f. 409–12, 418–23.

5 Don, 9 May 1944. Lang to Todd, 17 Nov. 1945: family papers of Mr David Malcolm.

6 Don, 3 May 1944.

7 Canon Ingram Hill, interview, 8 May 2002. Don, 27 Oct. 1944, 29 Oct. 1944.

8 Don, 24 Jul. 1941, 28 Feb. 1942, 29 Oct. 1944. Lockhart, *Lang*, 447.

9 E. Ford, interview 16 Nov. 2001. Todd, *Eighth Veil*, 44. Lockhart, *Lang*, 453.

10 J. Cox, *The English Churches in a Secular Society, Lambeth 1870–1930* (Oxford, 1992), 272–3. J. Morris, *Religion and Urban Change, Croydon 1840–1914* (London, 1992), 177. R. McKibbin, *Classes and Cultures, England 1918–1951* (Oxford, 2000), 273–6.

11 H. McLeod, *The Religious Crisis of the 1960s* (Oxford, 2007), 257, 262, 264–5.

12 Ziegler, *King Edward VIII*, 93–4.

13 LP, vol. 21, f. 34–5. Undated memorandum: LP, vol, 21, f. 77. Memorandum, 19 Nov. 1936: LP, vol. 21, f. 134. O.S. Cleverly to Don, 16 Mar. 1937: LP, vol. 22, f. 17.

14 Hastings, *English Christianity* , 444.

15 Hastings, *English Christianity*, 444–7.

16 Lockhart, *Lang*, 291.

17 Don, 15 Jan. 1942. A.J.C. was A.J. Clements, stenographer at Lambeth Palace.

18 Lockhart, *Lang*, 455–6.

Bibliography and Broadcast Sources

Primary Sources

Bodleian Library, Oxford
Papers of Herbert Asquith, the first Earl of Oxford and Asquith; the Bickersteth Family; Lionel George Curtis; Geoffrey Dawson; Sir James Marchant; Sir Walter Monckton, the first Viscount Monckton of Brenchley; the first Viscount Sankey; the third Earl of Selborne

Borthwick Institute for Archives, York
Papers of Archbishop Cosmo Lang; Archbishop William Temple; the second Viscount Halifax; the first Earl of Halifax

British Library, London, Sound Archives
Funeral of King George V, 28 January 1936

Religious service including abdication address by Archbishop Lang, 13 December 1936

Coronation preparation service and address by Archbishop Lang, 9 May 1937

New Year address by Archbishop Lang, 29 December 1940

'Christian Foundations', speech by Archbishop Lang at Sword of the Spirit meeting, 11 May 1941

Cambridge University Library
Papers of Stanley Baldwin, the first Earl Baldwin of Bewdley

Canterbury Cathedral Archives
Chapter Act Book, 1924–31

Correspondence of the Dean and Chapter

Federal Bureau of Investigation, Washington DC, USA
File on the Duke and Duchess of Windsor

Imperial War Museums
Private Papers 11987, Diary of Hilda Neal

Institute of Historical Research, University of London
Parliamentary Debates (Lords)
The Times

Lambeth Palace Library
Church of England Newspaper
Chronicle of Convocation
Diaries and papers of the Rev. Alan C. Don
Papers of Bishop George Bell; Archbishop Edward Benson; Archbishop Randall
    Davidson; Canon John Douglas; Archbishop Geoffrey Fisher; Archbishop
    Cosmo Lang; Archbishop Frederick Temple; Archbishop William Temple
Proceedings of the Church Assembly

Lincolnshire Archives
Papers of Perry, Lord Brownlow

The National Archives, Kew
Records of the Home Office
Records of the Prime Minister's Office

National Library of Scotland, Edinburgh
Papers of Sir Charles Dalrymple, Newhailes Collection; Seton Gordon; Hugh
    Pattison Macmillan

Rhodes House Library, Oxford
Papers of Lord Lugard

Ripon College Cuddesdon, Oxfordshire
Church Times
Guardian

Royal Archives, Windsor Castle
Papers of King George V
Papers of Queen Mary
Queen Victoria's Journal

Sir Edward Ford
Diaries of Mary Catherine Talbot

Mr John Green-Wilkinson
Papers of Bishop Oliver Green-Wilkinson

Mr David Malcolm
Correspondence between Archbishop Lang and Ann Todd

Sir John Maxwell Macdonald
Papers of John Morton Macdonald

Sir Clive Rose
Papers of the Right Rev. Alfred Rose, Bishop of Dover

INTERVIEWS

Sir Edward Ford, 19 October 2001
H.M. Queen Elizabeth The Queen Mother, 4 December 2001
The Rt Rev. John Perry, 11 January 2002
Mr David Malcolm, 7 February 2002
Canon Derek Ingram Hill, 8 and 9 May 2002
Mr Irvine Watson, 10 July 2002
The Most Rev. and Rt Hon. Dr Rowan Williams, 17 July 2003
Sir John Maxwell Macdonald, 20 and 21 August 2003
Lady Alethia Eliot, 3 October 2003
Mr John Green-Wilkinson, 11 February 2004
The Rt Rev. Christopher Hill, 1 July 2004
Sir Clive Rose, 9 August 2006

PRINTED PRIMARY SOURCES

Alcuin Club Prayer Book Revision Pamphlets, *Reservation, Its Purpose and Method, With a Letter on Reservation by Walter Howard Frere*, Mowbray, London, 1953.
Aquinas, St Thomas, *The Summa Theologica*, Benzinger Brothers, New York City, 1947.
Braley, E.F., *Letters of Herbert Hensley Henson*, SPCK, London, 1950.
Church and State: The Report of the Archbishops' Commission on Relations Between the Church and the State, London, 1936.
Church of England Liturgical Commission, *Prayer Book Revision in the Church of England, A Memorandum of the Church of England Liturgical Commission*, SPCK, London, 1957.
Cranage, D.H.S., *Loyalty and Order: Being Three Sermons Preached Before the University of Oxford 1932–33, to which are Added Two Sermons Preached in the Cathedral Church of Norwich, July, 1933*, OUP and Humphrey Milford, London, 1934.
Daniel, E., *The Prayer Book: Its History, Language and Contents*, Wells, Gardner, Darton and Co., London, 1894.
Dix, G., *A Detection of Aumbries*, Dacre Press, London, 1942.

—— *The Shape of the Liturgy,* A. and C. Black, London, 1982.

English Church Union, *Religious Ministrations in the Army,* London, 1916.

Erickson, J., *Invasion 1940: The Nazi Invasion Plan for Britain by SS General Walter Schellenberg,* St Ermins, London, 2000.

Freestone, W.H., *The Sacrament Reserved,* Alcuin Club, Mowbray, London, 1917.

Garbett, C., *The Claims of the Church of England,* Hodder and Stoughton, London, 1947.

Hart-Davis, D. (ed.), *King's Counsellor, Abdication and War: The Diaries of Sir Alan Lascelles,* Weidenfeld and Nicolson, London, 2006.

Hardinge, H., *Loyal to Three Kings,* William Kimber, London, 1967.

Harrison, B. (ed.), *Oxford Dictionary of National Biography,* OUP, Oxford 2004.

Henson, H.H., *Retrospect of an Unimportant Life,* 3 volumes, OUP, London, 1942, 1943, 1950.

Herbert, C., *Twenty Years Aschbishop of York,* Wells, Gardner, Darton and Co., London, 1929.

Hughes, A., *The Rivers of the Flood, A Personal Account of the Catholic Movement in the 20th Century,* Faith Press, London, 1961.

Inge, W.R., 'The Future of Protestantism', *Modern Churchman,* XXII, London, 1932.

Iremonger, F.A., 'The Old Archbishop and the New,' *Theology,* London, May 1942.

James, R.R. (ed.), *Chips: The Diaries of Sir Henry Channon,* Weidenfeld and Nicolson, London, 1967.

Jardine, R.A., *At Long Last,* Murray and Gee, Hollywood, 1943.

Jones, T., *A Diary with Letters,* OUP, Oxford, 1954.

King-Hall, S., *The Crowning of the King and Queen,* Evans Brothers, London, 1937.

Lang, C.G., *The Miracles of Jesus as Marks of the Way of Life,* Isbister, London, 1904.

—— *The Opportunity of the Church of England: Lectures Delivered in the Divinity School of the University of Cambridge in 1904,* Longmans, Green, London, 1905.

—— *The Young Clanroy: A Romance of the '45,* Smith Elder, London, 1897.

——*Thoughts on Some of The Parables of Jesus,* Pitman, London, 1906.

—— *Tupper (Canon A.D. Tupper-Carey): A Memoir of the Life and Work of a Very Human Parish Priest,* Constable, London, 1945.

Lowther Clark, W.K. and C. Harris (eds), *Liturgy and Worship,* SPCK, London, 1936.

Mackenzie, C., *The Windsor Tapestry, Being a Study of the Life, Heritage and Abdication of HRH The Duke of Windsor, KG,* Book Club, London, 1939.

Mallet, V. (ed.), *Life with Queen Victoria: Marie Mallet's Letters from Court 1887–1901,* John Murray, London, 1968.

Phillimore, R., *The Ecclesiastical Laws of the Church of England,* Sweet and Maxwell, Stevens, London, 1895.

Pullman, L., 'Prayer Book Revision', *All Saints' Margaret Street Parish Paper*, London, March 1911.

Pope Pius XII, *Address (In Questo Giorno) of Pope Pius XII to the Sacred College of Cardinals on Christmas Eve 1939 (The Pope's Five Peace Points)*, CTS, London, 1940.

Ponsonby, F., *Recollections of Three Reigns*, Eyre and Spottiswood, London, 1951.

Stone, Darwell, *The Faith of the English Catholic*, Longmans, Green and Co., London, 1926.

Storrs, R.A.H., *Orientations*, Nicholson and Watson, London, 1943.

Todd, A., *The Eighth Veil*, William Kimber, London, 1980.

United States War Department, *Instructions for American Servicemen in Britain*, Washington, DC, 1942.

Vincent, J., *The Crawford Papers: The Journals of David Lindsay, Earl of Crawford and Balcarres*, MUP, Manchester, 1984.

Wells, W.B., *Why Edward Went: Crown, Clique and Church*, Robert M. MacBride, New York, 1937.

Williams, N.P., *For the Present Distress: A Suggestion for an Interim Rite*, London, 1932.

Williamson, P. and E. Baldwin (eds), *Baldwin Papers: A Conservative Statesman, 1908–1947*, CUP, Cambridge, 2004.

Windsor, Duke of, *A King's Story: The Memoirs of HRH the Duke of Windsor, KG*, Cassell, London, 1951.

Windsor, Duchess of, *The Heart Has Its Reasons*, Companion Book Club, London, 1958.

Secondary Sources

Bailey, S., *A Tactful God*, Gracewing, Leominster, 1995.

Baldwin, S., *The Chapel Royal: Ancient and Modern*, Duckworth, London, 1990.

Barber, M., 'Randall Davidson: A Partial Retrospective', in S. Taylor (ed.), *From Cranmer to Davidson: A Church of England Miscellany*, Church of England Records Society, 7, Boydell, Woodbridge, 2002.

—— 'Tales of the Unexpected: Glimpses of Friends in the Archives of Lambeth Palace Library', *Journal of the Friends' Historical Society*, London, 2004.

Barnes, J., *Ahead of His Age: Bishop Barnes of Birmingham*, Collins, London, 1979.

Barry, F.R., *Mervyn Haigh*, SPCK, London, 1964.

Beeson, T., *The Bishops*, SCM, London, 2002.

Bell, G.K.A., *Randall Davidson, Archbishop of Canterbury*, OUP, Oxford, 1935.

Bellenger, D.A. and S. Fletcher, *The Mitre and the Crown: A History of the Archbishops of Canterbury*, Sutton, Stroud, 2005.

Bibbee, J., *Anglo-Catholicism and the Orthodox East: William Birkbeck and the Quest for Unity 1888–1916*, Anglo-Catholic History Society, London, 2007.

Bloch, M., *The Duchess of Windsor*, London, 1996.

Bradford, S., *George VI*, Penguin, London, 1989.

Bradley, I., *God Save the Queen: The Spiritual Dimension of Monarchy*, DLT, London, 2002.

Brendon, P., *The Dark Valley: A Panorama of the 1930s*, Pimlico, London, 2001.

Bromhead, P.A., *The House of Lords in Contemporary Politics, 1911–1957*, Routledge and Paul, London, 1958.

Brown, C.G., *Religion and Society in Twentieth-Century Britain*, Pearson Longman, Harlow, 2006.

—— *The Death of Christian Britain*, Routledge, London, 2001.

Buchanan, T., *Britain and the Spanish Civil War*, CUP, Cambridge, 1997.

Burns, A., 'W.J. Conybeare: Church Parties', in S. Taylor (ed.), *From Cranmer to Davidson: A Church of England Miscellany*, Church of England Records Society, 7, Boydell, Woodbridge, 2002.

Cannadine, D., 'The Context, Performance and Meaning of Ritual: The British Monarchy and the "Invention of Tradition", c. 1820–1977', in E. Hobsbawm and T. Ranger (eds), *The Invention of Tradition*, CUP, Cambridge, 1983.

Carpenter, E., *Cantuar: The Archbishops in their Office*, Cassell, London, 1971.

—— *Archbishop Fisher: His Life and Times*, Canterbury Press, Norwich, 1991.

Carpenter, S.C., *Winnington-Ingram*, Hodder and Stoughton, London, 1949.

Chadwick, O., *Hensley Henson, A Study in the Friction between Church and State*, Canterbury Press, Norwich, 1994.

—— *Michael Ramsey: A Life*, Clarendon Press, Oxford, 1990.

—— 'The English Bishops and the Nazis', *Friends of Lambeth Palace Library Annual Report*, 1973.

—— *The Victorian Church, Part Two, 1860–1901*, SCM Press, London, 1987.

Chandler, A., 'A Question of Fundamental Principles: The Church of England and the Persecution of the Jews in Germany, 1933–1937', *Leo Baeck Institute Handbook*, XXVIII, London, 1993.

—— (ed.), *Brethren in Adversity: Bishop George Bell, the Church of England and the Crisis of German Protestantism 1933–1939*, Church of England Records Society, 7, Boydell, Woodbridge, 1997.

—— 'Munich and Morality: The Bishops of the Church of England and Appeasement', *Twentieth Century British History*, 5, London, 1994.

Clarke, P., *Hope and Glory, Britain 1900–2000*, Penguin, London, 2004.

Coombs, J., *Judgement on Hatcham: The History of a Religious Struggle, 1877–1886*, Faith Press, London, 1969.

Cox, J., *The English Churches in a Secular Society, Lambeth 1870–1930*, OUP, Oxford, 1992.

Crawley, A., *Look Before You Leap: A Memoir*, Collins, London, 1988.

Davidson, R.T. and W. Benham, *Life of Archbishop Tait*, Macmillan, London, 1891.

Davie, G., *Religion in Modern Europe: A Memory Mutates*, OUP, Oxford, 2000.

Davies, H., *Worship and Theology in England: From Newman to Martineau*, OUP, Oxford, 1962.

—— *The Ecumenical Century, from 1900 to the Present*, Erdmans, Michigan, 1996.

De la Noy, M., *Michael Ramsey, A Portrait*, Collins, London, 1990.

—— *The Queen Behind the Throne*, Arrow, London, 1994.

Dearmer, Percy, *The Parson's Handbook*, Grant Richards, London, 1899.

Dickens, A.G., *The English Reformation*, Fontana, Glasgow, 1981.

Donaldson, F., *Edward VIII*, Weidenfeld and Nicolson, London, 1974.

Dunlop, C., *Anglican Public Worship*, SCM Press, London, 1953.

Eason, R.E. and R.A. Snoxall, *The Last of their Line, the Bible Clerks of All Souls College, Oxford, Some Notes and Reminiscences*, All Souls College, Oxford, 1976.

Edwards, A., *Matriarch: Queen Mary and the House of Windsor*, Hodder and Stoughton, London, 1984.

Edwards, D.L., 'Archbishop Randall Davidson', in *Armchair Athenians: Essays from the Athenæum*, The Athenæum, London, 2001.

Ellis Roberts, R., *H.R.L. Sheppard: Life and Letters*, John Murray, London, 1942.

Ferguson, N., *The War of the World*, Penguin, London, 2007.

Gilbert, A., *The Making of Post-Christian Britain: A History of the Secularisation of Modern Britain*, Longman, London, 1980.

Gilbert, M. and R. Gott, *The Appeasers*, Phoenix, London, 2000.

Gray, D., *Earth and Altar*, Canterbury Press, Norwich, 1986.

—— *The 1927–28 Prayer Book Crisis*, 2 volumes, Alcuin Club, SCM-Canterbury Press, Norwich, 2006.

Green-Wilkinson, J., *Bishop Oliver, Letters and Reminiscences*, Wilton 65, York, 1998.

Gregory, A., *The Silence of Memory: Armistice Day 1919–1946*, Berg, Oxford, 1994.

Grimley, M., *Citizenship, Community and the Church of England: Liberal Anglican Theories of the State between the Wars*, Clarendon, Oxford, 2004.

Gummer, S., *The Chavasse Twins*, Hodder and Stoughton, London, 1963.

Hastings, A., *A History of English Christianity, 1920–2000*, SCM Press, London, 2001.

Heenan, J.C., *Not The Whole Truth*, Hodder and Stoughton, London, 1971.

—— *Crown of Thorns*, Hodder and Stoughton, London, 1974.

Higham, C., *Mrs Simpson: Secret Lives of the Duchess of Windsor*, Sidgwick and Jackson, London, 2004.

Hinchcliffe, P., *Frederick Temple, Archbishop of Canterbury: A Life*, Clarendon, Oxford, 1998.

Iremonger, F.A., *William Temple, Archbishop of Canterbury*, OUP, Oxford, 1949.

Jasper, R., *Arthur Cayley Headlam: The Life and Letters of a Bishop*, Faith Press, London, 1960.

—— *George Bell, Bishop of Chichester*, OUP, Oxford, 1967.

Jenkins, R., *Baldwin*, Collins, London, 1987.

Kemp, E.W., *Kenneth Escott Kirk*, Hodder and Stoughton, London, 1959.

Kent, J., *William Temple: Church, State and Society in Britain 1880–1950*, CUP, Cambridge, 1992.

Kershaw, I., *Making Friends with Hitler: Lord Londonderry and Britain's Road to War*, Penguin, London, 2005.

Lawson, T., *The Church of England and the Holocaust: Christianity, Memory and Nazism*, Boydell Press, Woodbridge, 2006.

Leeder, L., *Ecclesiastical Law Handbook*, Sweet and Maxwell, London, 1997.

Lloyd, R., *The Church of England, 1900–1965*, SCM Press, London, 1966.

Lockhart, J.G., *Cosmo Gordon Lang*, Hodder and Stoughton, London, 1949.

Lowther Clarke, W.K., and C. Harris, *Liturgy and Worship: A Companion to the Prayer Books of the Anglican Communion*, SPCK, London, 1933.

MacCulloch, D., 'The Myth of the English Reformation', *Journal of British Studies*, 30 (1991).

—— *Thomas Cranmer, A Life*, Yale University Press, New Haven, CT, and London, 1996.

Machin, G.I.T., 'Marriage and the Churches in the 1930s: Royal Abdication and Divorce Reform', *Journal of Ecclesiastical History*, 42, London, 1991.

McKibbin, R., *Classes and Cultures, England 1918–1951*, OUP, Oxford, 2000.

McLeod, H., *Religion and Society in England, 1850–1914*, Macmillan, Basingstoke, 1996.

—— *The Religious Crisis of the 1960s*, Clarendon, Oxford, 2007.

Maiden, J., *National Religion and the Prayer Book Controversy, 1927–1928*, Boydell Press, Woodbridge, 2009.

Mansbridge, A., *Edward Stuart Talbot and Charles Gore*, Dent, London, 1935.

Marrin, A., *The Last Crusade: The Church of England and the First World War*, Duke University Press, Durham, NC, 1974.

Matthews, W.R., *Memories and Meanings*, Hodder and Stoughton, London, 1969.

Maynard Smith, H., *Frank, Bishop of Zanzibar*, SPCK, London, 1926.

Medhurst, K.N. and G.H. Moyser, *Church and Politics in a Secular Age*, Clarendon, Oxford, 1988.

Mews, S., 'The Sword of the Spirit', *Studies in Church History*, XX, London, 1983.

Middlemas, K. and J. Barnes, *Baldwin: A Biography*, Weidenfeld and Nicholson, London, 1969.

Moloney, T., *Westminster, Whitehall and the Vatican: The Role of Cardinal Hinsley, 1935–1943*, Burnes and Oates, London, 1985.

Montgomery Hyde, H., *Baldwin, the Unexpected Prime Minister*, Hart-Davies, MacGibbon, London, 1973.

Moorman, J., *The Anglican Spiritual Tradition*, DLT, London, 1983.

—— *History of the Church in England*, Adam and Charles Black, London, 1976.

Morris, J., *Religion and Urban Change, Croydon 1840–1914*, Royal Historical Society, London, 1992.

Morrow, A., *Without Equal*, Stratus, Thirsk, 2000.

Muggeridge, M., *The Thirties, 1930–1940 in Great Britain*, Hamish Hamilton, London, 1940.

Nicolson, H., *King George V: His Life and Reign,* Constable, London, 1952.

Nockles, P.B., *The Oxford Movement in Context*, CUP, Cambridge, 1994.

Norman, E.R., *Church and Society in England, 1770–1970: A Historical Study*, Clarendon, Oxford, 1976.

Pawley, B. and M., *Rome and Canterbury Through Four Centuries*, Mowbray, London, 1981.

Peart-Binns, J.S., *Blunt,* Mountain Press, Queensbury, 1969.

Pigott, A., *Donnish, Unrealistic, or Even Insincere: Sir Will Spens and Liberal Anglo Catholicism 1900–1940*, Anglo-Catholic History Society, London, 2004.

Pinnington, J., *Anglicans and Orthodox, Unity and Subversion 1559–1725*, Gracewing, Leominster, 2003.

Ponsonby, F., *Recollections of Three Reigns*, Eyre and Spottiswood, London, 1951.

Pope-Hennessy, J., *Queen Mary, 1867–1953,* George Allen and Unwin, London, 1959.

Purcell, W., *Fisher of Lambeth: A Portrait from Life,* Hodder and Stoughton, London, 1969.

Ramsey, M., *Canterbury Pilgrim*, SPCK, London, 1974.

Roberts, A., *The Holy Fox: The Life of Lord Halifax*, Phoenix, London, 1997.

Rose, K., *King George V*, Weidenfeld and Nicolson, London, 1983.

Smyth, C., *Cyril Foster Garbett, Archbishop of York*, Hodder and Stoughton, London, 1959.

Snape, M., *God and the British Soldier: Religion and the British Army in the First and Second World Wars*, Routledge, London, 2005.

Spencer, S., *William Temple: A Calling to Prophecy*, SPCK, London, 2001.

Squibb, D.G., *Order of Precedence in England and Wales*, Clarendon Press, Oxford, 1981.

Starkey, D., *Monarchy: England and her Rulers from the Tudors to the Windsors*, Harper Perennial, London, 2007.

Watson, F., *Dawson of Penn*, Chatto and Windus, London, 1950.

Wheeler-Bennett, J.W., *King George VI: His Life and Reign*, Macmillan, London, 1958.

Williams, S., *The People's King: The True Story of the Abdication,* Allen Lane, London, 2003.

Wilkinson, A., 'Changing English Attitudes to Death in Two World Wars', in P.C. Jupp and G. Howarth (eds), *The Changing Face of Death: Historical Accounts of Death and Disposal*, Macmillan, London, 1997.

—— *Dissent or Conform? War, Peace and the English Churches 1900–1945*, SCM Press, London, 1986.

—— 'Lang, (William) Cosmo Gordon', in B. Harrison (ed.), *New Oxford Dictionary of National Biography*, OUP, Oxford, 2004.

—— *The Church of England and the First World War*, SCM Press, London, 1996.

—— *The Community of the Resurrection*, SCM Press, London, 1992.

Williamson, P., *Stanley Baldwin: Conservative Leadership and National Values,* CUP, Cambridge, 1999.

—— 'The Doctrinal Politics of Stanley Baldwin', in M. Bentley (ed.), *Public and Private Doctrine*, CUP, Cambridge, 1993.

Wolffe, J.R., *God and Greater Britain: Religion and National Life in Britain and Ireland, 1843–1945*, Routledge, London, 1994.

Wollheim, R., *Germs: A Memoir of Childhood,* Black Swan, London, 2005.

Yates, N., *Anglican Ritualism in Victorian Britain, 1830–1910*, Clarendon, Oxford, 1999.

Ziegler, P., *King Edward VIII, The Official Biography*, Collins, London, 1990.

BROADCAST SOURCES

Canterbury Tales, Twenty Twenty Television, Channel 4, 26 September 1996.

Reinventing the Royals, Granada Television, Channel 4, 22 December 2002.

Edward VIII: The Plot to Topple a King, Blakeway, Channel 4, 9 May 2012.

Index